CW01647206

Mary Weatherford

LUND HUMPHRIES | CONTEMPORARY PAINTERS

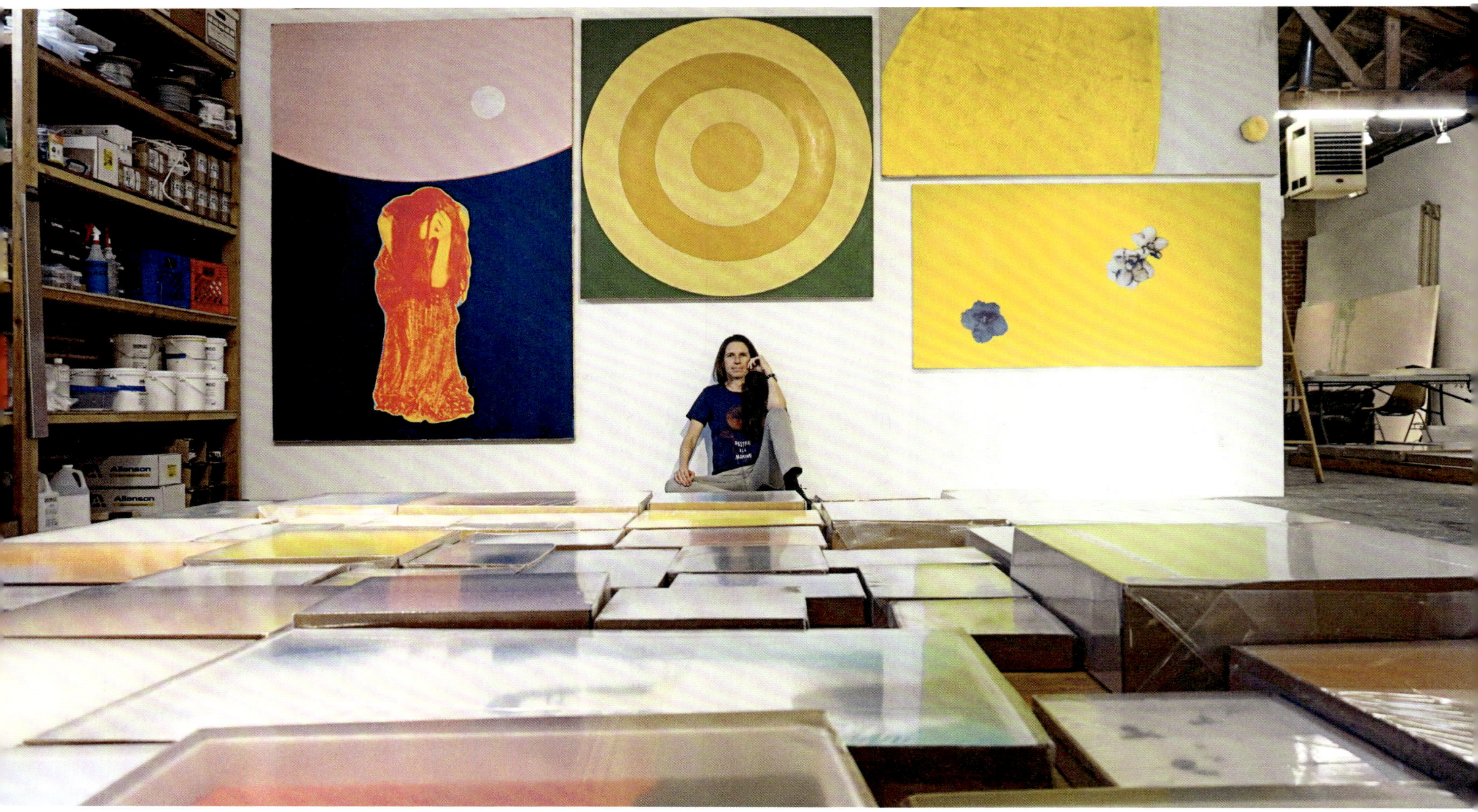
Allenson
Allenson

Suzanne Hudson

Mary Weatherford

LUND HUMPHRIES | CONTEMPORARY PAINTERS

Contemporary Painters Series

Series Editor: Barry Schwabsky

The Contemporary Painters Series is a new, curated series of accessible, authoritative, and highly illustrated monographs on the world's leading living painters, which locates painting as a vibrant and vital part of contemporary art.

The series is edited by American art critic Barry Schwabsky, supported by an international advisory board with a specialist interest in contemporary painting. It aims to redefine 'painting' in the contemporary context as work which is done within the conventions and history of painting, but which may incorporate other materials or techniques.

Advisory Board
Paco Barragán, independent curator and arts writer and Contributing Editor of *Artpulse*
Tony Godfrey, freelance writer and curator based in Singapore and Philippines
David Pagel, Los Angeles-based art critic, curator, and writer
Ida Panicelli, former Editor-in-Chief of *Artforum*
Simon Rees, former Director of the Govett-Brewster Art Gallery/Len Lye Centre, New Zealand
Beatrix Ruf, former Director of the Stedelijk Museum, Amsterdam
Philip Tinari, Director of the Ullens Center for Contemporary Art, Beijing
Gilda Williams, art critic, writer, lecturer, and London correspondent for *Artforum*
John Yau, poet, art critic, and curator

Also available in the series:
Amy Sillman by Valerie Smith
Bernard Frize by David Rhodes
Etel Adnan by Kaelen Wilson-Goldie
Lois Dodd by Faye Hirsch
Neo Rauch by Michael Glover
Philip Taaffe by John Yau
Thomas Nozkowski by John Yau
Verne Dawson by John Hutchinson

Contents

Foreword

For more than twenty-five years, Mary Weatherford has been delving relentlessly into the politics of visual pleasure, producing paintings whose intelligence and intransigence have revealed themselves, not in spite of or even simply alongside her work's lyrical sensibility, coloristic richness, and heart-on-the-sleeve emotional openness, but precisely through those things. As Suzanne Hudson points out, Weatherford has been a strong if sometimes inconspicuous influence on fellow painters, among them Laura Owens and Monique Prieto – all those, in fact, who got the point of her 'excessively, aggressively feminine work'. In a searching account of the development of Weatherford's art and its manifold sources, Hudson traces the artist's geographical peregrinations, from California (part of her childhood was spent in the bohemian enclave of Ojai, in the mountains above Los Angeles) to New York, where she was received as part of an emerging group of young painters that also included John Currin and Sean Landers, among others, and back again to California; perhaps Weatherford's bicoastal perspective helps account for her ever-greater ability to synthesize multiple strands of the American modernist tradition, including the once-dominant ones that were cultivated in New York and the dissenting ones that managed to thrive out west. To this end Weatherford has essayed a range of techniques, including silk-screening, staining, and assemblage; since 2012 she has been mounting neon tubes to her canvases, marrying blatant artifice and expressive naturalism in such a way that, as Hudson says, 'Every painting contains its own atmosphere, evoking "shifting time of day and changing seasons", so fully accomplished and non-selfsame does each become.' Hudson's writing grows particularly eloquent in the vicinity of these extraordinary recent works, and it becomes apparent that what she writes about Weatherford's art is equally true of her own work here as a critic-historian: that it is 'less motivated by some belated modernist ambition than underwritten by a liberal, manifold curiosity: about the natural world, pictures and the stories that have been told about them, and sensible apprehension of place and one's implication within it, most intimately but also most broadly.'

Barry Schwabsky

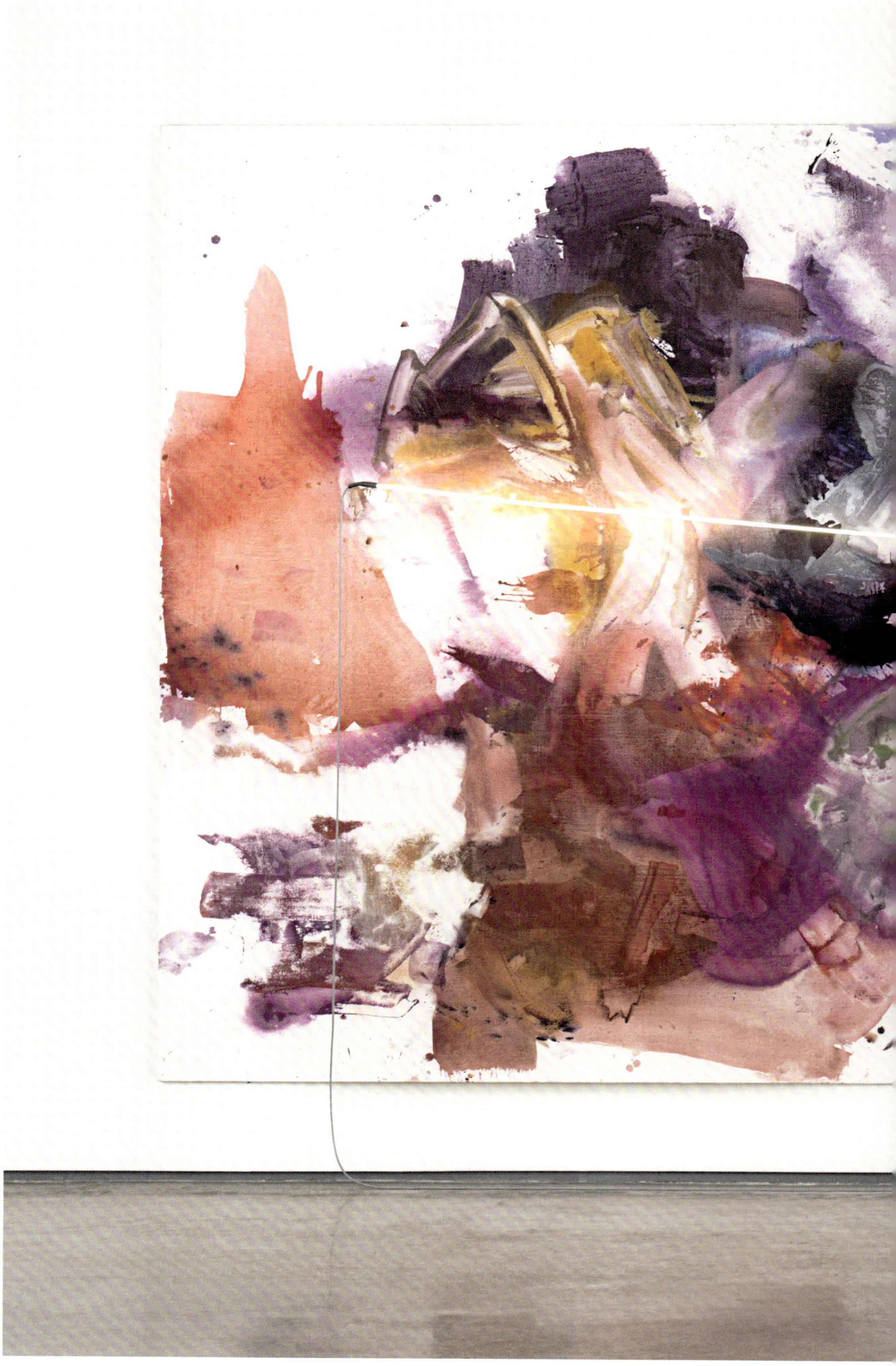

1. Butterfly 2017

Flashe and neon on linen
297.2 × 594.4 cm (117 × 234 in.)
Fondation Louis Vuitton, Paris

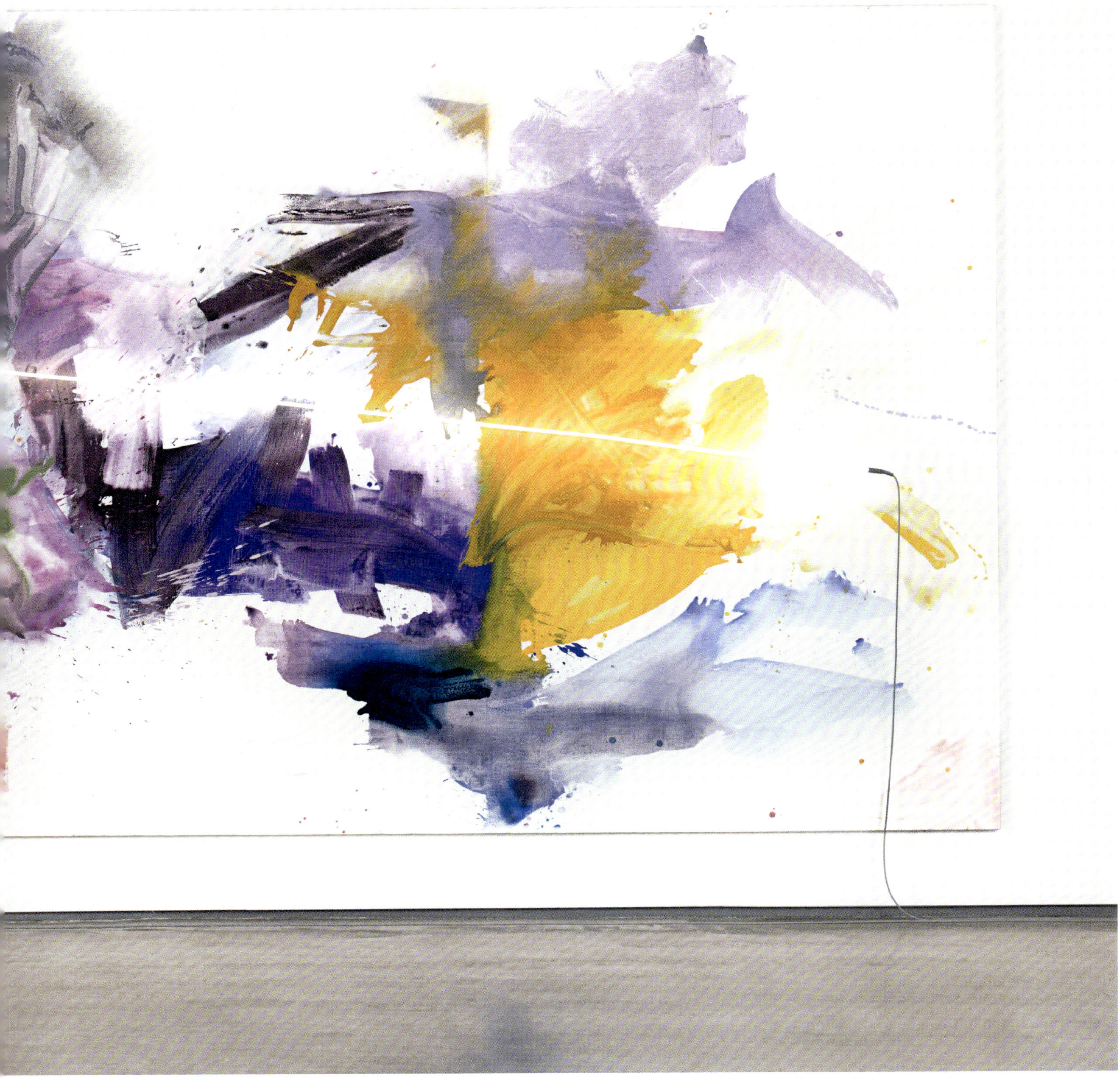

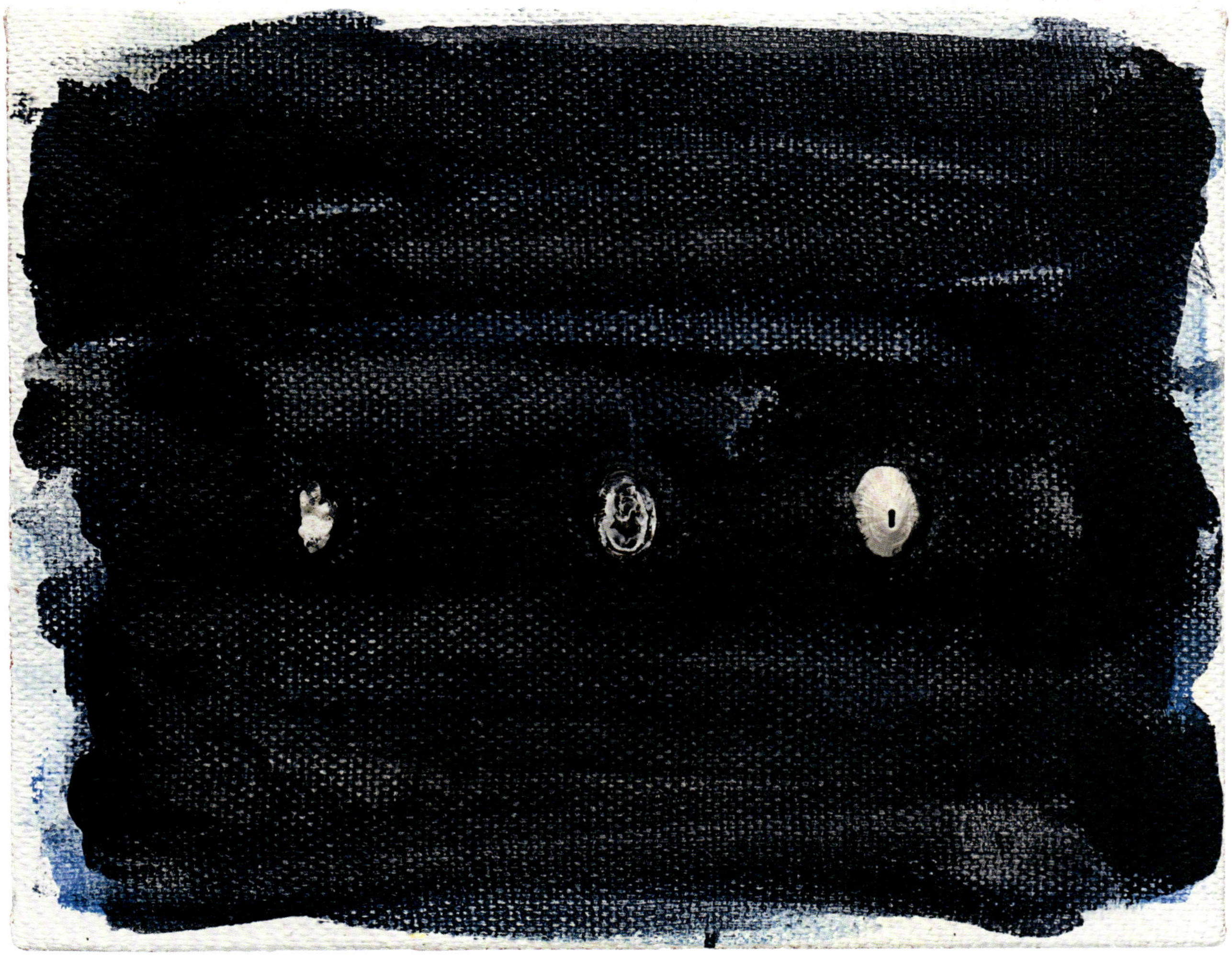

2. el mar 2014

Flashe and found objects on cleaning rag
40.6 × 50.8 cm (16 × 20 in.)
Collection of the artist

Introduction

As I worked on the text that would become this essay, life was interrupted by wildfires burning very close, in disobedient conflagrations of eucalyptus and pine needles, manzanita and wild mustard, dry brush and human debris. North of Los Angeles, flames circled Ojai, a small town at the foot of the Topatopa Mountains, where, in 1963, Mary Weatherford was born. The city survived even the rains and mudslides that followed, an exceptionalism befitting its (apocryphal) role as a stand-in for Shangri-La in Frank Capra's 1937 film adaptation of James Hilton's *Lost Horizon*. The history of fire and water is intertwined with the making of modern California, something Joan Didion, its great native chronicler, reads deterministically. Quoting Raymond Chandler, she recognizes a strained illusion in the 'weather of catastrophe, of apocalypse'.[1] Much has been made of Didion's own family's Manifest Destiny, of their crossing the continent and then the Sierra Nevada near Donner Pass before splitting from the party that would, marooned in a blizzard encampment, eat its own dead. Apropos of an unpredictable geography and the cupidity of its pilgrims, Didion later remarked on her characters' finding 'salvation . . . in extreme and doomed commitments'.[2] One might put the themes a bit differently for Weatherford's work – she claims 'love and tragedy'[3] – but the sentiment holds.

Weatherford grew up aware of William Weatherford, her enigmatic mixed-race Creek chief ancestor, whose sobriquet was established years after his death in the romanticizing cantos of *The Red Eagle: A Poem of the South*, which antebellum orator and litterateur A. B. Meek published in 1855. A deer hide and cattle trader, he was swept into the civil war among the Creeks in 1813. He seems to have participated as a reluctant nativist leader in the infamous Red Stick Creek attack against Fort Mims, a massacre of military conscripts and civilians that made news, provoked public sentiment, and created support for retaliation against the Creek Nation. It was a milestone in the United States' suppression and attempted eradication of indigenous peoples from the fertile fields of the Southeast, where – not incidentally – gold was discovered in the foothills of Georgia's Blue Ridge Mountains in 1828. The federal government's response was the Indian Removal program, forced displacement meant to keep land available for white farmers and miners (until the latter took off for bigger lodes in Sacramento in 1848).

William Weatherford's life is elsewhere encapsulated in a surprisingly genteel image of his surrender to Andrew Jackson. Happening upon it in a high-school history book, Mary Weatherford encountered in this representation a man with the same name as her father, a relative who was born in the South before the American

Revolution and died there in 1824, and who had been witness to some of the most decisive events in Native American history. His descendants had made their way to California by the 1920s. They came in plenty of time to live through the Depression and to welcome Dust Bowl refugees fleeing the desiccated Southern Plains, where so many of the 'civilized tribes' – Cherokee, Chickasaw, Choctaw, Creek, and Seminole – had been resettled. Weatherford's grandfather water-blasted rock face for the construction of the Morris Dam in Azusa. A feat of civil engineering, the dam survived the great flood of 1938, and the Morris Reservoir soon was put to use as a naval weapons test station for torpedoes and ballistic missiles during World War II.

In 1890 the director of the United States Census Bureau had announced the closing of the American frontier, explaining that the moving line of population density had reached its terminus. On the announcement of this fact, the historian Frederick Jackson Turner posited that the existence of the frontier had been constitutive of American democracy. Despite the arrival of the nation's people at the far sea, the narrative drive of the homesteading pioneer never really went away, nor did the less than tacit affirmation of rugged individualism and self-sovereignty that the subjugation of terrain and extermination of populations required along the way.[4] Before but also after the boundary was met, the work of establishing order against inevitable chaos found comparable expression in so much American art predicated upon an Edenic landscape that in reality had long since been tilled. The closure of the frontier and Turner's thesis about its significance justified unending imperialism; its metaphorics expanded to the colonizing of other domains but also of inner space.

In response to a *Time* magazine article undermining the intentionality of his actions, Jackson Pollock famously proclaimed, 'No chaos, damn it.'[5] The contemporary grasp of the unconscious exposed the adversarial within. Pollock's admonition then might be understood as not just declarative but performative. In his work – in his wrangling of drips into precisely layered and undulating skeins – this mustering of control over mind and matter assumes pictorial form. Many standard narratives of art history from 1945 on take Pollock as the ur-figure of vanguardism.[6] A child of the American West, he made marks, as though for the first time, on canvas after canvas that he would keep calling *Number 1*. He took precedence in an art scene newly and disproportionately wedded to New York, in a world decimated by a war whose bombs fell far away, still subject to the same laws of gravity as his dripped paint. Writers including Clement Greenberg and Harold Rosenberg shored up his primacy alongside their own. For the former, Pollock exemplified his theories of self-critical medium specificity in which painting consisted of colors and shapes on a flat support as composition and subject; for the latter, Pollock made the canvas a space of existentialist combat – 'an arena in which to act', in Rosenberg's tremendous formulation of the picture-become-event.[7] Rosenberg believed in the inextricability of work and biography, while Greenberg furthered ideas about illusionistic space as nascent modernist 'opticality', an autonomous representational scheme that, unlike three-dimensional sculpture, could be traversed 'with the eye'.[8]

Nevertheless, if Pollock was an origin, he was also an apotheosis. It was only with the rise of Color Field painting – and through the example of Helen Frankenthaler's coruscating stains of color seeping into unprimed supports – that Pollock's legacy was extended. Morris Louis famously summarized this position, proclaiming that Frankenthaler was 'the bridge between Pollock and what was possible'.[9] Even if this formulation established Frankenthaler as but a linkage between two exultant men, it nevertheless marked a generational shift with implications for the gendered economy of abstraction. In 1952 Frankenthaler completed *Mountains and Sea*, pouring turpentine-thinned oil paint onto raw canvas unfurled beneath her feet, and discovering Nova Scotia in the resulting puddles of dirty salmon and cerulean. This abstract evocation of landscape happened in the studio; nature was prior to it, and also beyond the representational act that it retroactively framed. She later described her paintings as 'full of climates, abstract climates and not nature per se, but a feeling, and the feeling of an order that is associated with nature. Nature in seasons, maybe; but nature in, well, an order. I think art itself is order out of chaos, and nature is always fighting the same battle.'[10]

Only a year before Frankenthaler's breakthrough picture, *Life* magazine had published a spread on the so-called 'irascibles', a group consolidated, if equivocally, as Abstract Expressionists. Hedda Sterne is the only woman included in Nina Leen's accompanying black-and-white photo of the hypermasculinized cohort smartly dressed in suits and ties – Pollock, Adolph Gottlieb, Willem de Kooning, Robert Motherwell, Barnett Newman, Ad Reinhardt, and others.[11] When *Life* turned to the women of the Second Generation in 1957, Gordon Parks captured Frankenthaler in color, demurely sitting on one of her paintings, legs tucked and ankles crossed, head knowingly cocked. That she dons an outfit coordinating with *Mountains and Sea*, which forms a backdrop-like wall behind her, only patronizes, even (or somehow especially) if she had agency in the choice.[12] Rosenberg, who was no fan, similarly subjected her to a crippling femininity. He characterized her work as visually insubstantial, akin to the 'customary procedure in watercolor', and also to 'Georgia O'Keefe [*sic*] painting with absorbent cotton'.[13] He further accused her of failing to grasp the 'moral and metaphysical basis of Action painting', writing, 'With Frankenthaler, the artist's action is at a minimum; it is the paint that is active.'[14]

Perhaps it goes without saying, but the aleatory method that Frankenthaler utilized for the soak-stain did not preclude decision making to follow: to pick up the painting from the ground; to hang it on the wall (in a certain orientation); to decide whether it was a painting, and then a good one; to keep it and to name it and to let it out of the studio; and so on. Frankenthaler assigned significance to the critical act of judging the work after the materials self-organized within the bounds of the technique that she established. Even as she abjured the autographic mark for the pour, her traces betrayed her presence, and to an extent greater than Rosenberg would acknowledge; his anxiety about the works' femininity admits as much. Color is not exclusively perceptual.

Of his safeguarding of Greenbergian opticality after Abstract Expressionism and into the 1960s and beyond, Michael Fried would write that what was at stake was 'nothing less than the continued existence of painting as a high art'.[15] Yet the art of pure, flat hue, Greenberg's 'Post-Painterly Abstraction', flaunted the decorative. Merely 'pretty' is how Arthur Danto disparagingly described Louis's luminous paintings, comparing the experience of seeing them to 'walking through racks of negligees at Bendel'.[16] For artists distancing themselves from formalist modernism, though, the source of Danto's contempt became the basis for production that welcomed the implications of dyeing and domesticity, handicraft and manual labor. The peerless *Womanhouse*, organized by Judy Chicago and Miriam Schapiro in Los Angeles in 1972, built a liberation politics. Meanwhile in New York, gallerist Holly Solomon supported artists associated with the Pattern and Decoration movement. These artists sourced designs from quilts, mosaics, and textiles; they unapologetically draped paintings with swags of fabric and covered them in hearts and flowers.

This is the broader background of gestural abstract painting and its evaluative gendering in postwar American art, and the discourses that proliferated alongside it, against which Weatherford must be read. To be sure, her experience in California across some of these years (from 1963 to 1980, when she left for college) necessarily altered the terms of her reception of this bequest, emphasizing the tug of war between contingency and mastery; yet so too did her staying on the East Coast for two decades, from the fall of 1980 to the spring of 1999. Then came her repatriation to Los Angeles, and with it an accommodation and then embrace of the imperative of landscape, but even more, an equivocating regard of the American tradition as it traveled headlong to the Pacific. Weatherford moved from painting targets with concentric circles of repeating colors in the 1980s to flowers, winged insects, and collages with sea creatures in the 1990s, and through both decades she painted women, first as tragedy and then as monument. Then came caves yawning at the edge of the continent, and motifs that blocked vision beyond the surface: vines and weeds, brick walls, and rock masses formed by erosion, all in the 2000s. In 2012 she arrived at elemental, ambient atmospheres interrupted by rods of neon mounted to the color-washed surfaces, power cords hanging heavy and crude, plugged into anchoring transformers. If her first targets serve as emblems of calculation and risk, these more recent light-studded stains of liquefied paint embody a language of potential failure and exercised command over a fragile, surprisingly resplendent environment of one's making.

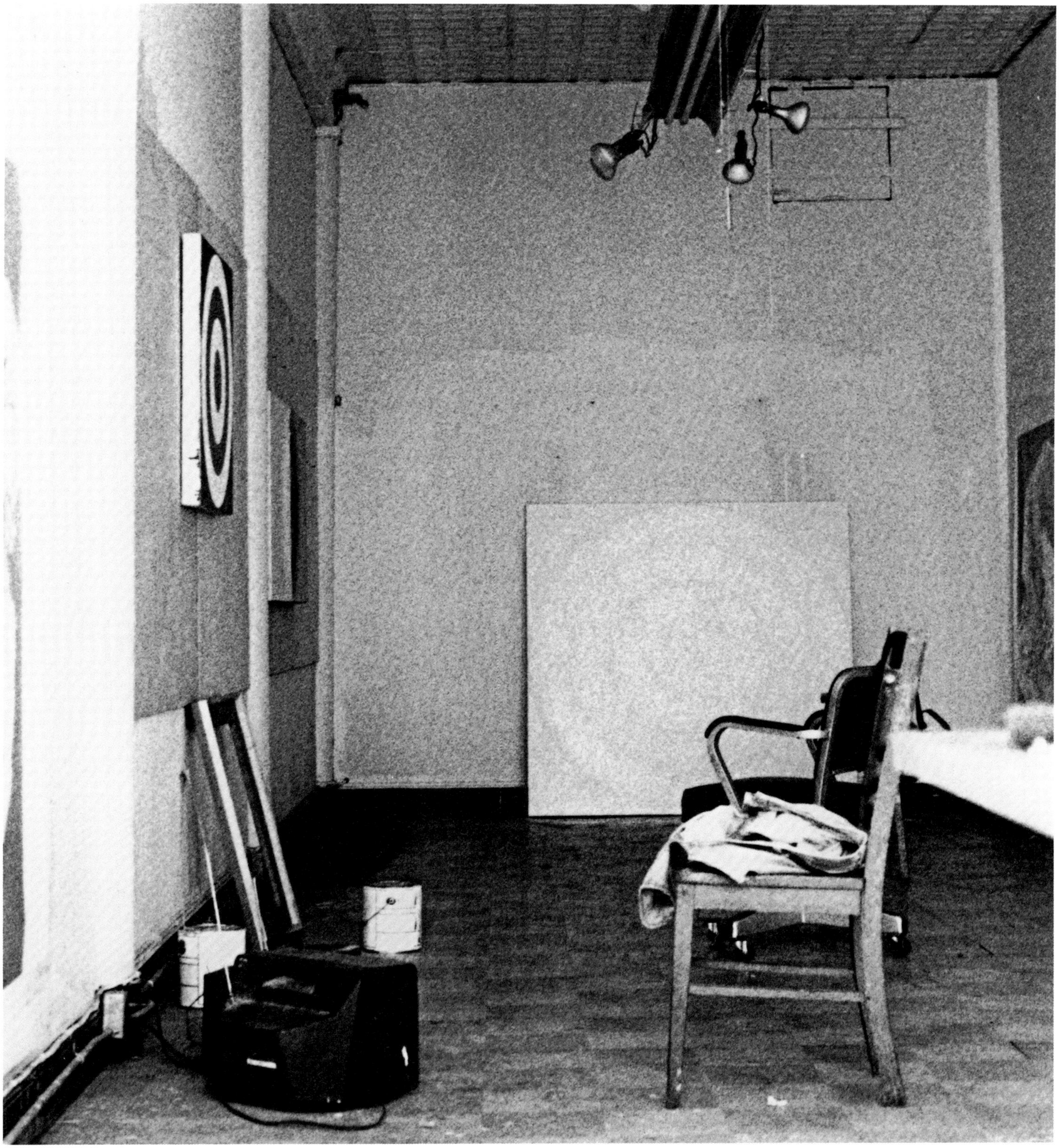

3. Weatherford studio at
12 Warren Street, New York,
1990

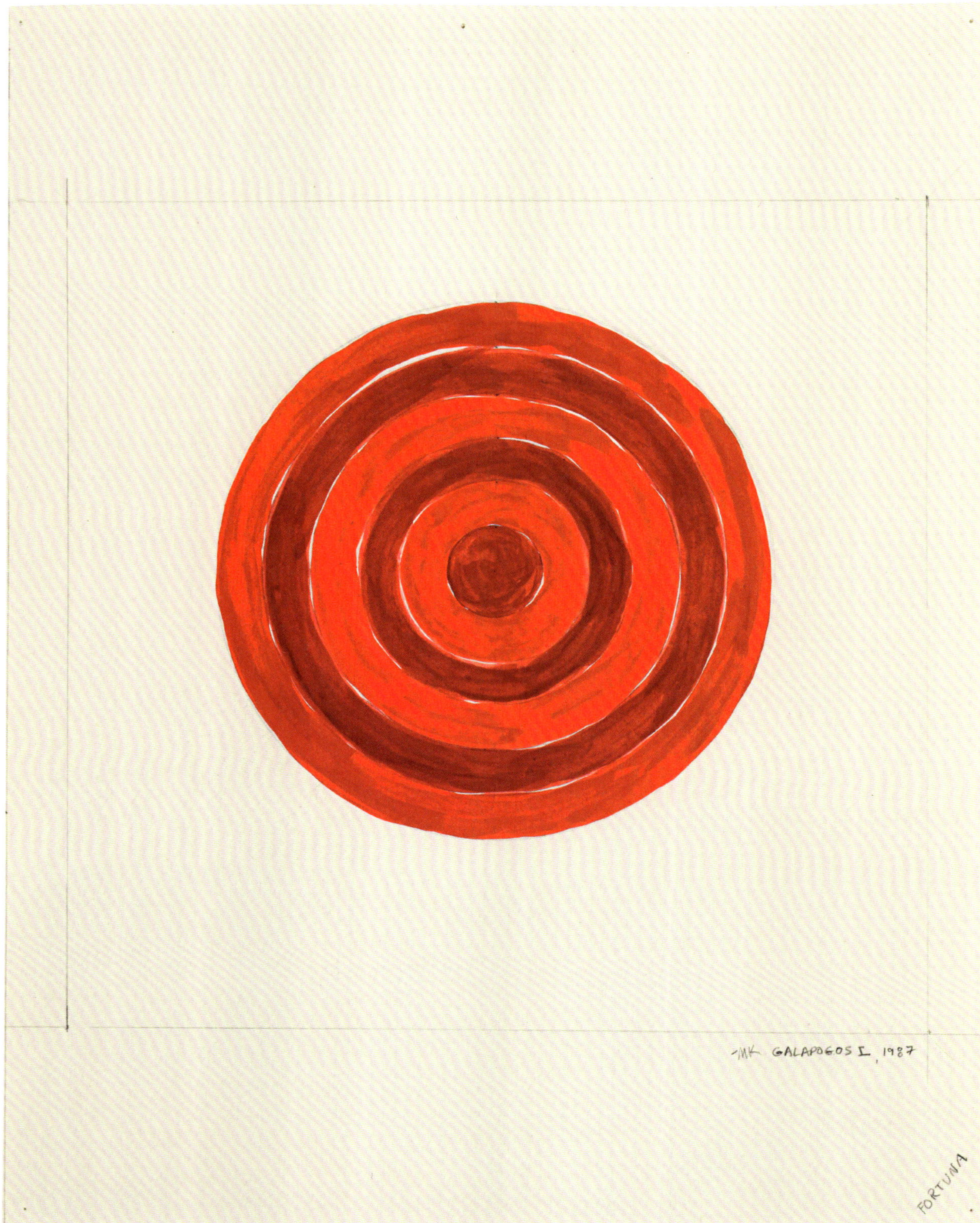

4. Galapagos I 1987

Gouache and pencil on paper
26 × 20.3 cm (10¼ × 8 in.)
Collection of the artist

1 Origins: 1963–1980s

Mary Weatherford was the first child for William and Regina (née Kunzel) Weatherford, born before her sister, Margaret, and her brothers, John, Stephen, and Billy. In Ojai, where her father served as vicar of St Andrew's Episcopal Mission, the family was surrounded by a group of what the artist calls 'interesting people', including the entrepreneur-activists Verne and Anne Johnson and their eight children, and artists Leon Salter and Franklin Fireshaker. Fireshaker was a Ponca elder who was responsible for the first paintings that Weatherford ever saw, dreamscapes of tribal legends and history, testaments to communion and peyote. Beatrice Wood lived nearby, affiliated with a colony of Theosophists (some of whom had settled in the area as early as the 1940s to be near Krishnamurti), and is fondly remembered by the Weatherfords for her sympathetic participation in a daylong search for the family's lost poodle.

Glamorized as a holistic New Age sanctuary, the hamlet was decidedly less idyllic, in Weatherford's experience, beyond this circle of family friends. The Rumford Fair Housing Act had been passed by the California legislature in 1963, but conservative groups had immediately moved to counteract this legislation aimed at ending racial discrimination by property owners and landlords by putting forth Proposition 14, an amendment to the state's constitution that relegalized it. The successful passage of this amendment in 1964 was a key event for ever-deteriorating race relations in the Southland, and directly contributed to the massive uprising that took place in South Central Los Angeles in 1965. In the riots' wake, Weatherford's father asked the Episcopal diocese to transfer him from his post at St Andrew's, where his stand against discrimination had not been popular. (His decisions to support voter registration in the South and to join the civil rights march from Selma to Montgomery, capital of the Old Confederacy, in 1965 had not been, either.) An overtly political sermon in support of fair housing consolidated the mounting sentiment against him.

The family moved to Los Angeles and settled in the Crenshaw District for five years, from 1967 to 1972. During this time Weatherford's father worked with a consortium of many denominations serving an area conveniently defined as lying under the Los Angeles International Airport's landing pattern. He also matriculated in an urban ecology studies program at the University of Southern California, working with the Los Angeles Planning Department to organize public forums for community input into long-range plans for future metropolitan growth and public transportation.

In an anecdote she has told in interviews, Weatherford narrates becoming aware of art in local museums:

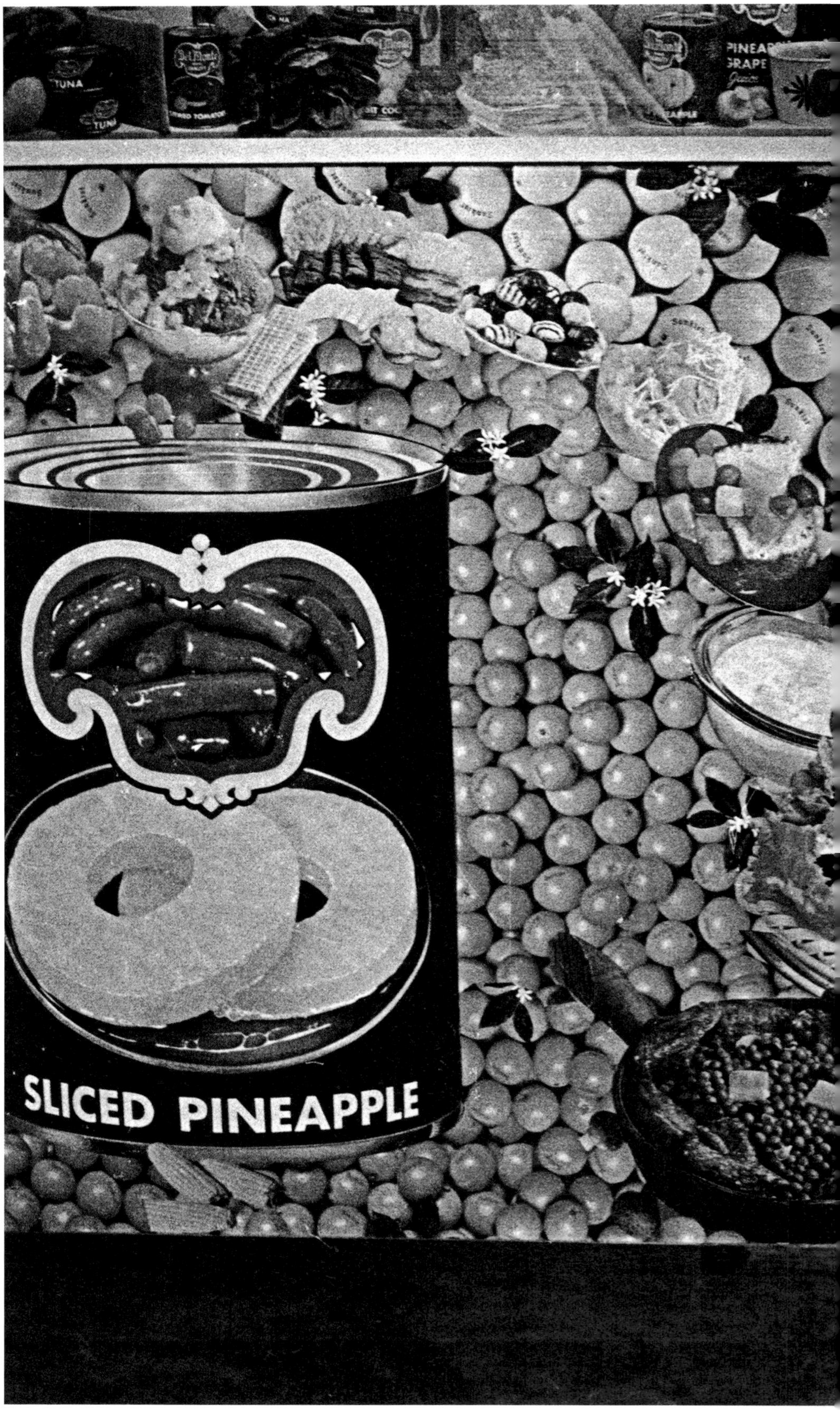

5. *Fruit Room*, created by Kim Boutelle (now Sigrid Jardin), Jonathan Boutelle, Philip Thompson, and Beatrice Thompson, in a room under the Cowell College dining hall, 1969

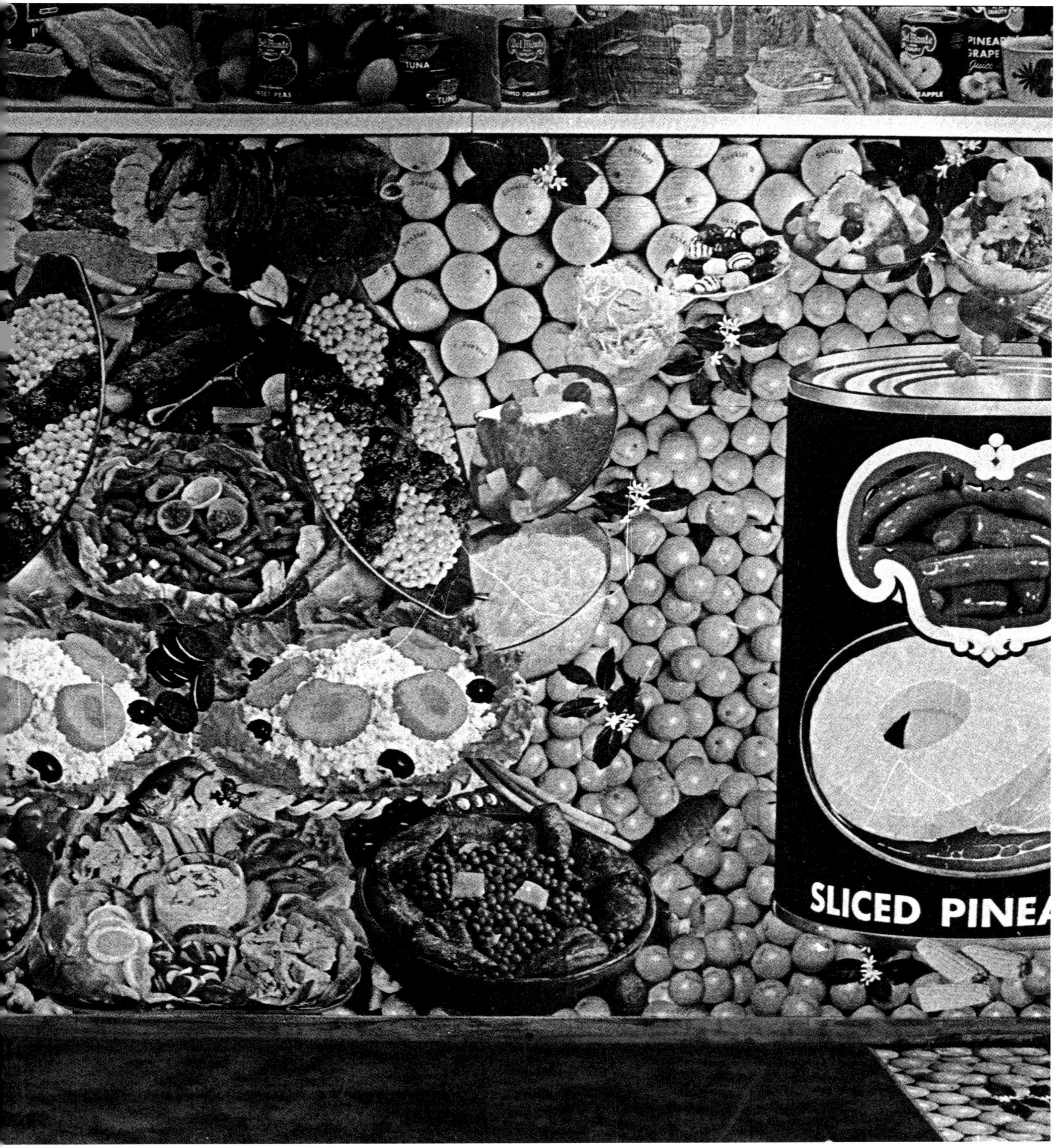
TUNA
SLICED PINEA

> The first art show I ever saw was the [Vincent] van Gogh show at LACMA [the Los Angeles County Museum of Art] in 1969. I was small enough that my father could pick me up like this. [Demonstrates dangling a child in front of body.] He thought if he could hold me in front of the painting long enough, that it would soak in. He held me in front of *Wheat Field with Crows*, which is a double square . . . So he holds me in front of *Wheat Field with Crows* and says this is the most frightening painting I've ever seen in my life. I hung there for the requisite amount of time while I took in why this painting might be terrifying.[1]

She also happened to see the Willy Wonka-esque *Fruit Room* in 1969 at the University of California, Santa Cruz, where her aunt and namesake, Mary Katherine Kunzel, and Mary's boyfriend, Keith Christiansen, were students. Spearheaded by Beatrice Thompson, with Kim Boutelle (now Sigrid Jardin), Jonathan Boutelle, and Philip Thompson, *Fruit Room* grew out of a shell mirror project (Weatherford had gone along to choose the seashells at a local shell shop); the artists papered an unused space with a dense mosaic of supermarket advertisements featuring fruits and vegetables, the cornucopia grounded by a green Astroturf carpet.

All along, she made art. Weatherford took classes at LACMA and at Barnsdall Art Park in Hollywood, where, as she narrated in a grant application many years later, the 'children's projects were versions of LA Fetish Finish and the La Cienega scene'.[2] She further recalls:

> In 1971 I saw Maurice Tuchman's *Art and Technology* show at LACMA. I *vividly* remember Rauschenberg's mud table, Samaras' mirror room, Matta-Clark's algae beds, Rockne Krebs' laser show, Robert Morris' cardboard sculptures, and Warhol's 3-D daisies with water showers at the exit. My thoughts on Warhol at the time: 'This guy didn't try very hard.' Ten years later, thumbing through old *ArtForum* [*sic*] magazines at Marquand Library [at Princeton University], I realized how lucky I am to have seen that show.[3]

Her mother, Gina, a Stanford-trained historian in charge of the five children, fostered resourceful ventures in a range of media: Weatherford experimented with macramé, batik, and tie-dye, and fashioned Ukrainian eggs – the last tendered from a European Jewish heritage that they had not yet recovered, so assimilated had the family become in the decades since coming to America. They made their own Clacker balls with resin and molds for fabricating decorative grapes. Weatherford's mother indulged her, allowing her to begin the next design even if she hadn't completed the last. Coloring books were outlawed. Weatherford compensated by making her own version of a DoodleArt poster, drawing butterflies and flowers sourced from library books in India ink and filling them in with felt-tipped pens. This child's play foreshadows her butterfly paintings three decades later.

In 1972 the family relocated to the San Diego neighborhood of Tierrasanta, a brand-new, master-plan housing tract on land once occupied by a Spanish mission and more recently by a military base. The development spread across hills and ravines still littered with ordnance and debris. 'Wild' is how Weatherford describes it, lacking civic infrastructure; there was no library or grocery store, and the playground – a shaved-off hill with parked trailers that constituted the elementary school – teemed with rattlesnakes that the janitor would decapitate with a shovel. Kids roamed the canyons and made forts in storm drains. It was only after Weatherford transferred to Lewis Junior High at the age of twelve that she discovered a peer group. They went to Shakespeare productions in Balboa Park and discussed books, notably including plays that she studied and turned into dramatic-interpretation monologues for the speech team. She decided on Princeton University. Her father had studied at the seminary there, but even more compelling was the school's proximity to Broadway (she was awarded a theatre scholarship) and access to New York more generally.

Weatherford made it to the city for the first time in 1980. She had never been to the East Coast and was unprepared for the concentrated humidity that greeted her upon deplaning. She had a few days in New York, where she stayed with her aunt Mary, now married to Keith Christiansen; the two had moved there from Santa Cruz in 1977 (he took a job as a curator at the Metropolitan Museum of Art, and she became an art educator and later took up botanical illustration). As Weatherford recalls, her uncle picked her up at the airport and showed her the subway and their life uptown, where she stayed until getting on a Port Authority bus bound for New Jersey. In these first catalytic days in Manhattan, he took her to the Museum of Modern Art, where that season the entire exhibition space was given over to the nearly one thousand artworks assembled for *Pablo Picasso: A Retrospective*. Since historicized as the museum's first blockbuster, it broke attendance records, necessitated the hiring of additional security staff, and required modifications to the building to improve its climate control. It proved a near-cultic exaltation of the modern master – and in so many ways, too, its bell tolling.

6. Simon Rodia
Watts Towers 1921–54

Los Angeles

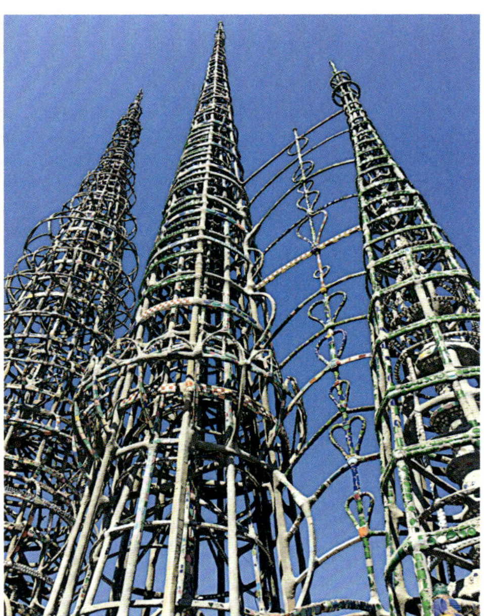

Over the next year, Weatherford would visit shows in New York with her roommate Tina Kachele, and subsequently on her own, with her art classes, or with other friends. She saw Walter De Maria's *Earth Room* on Wooster Street and his nearby installation of brass rods, *Broken Kilometer*, amid regular trips to SoHo galleries, among them Paula Cooper, Leo Castelli, and Holly Solomon. On campus, Weatherford auditioned for plays and began studying architecture. Even after she transitioned into fine arts, she took an engineering course on bridges and thin-shell concrete structures, for which she wrote a paper on the Watts Towers in Los Angeles and calculated the sway at their apex. (Weatherford still regards this as a defining experience, one that prepared the way for the catenary drape of electrical cords becoming part of her art in 2012.)

At Princeton, one could not major in studio art without fulfilling the requirements for art history, so Weatherford did exactly that, enrolling in upper-division seminars that stressed writing over memorization after she bombed an exam in Renaissance Architecture and decided that she was through taking tests. Meanwhile, Weatherford was one of eight in her tiny Visual Arts Department. Her instructors included Andrea Blum, Jerry Buchanan, Heidi Glück, and James Seawright; Harvey Quaytman, Sean Scully, and Merrill Wagner all passed through. Thomas Crow, Sam Hunter, and P. Adams Sitney were also mainstays, each differently significant for her. Weatherford seems to have made the most of her time at Princeton; an early CV she kept in her papers dutifully records her receiving awards and recognition including a John Adams Schuman Scholarship in Theatre Arts, Honorable Mention in the Francis Lemoyne Page Visual Arts Award, a Thesis Prize, and the Louis Sudler Award in the Arts. The $1,500 cash award that came with the last allowed her to move to New York after graduation.

In Weatherford's words, 'By the age of eighteen I was all studied up on the New York School',[4] thanks to Sam Hunter, an eminent critic, art historian, curator, and museum director. Hunter's many achievements in the 1960s alone include his tenure as founding director of the Rose Art Museum at Brandeis University and as the director of the Jewish Museum in New York. He became a professor of art and archaeology and faculty curator at Princeton at the decade's end, and retired from the university only in 1991. While he presided over the Jewish Museum's institutionalization of Minimalism in the landmark survey *Primary Structures*, he was more forthrightly aligned with Abstract Expressionism. Earlier, while at the Museum of Modern Art, he had organized Jackson Pollock's first museum show – in 1956, the year of the artist's death – and the following year he selected a grouping of Pollock's work to represent the United States at the 1957 São Paulo Biennial. Even while at the Jewish Museum, Hunter mounted exhibitions of Ad Reinhardt and Philip Guston. The author of a canon-making textbook on modern art, he carried these commitments into his teaching. Weatherford became his research assistant, and they kept in touch long after her graduation, with Hunter including her in a show in 1990 and writing the first sustained scholarship on her art.

A chance encounter with critic and art historian Rosalind Krauss also proved key. During Weatherford's senior year, Krauss was a fellow at the Institute for Advanced Study in Princeton, where she was at work on her watershed volume *The Originality of the Avant-Garde and Other Modernist Myths*, which appeared in 1985. Weatherford attended a public talk Krauss gave on Auguste Rodin's multiples (in dialogue with a 1981 retrospective at the National Gallery of Art, Washington, DC) and the logic of postmodernism. Krauss had already published a version of this material in the journal *October* that same year as 'The Originality of the Avant-Garde: A Postmodern Repetition', which became the titular essay in the collected volume. Weatherford remembers her discussion of Sherrie Levine and the threat her reproductions posed to a long-standing model of avant-gardism. Weatherford raised her hand and asked why Levine's appropriation-based photography was art, much to Krauss's frustration. 'Can't go on, must go on' is how Weatherford summarizes the argument. Unwittingly, Weatherford had bracketed her education with mastery hallowed in the name of Picasso and hollowed out by Levine, who discovered in it only a gloriously unredeemed misogyny.

When she graduated in 1984, Weatherford moved to New York and entered the Independent Study Program (ISP) at the Whitney Museum of American Art. Artists in the studio program that year included Ashley Bickerton, Mark Dion, Andrea Fraser, and Glenn Ligon. Having been accepted for the curatorial track, Weatherford worked collaboratively with Joshua Decter, David Lurie, and Vicente Todolí, organizing and installing a sculpture exhibition for the Whitney's branch in Stamford, Connecticut. In what would become a recurring theme for many years, it was, as Weatherford puts it, 'me and just men',[5] even though ISP was hosting women in other tracks of the program at the same time. The program had by then embraced, more fully than most, the feminist interventions of the previous decade. As its longtime director, Ron Clark, summarized in 2008, for the ISP's fortieth anniversary, the 'defining characteristic of the program is the recognition that there are always social and political stakes involved in cultural practice . . . Many of the artists have been committed to a socially engaged critical art practice of a critique of the ideological effects of existing forms of cultural representation, such as advertisements, Hollywood films, or the high art canon itself.'[6]

Following the exhibition *Pictures*, organized by Douglas Crimp at Artists Space in New York in 1977, such a theoretical orientation as the one Clark describes commonly assumed appropriation as its method; an artist might forgo making, instead finding sources in extant images and objects. For her first solo outing at the newly opened Metro Pictures gallery in New York in 1981, Levine photographed a highly recognizable Farm Securities Administration series by Walker Evans. She offered the following in the show's press release: 'I am interested in issues of identity and property – i.e. What is the same? What do we own? I suspect auratic notions about art: "authenticity," "the genius," "the masterpiece," "the hand." When every image is leased and mortgaged, a photograph of a photograph is no more remarkable than a photograph of a nude.'[7] But *After Walker Evans* is only a single example of Clark's 'high art canon itself' being subject to revision. Others appear in Levine's related paintings: she mimicked specific exemplars of Piet Mondrian scaled to printed reproduction, while in her more generic checkers or stripes she also abrogated originality and undermined period style as such.

Levine's works became important touchstones for contemporary discourses around painting. One appraisal following Crimp and Krauss came in the form of *Endgame: Reference and Simulation in Recent Painting and Sculpture*, curated by Elisabeth Sussman and David Joselit at the Institute of Contemporary Art, Boston, in 1986. The show and its catalogue posed in relation to modernist painting a cultural revaluation rather than a literal stoppage. Referencing Samuel Beckett's play of the same title, the show, as David A. Ross explains in the catalogue's preface, drew on chess for its guiding metaphor:

> Endgame is a term which describes the final set of moves which will lead to the mating of the King – the ritual killing which (out of respect) is never in fact carried out – but the indication of its inevitability signifies the termination of play. The endgame is most often played with a severely reduced number of pieces, creating need for a subtle yet effective strategy based on an economy of means. It is a time for desperate measures when, fighting against the odds and outnumbered, you freely invent as you struggle to survive. And then, it's over, and you quit the play perhaps to start again, recapitulating old patterns to evolve a new approach to an ancient game.[8]

The medium could elude the 'end' by self-reflexively marking its own concessions. Even so, death was ubiquitous in contemporary debates about the meaning of representation. It is hard to imagine things having been otherwise, given the Reagan administration's malignant disregard of the AIDS epidemic, in health and social policies that abetted the burgeoning virus. (Ronald Reagan would not utter the term 'AIDS' until 1987, when tens of thousands had already died from the disease.) The question became whether painting could effectually communicate such urgent content.

This concern had much to do with the insurgence of neo-Expressionist painting: symptomatic of a booming economy and a solvent collector base eager to own virtuosity, it explicitly courted commodity status. Many painters identified with this trend maintained a posture of expressivity through exaggerated facture as a would-be correlate of the self. Moreover, they assumed a distinctly prelapsarian attitude in large-scale panels given over to adolescent sexual fantasies and hyperbolic imaginings of olden myths. These recuperative acts achieved the look of spontaneity and were meant to signify catharsis – the work of men strong enough to play at emoting and be rewarded for the advantage that they so freely exploited. Supporters downplayed what might be construed as suspect motivations and instead charted a triumphal transhistorical humanism that connected the whole of human creativity as founded in paint and regarded the topical avoidance of painting for photo-based appropriation and activist polemic as an insignificant blip in the longer course.[9] Where postmodernists like Levine insisted that they were coming to modernism too late, these artists claimed that lineage and its extensibility as their patrimony.

As much as some of the neo-Expressionism was packaging, so were Levine and Crimp similarly positioned against that other. Weatherford's experience of this field is more nuanced than the broad museum takes at the time in recognizing the mutuality

7. Untitled 1986

Oil stick and charcoal on linen on panel
35.6 × 35.6 cm (14 × 14 in.)
Collection of the artist

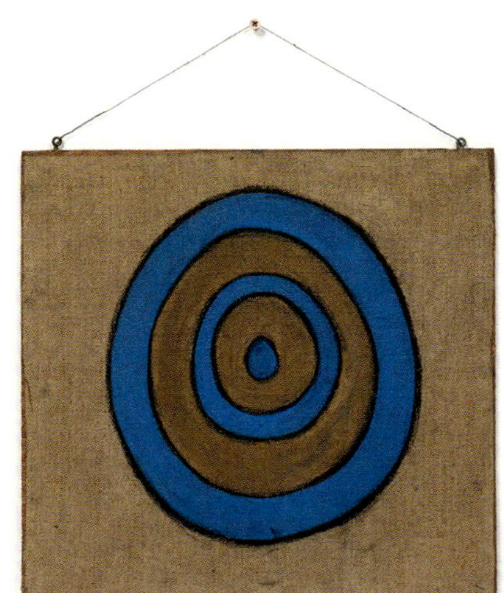

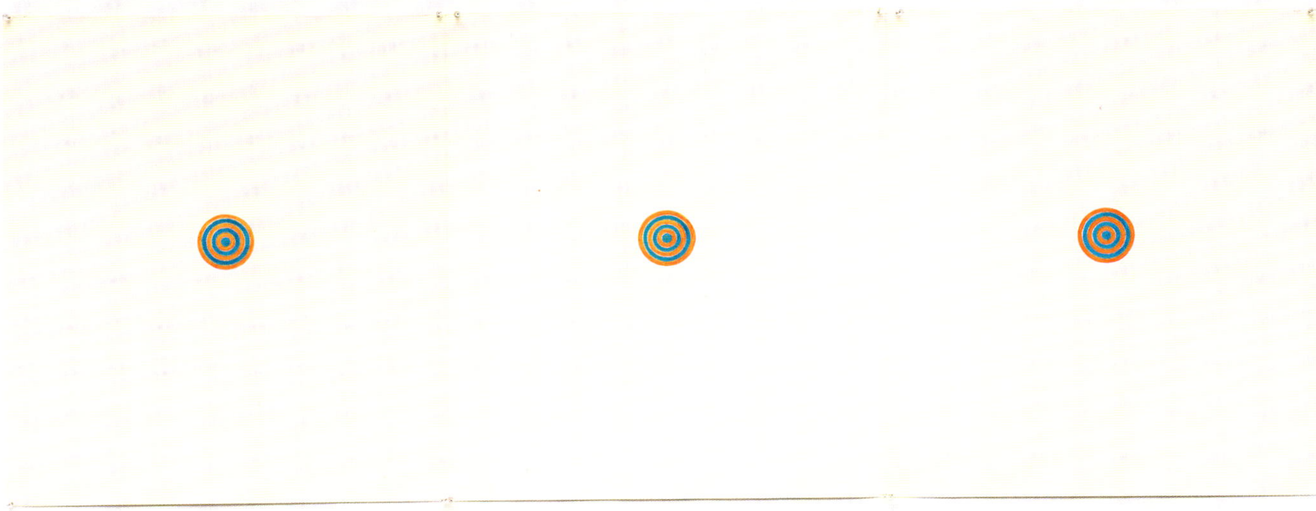

8. A Brief History of Time 1987

Gouache and pencil on paper
66 × 175.3 cm (26 × 69 in.)
Collection of the artist

of reciprocal self-definition between neo-Expressionism and the postmodernism of Crimp and Levine. Weatherford's earliest paintings from the 1980s posed neither the obviating foreclosure of critical, and often anti-aesthetic, postmodernism nor the opportunism of ahistorical revivalism. Instead her position admitted the pragmatism of someone aware that artists, regardless of clique, were all sourcing images. While Weatherford was at Princeton, Andrea Blum had helped her get a job working at Untitled, a famed postcard and photography bookstore on Lower Broadway run by photographer Bevan Davies. The store was empty when she began, save for the copious postcards arranged by artist or theme, and Weatherford read each book as it arrived for shelving – an exercise that made for a masterclass in the history of the reproductive medium. Even before the books filled the displays, with thousands of postcards priced under a dollar each, Untitled was a magnet for those seeking readymade material to mediate in their artworks, especially given the proximity of the shop to so many artists' studios. Weatherford names Jean-Michel Basquiat, Francesco Clemente, and Alexis Rockman as regular customers; Keith Haring would approach the register with postcards by the handful. Robert Mapplethorpe ate lunch in the window of the diner across the street. She watched him get physically weaker and Haring grow covered by telltale spots, and she saw a generation of artists around her die. In the meantime, she rang up their purchases, noting their selections. Arnold Böcklin's *Island of the Dead* (1880), a foreboding, Symbolist scene of a rocky islet, for example, was in high demand.

Weatherford began painting targets on paper this same year, 1984, while working at Untitled and participating in the ISP. The choice of subject matter nodded deliberately

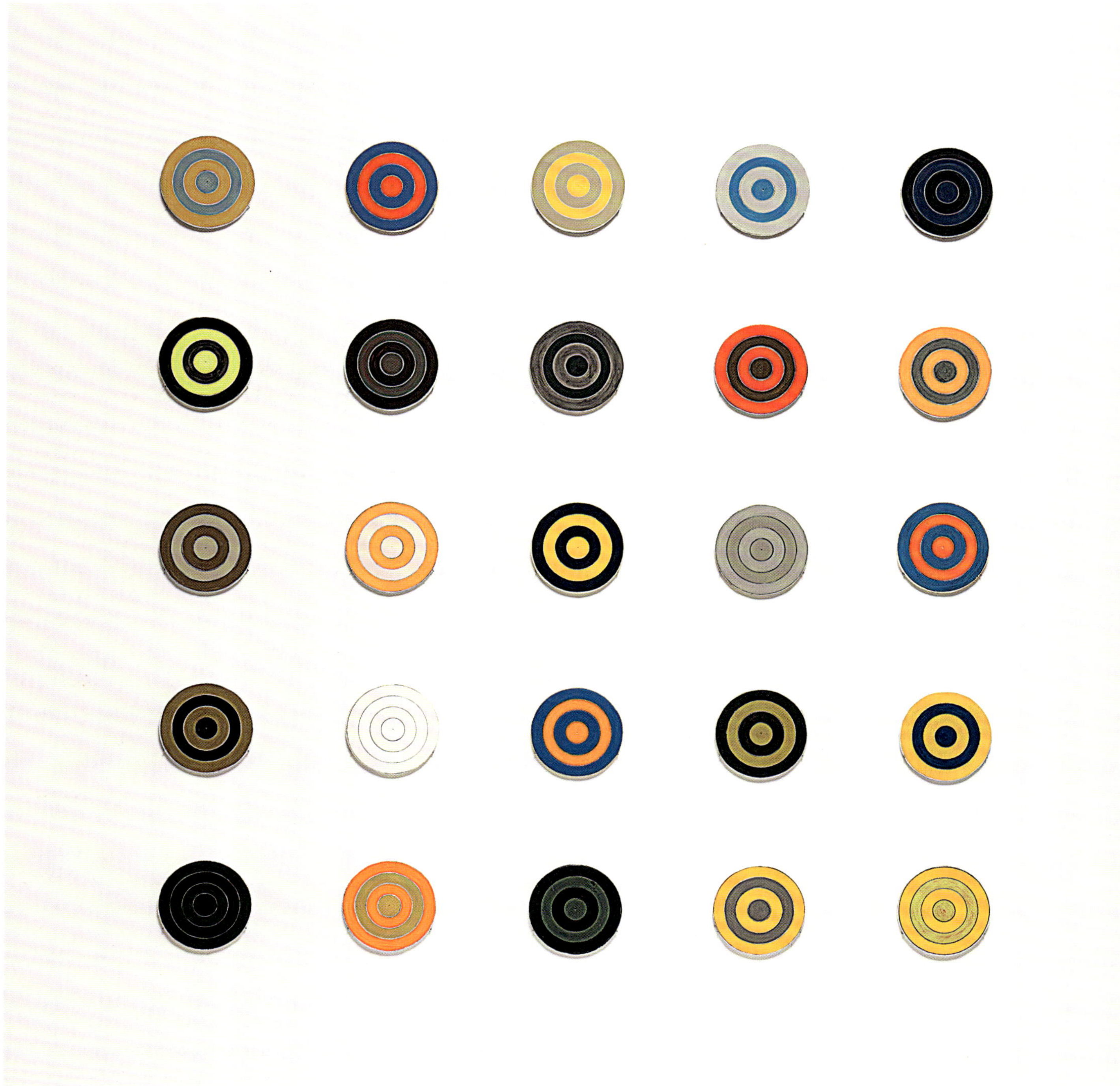

9. Untitled 1988

Gouache and pencil on plasterboard discs
25 discs, each 17.8 cm (7 in.) diameter, mounted 17.8 cm
(7 in.) apart; overall 160 × 160 cm (63 × 63 in.)
Collection of the artist

to Jasper Johns and Kenneth Noland, even as her handling of it confirmed the distance between herself and them. In her various inflections, Weatherford showed the target's connotation to be conditional on discursive context rather than altered form, since each obeys the logic of rings in alternating A–B colors, with a third color filling in around the target to the edges of the canvas. The target was a readymade on the order of the grid (which Weatherford also exploited in works like *Galapagos II*, 1987 (fig.10), one such checkerboard acknowledgment of Levine made with stickers and paint). She used it thus in part as a vehicle for color study similar to the template Josef Albers maintained in his *Homage to the Square* series, begun in 1949.[10] As she had with her childhood butterfly poster, she drew the linear outlines of the targets freehand and filled them with combinations of hues. In later works she would inscribe these circular scaffolds with a small compass.[11] Perhaps owing to Weatherford's use of them across a span of a few years, the concentric rings also came to serve, significantly, as markers of time and narrative unfolding through it, a function they performed far more effectually than could the grid, which Rosalind Krauss argued in a 1979 essay on the theme as 'anti-developmental'.[12]

As evidenced in works like *Natural Selection*, 1986, an aggregation of targets and botanical renderings (pencil drawing versions of Karl Blossfeldt's photographs of plants), and *Untitled or Voyage of the Beagle*, 1987, a piece comprising multiple panels, each emblazoned with a slightly higher-than-centered target, Weatherford was reading the work of Charles Darwin: *The Voyage of the Beagle*, 1839, and his 1859 summa, *The Origin of Species*. These texts contributed to her thinking about evolution and adaptation within a given set of means – issues that may relate to institutions of art, and to painting at that historical juncture specifically, even as they come to it from without.

Writing in 1990, Sam Hunter stressed differently how Weatherford's painting emerged from other media. Like Cindy Sherman's culling of B-movies or European avant-garde cinema, Weatherford's practice related to 'a moment of epiphany during a viewing of Hitchcock's film, *Vertigo*', when 'modernist form and a viable deconstructive critique for unmasking antifeminist codes of representation first came together'.[13] He quotes Weatherford's description of her 'origin scene':

> In the film Jimmy Stewart and Kim Novak are walking in a forest. This is a woman pretending to be reincarnated, pretending to be another woman. She walks up to one of the trees and says, 'I was born here and I died there.' I felt it was the perfect place in the film, where time and place become one . . . I had found a model for a time line. Then I remembered those Natural History museums of my childhood where you see a slab of a tree with the dates marked off on its rings, and there I found a great physical metaphor for the passage of time and how things evolve. Then I began thinking in political terms, how things in the world change little by little: You start here and you end up there, and you're not quite sure how it happened but somehow as a woman you've

10. Galapagos II 1987

Stickers, gouache, and pencil on paper
36.8 × 34.3 cm (14 ½ × 13 ½ in.)
Collection of the artist

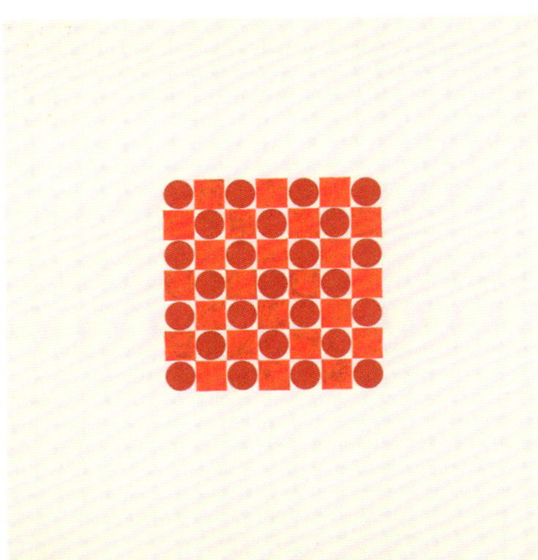

> been cheated out of your rights. So my paintings started out being historical time lines, and then I wondered why they couldn't go a step further and become personal histories.[14]

This move to the personal history is perhaps the most important aspect of the targets, even if Weatherford would not yet claim her own history as the basis for her (admittedly still rather oblique) subjects until 1992. In the interim, she painted women who had attained but also ceded agency, such as the model and photographer Lee Miller (*Painting for Lee Miller*, 1987, has a target on each of its four small linen panels), and men who had careers thanks to them (*Untitled*, 1988 (fig.9), is a five-by-five grid of gouache-on-plasterboard targets, each standing in for a Hitchcock actress).

As these last two examples indicate, Weatherford created surrogate portraits in various media, including the vinyl-based paint Flashe, which she used to make targets on paper in 1985. Resembling the look of gouache, Flashe scuffs easily once dried, its delicate surface like the nap of velvet, where a rub crushes the tiny upright bristles. Its fragility only adds to the appeal. It is, besides, a versatile and highly pigmented medium, and one that would become a mainstay for Weatherford as an antagonist to oil paint, which she ultimately eschewed for its pretension and historical baggage. (Acrylic was likewise rejected, for looking too plasticky, except in the first stains that she made, beginning in 1991, where she used it with raw canvas.)[15]

In the works on plasterboard, Weatherford underscored their status as stand-ins for likenesses through the addition of a name carefully typeset on the reverse, in an unusual font with dots in the centers of the *o*'s. The target portraits recall Frank Stella's *Purple Paintings* of 1963, shaped, non-objective canvases he nominated as distantiated portraits by virtue of his naming them after individuals: for example, a parallelogram for Carl Andre, a triangle for Leo Castelli. Yet more proximate are Felix Gonzalez-Torres's text-based datelines, which he began in 1987 (the same year he became affiliated with the New York art and activist collective Group Material). Gonzalez-Torres listed achronological dates interspersed with significant cultural and political events; he also completed dateline 'portraits', adding to the seemingly exogenous historical context items of a more private nature ('Ross 1983' appears with 'Black Monday 1987' and 'Berlin Wall 1989' in *Untitled*, 1989). In this milieu, the military target also assumed import in works dealing with AIDS – as in, for one, Donald Moffett's *He Kills Me*, 1987, a lithograph diptych with one half a pulsing orange-and-black target and the other a black-and-white photo of a smirking President Reagan overlaid with the text 'HE KILLS ME.'

However admiring she was of Gretchen Bender, Sarah Charlesworth, and Barbara Kruger, among others – artists who, like Sherman, were working in everything except painting – Weatherford came to understand media-based feminist appropriation as a saturated field. Effectively maintaining the logic of the chess game, she plotted out the next move. This amounted to her targets looming larger: she made scaled-up

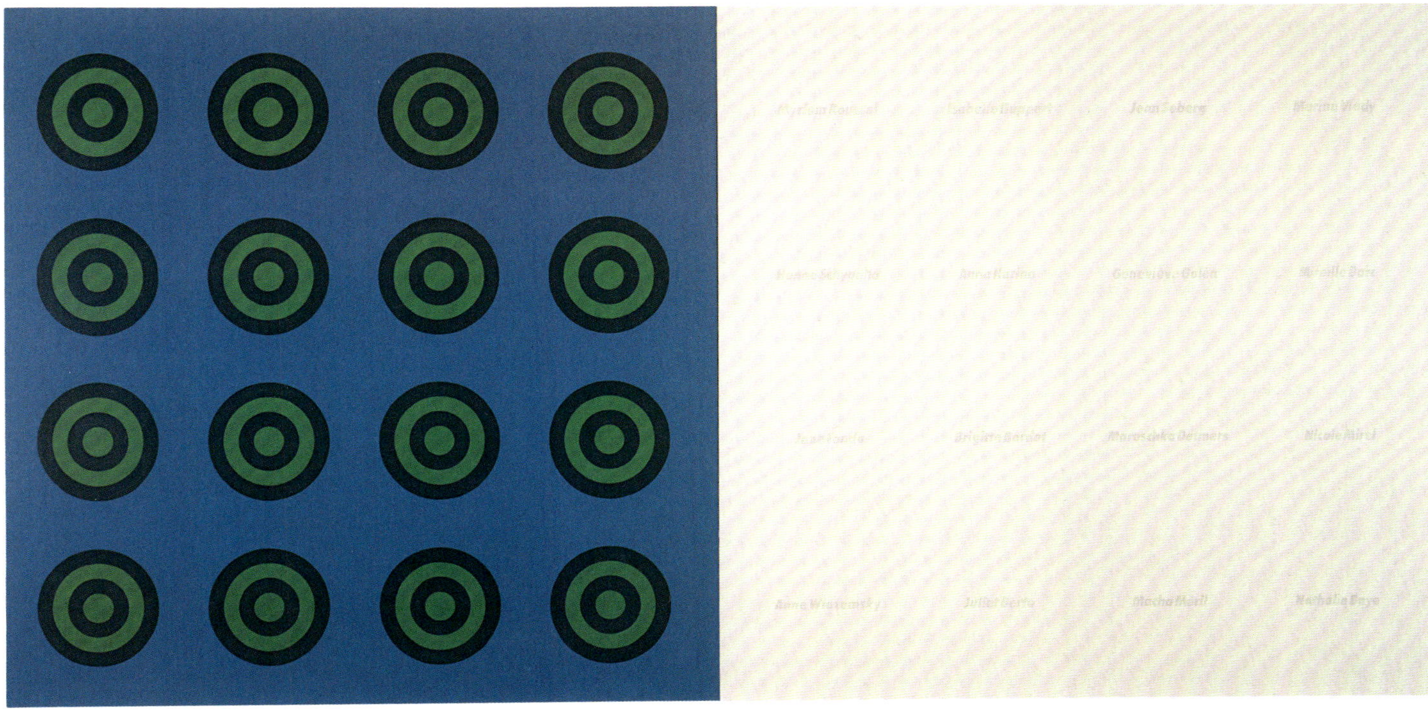

11. Portrait of Jean-Luc Godard 1988

Enamel on canvas
152.4 × 304.8 cm (60 × 120 in.)
Private Collection

abstract paintings in the heroic vein of Pollock's quasi-murals. (*La Traviata (Violetta)*, 1989 (fig.13), is around 150 × 300 centimeters; *Nagasaki*, 1989 (fig.14), is 208 × 208 centimeters; *Madame Butterfly*, 1989 (fig.15), reaches more than 150 centimeters square.) In notes for a talk that she gave to students at the University of Southern California in 2009, Weatherford wrote:

> I decided that the next logical move for a feminist artist was to walk straight into the house through the front door – to make big paintings. It *could* be a political move if one *considered* it *so*. So that is what I tried to do. Some other women had the same idea at the same time: Karin Davie, Jacqueline Humphries, Suzanne McClelland. (Kiki Smith had been working at it from the sculptural side – I think that when she is *closest* to Degas, she is at her finest, her most cutting.)[16]

In a public conversation with Katy Siegel at the Museum of Modern Art, New York, in 2015, she bluntly, succinctly recalled wanting to 'change from the inside'.[17] Thus did this decision to move from the page or plasterboard to the unapologetically looming support attend Weatherford's decision that she was a painter.

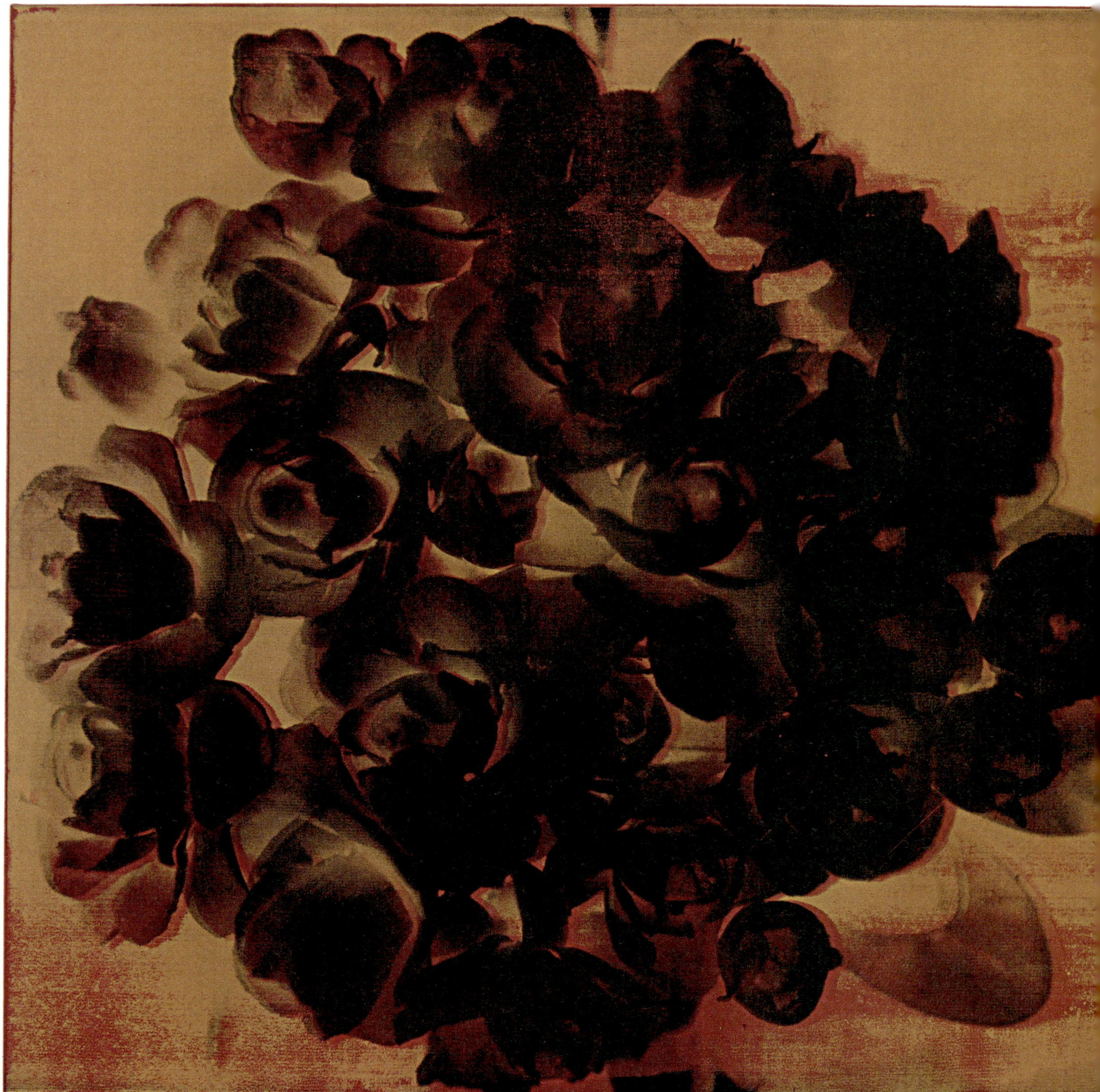

12. Camille 1989

Oil and ink on canvas
152.4 × 304.8 cm (60 × 120 in.)
Private Collection

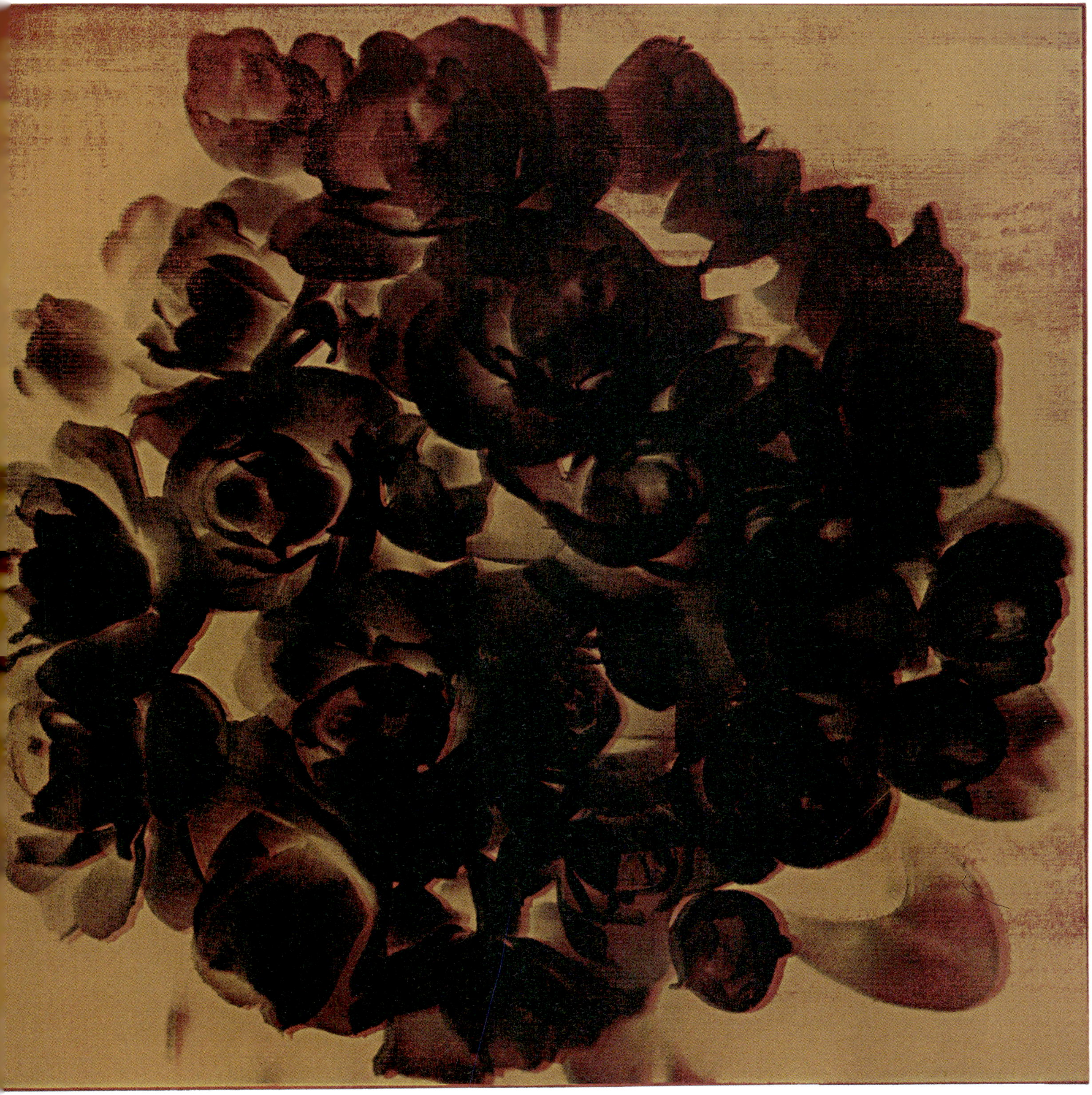

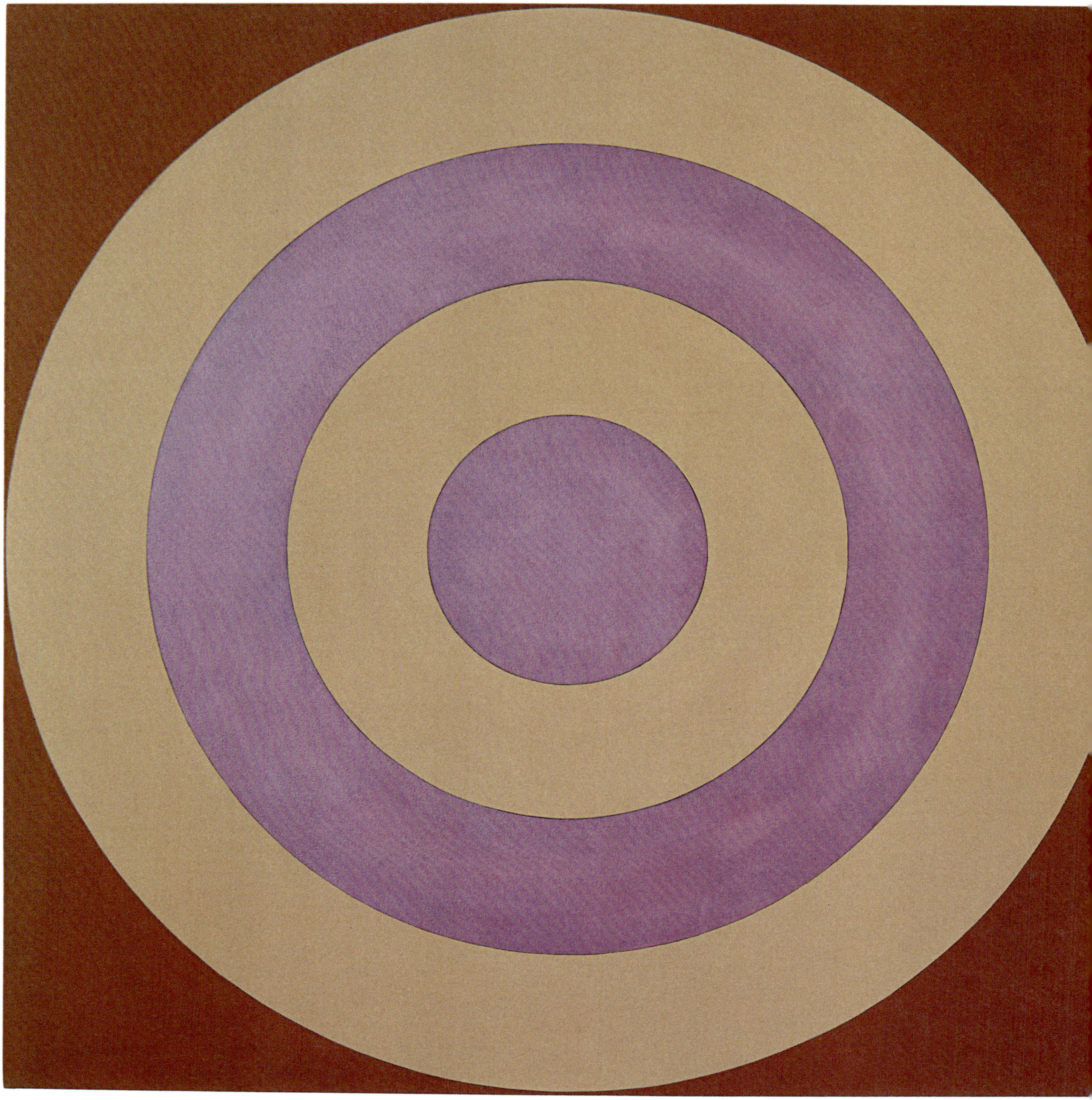

13. La Traviata (Violetta) 1989

Oil on canvas
152.4 × 304.8 cm (60 × 120 in.)
Private Collection

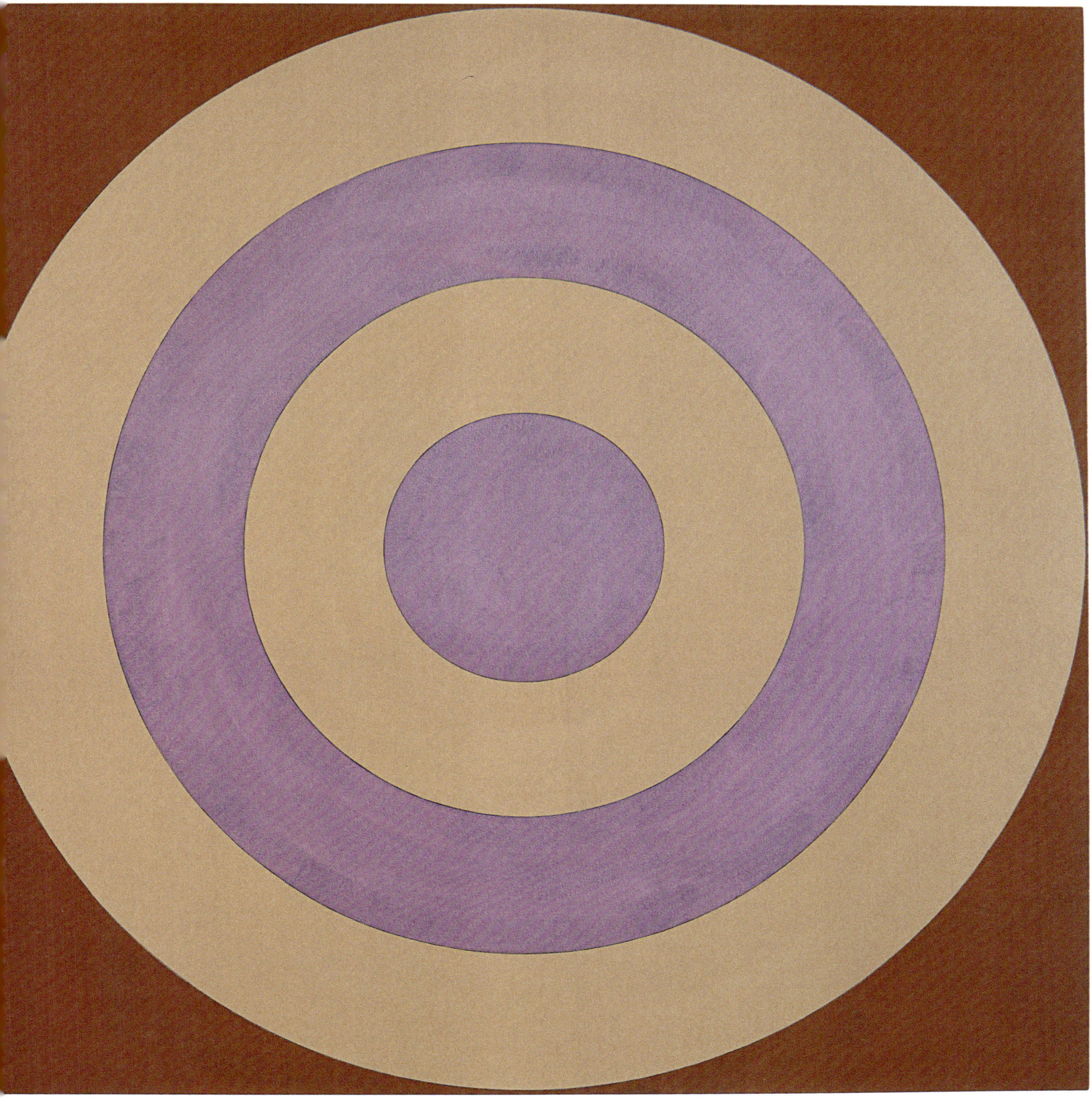

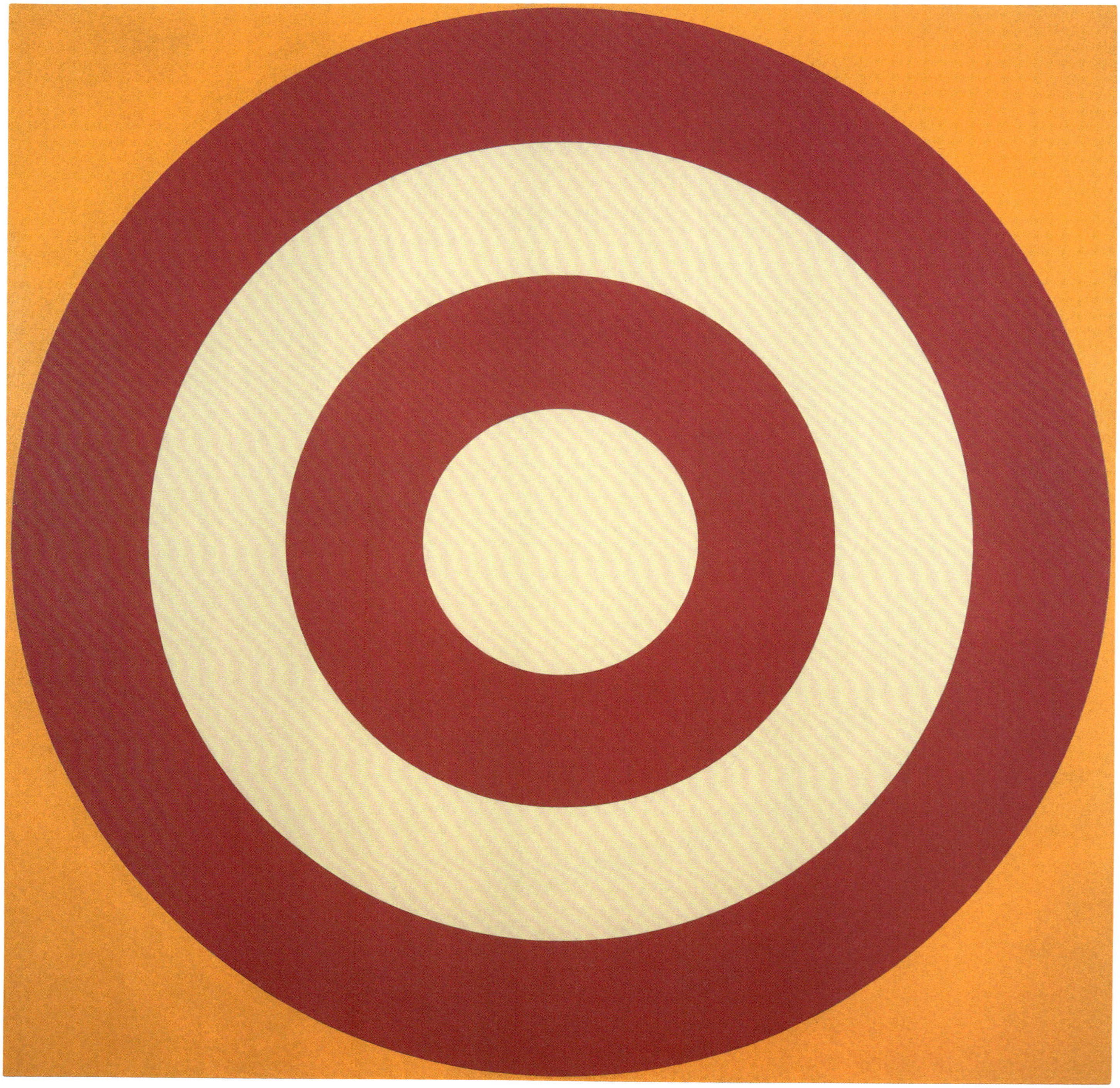

14. Nagasaki 1989

Oil on canvas
208.3 × 208.3 cm (82 × 82 in.)
Private Collection

2 Concentric Circular Timelines: 1985–1991

It is important to register that Weatherford neither identified as an artist nor showed her work until 1989, even as she manifested ambitions to challenge the legacy of American postwar painting by using and explicitly subverting its hallowed precepts. In between settling on the target and making it public, she led a 'double life' beset by relationship issues and other less than salutary personal circumstances, to say nothing of a general concern that her work was not yet good enough to hang. So she labored elsewhere. While in the ISP, she assisted Lee Jaffe, an artist who played harmonica with Bob Marley, managed the Wailers, and produced Peter Tosh's legendary album *Legalize It*. Weatherford credits him with teaching her how to properly stretch a canvas. In 1985 she started working at Paula Cooper Gallery, with Douglas Baxter, and Jacqueline Humphries took over her role with Jaffe. In a continuation of her time at Untitled, at Paula Cooper Weatherford organized image archives for the gallery's artists, including Carl Andre, Jennifer Bartlett, Robert Gober, Robert Grosvenor, Donald Judd, Robert Mangold, and Elizabeth Murray. Murray was one of the few to see her works on paper as they were being made. In Weatherford's telling, during a visit to her apartment Murray gamely climbed on her worktable to see them arrayed on the ground, from a vantage otherwise impossible within the small space. Murray also told Weatherford to read French philosopher Catherine Clément's *Opera, or The Undoing of Women*, 1979, which she bought at St Mark's Bookshop 'the next day and based the following four years of work on that book'.[1]

Within a year, Weatherford moved on to the Diane Brown Gallery, where she would be employed for the next three. In what is her first press mention, she is designated 'Best Supporting Actress' in a *New York Press* round-up of cheeky, yearbook-like accolades in their September 30, 1988, issue:

> They Broke the Mold. While dealers are off to lunch, making studio visits, wining and dining collectors, and seem to be 'out of the gallery' an awful lot of the time, the gallery director holds down the fort. It's a tough job, and the burnout rate is high. Usually, these days, the director is a woman – or at least this is our impression. Thus the title of this category. Mary K. Weatherford at Diane Brown (560 Broadway) is the most congenial, helpful, and non-threatening director around right now. She hasn't mastered attitude, or the withering glances of the high and mighty, she's always approachable, and friendly – but never a pushover. If you take your slides to her she'll probably say 'We're not looking at slides right now', but at least you won't feel like you've been skinned alive.[2]

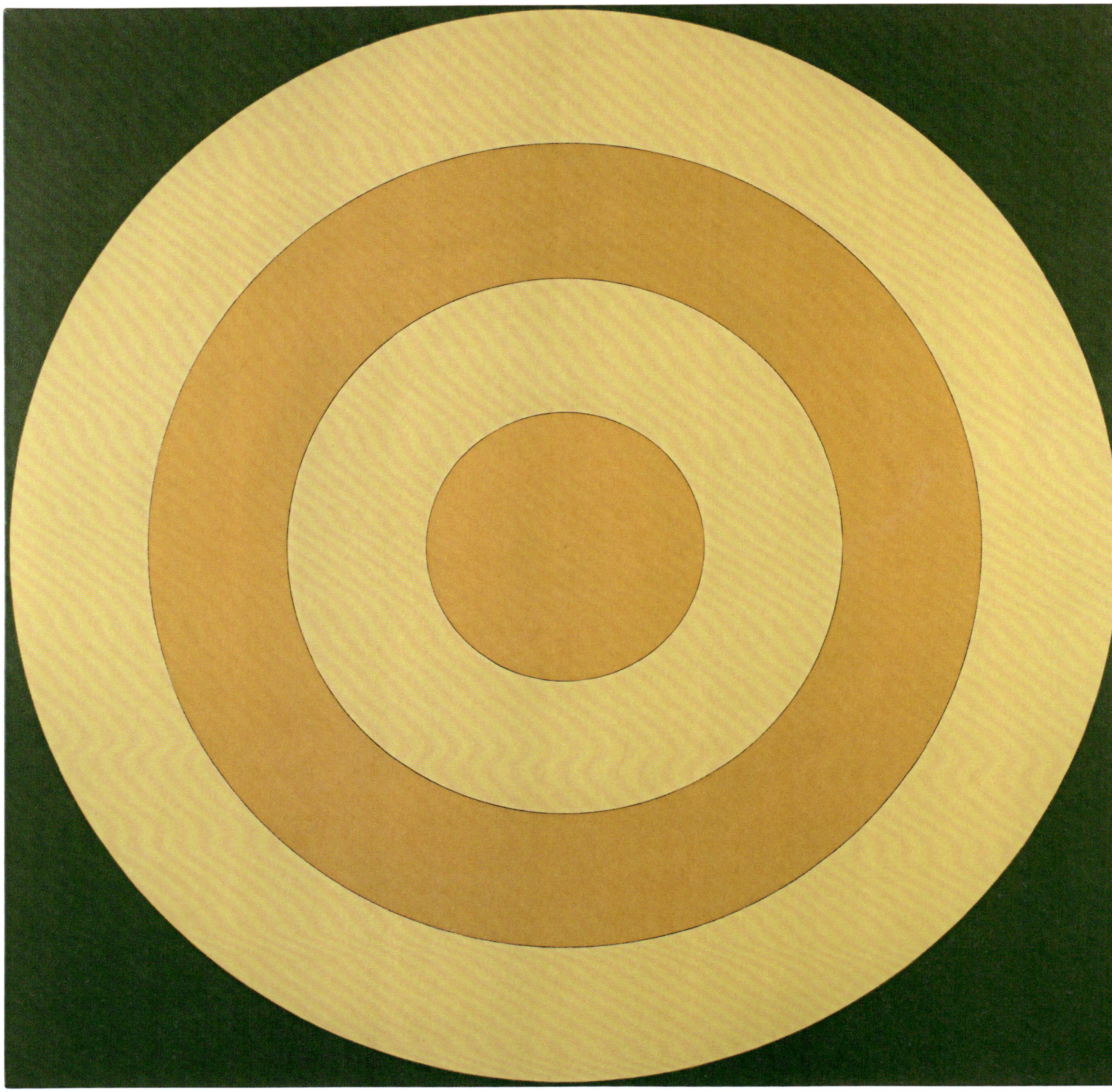

15. Madame Butterfly 1989

Oil and pencil on canvas
152.4 × 152.4 cm (60 × 60 in.)
Collection of the artist

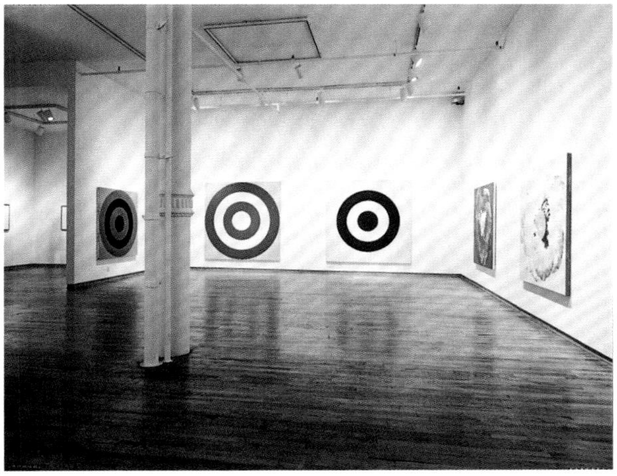

16. Diane Brown Gallery
New York
1990

Only in 1989 did she commit to working on her art full-time, a direct consequence of the successes of the previous months, which encompassed her moving into an apartment in the East Village, on Third Street between Avenue A and Avenue B (where she would stay until she returned to California in 1999), and opening her inaugural show at New York's PS1, where she presented paintings in a solo room. For years after, though, she still spoke of having worked in galleries, acknowledging that her perspective had been shaped by this involvement. In an *Art in America* feature in 1990, where Weatherford was one of thirteen artists interviewed by Lilly Wei and Cecile N. McCann for an issue on artists making money, she describes working for Cooper as a 'privilege', and comments on Cooper's professionalism, as well as on how hard Brown worked. She also – somewhat surprisingly in the company of an accusatory Carrie Mae Weems and Martha Rosler and comparably aggrieved peers, and against her own later reckonings with a far from benevolent system – justifies the sales split with dealers as being more equitable than some artists imagine because of the inordinately high operational costs that they incur, and notes the gift of galleries being free and open to the public.[3]

The PS1 opportunity came about because of Joshua Decter, who – aware of what she had been making since their time together in the ISP – offered her a solo room in his capacity as a curator there. Decter ended up leaving PS1 midcourse, but R. H. Quaytman took over his position, and Weatherford's contribution to *Special Projects '89* opened in January, downstairs from *The Secret Pictures by Hilma af Klint*.[4] Weatherford showed four enamel paintings on canvas. Two are untitled, one based on a large photo of Orson Welles and the other on a photo of Jean-Luc Godard; the directors' faces are inscribed with a grid of names of actresses with whom each worked.[5] The remaining two paintings, *Portrait of Orson Welles*, 1988, and *Portrait of Jean-Luc Godard*, 1988 (fig.11), are both diptychs: the left panels contain four-by-four grids of targets, while the right panels feature the same actresses' names in place of the targets – none too subtly assuming the position of marks for projection of another type. By then well schooled in Laura Mulvey's writings on the screen and the 'male gaze', Weatherford described the approach in a recent conversation as putting her 'heart on her sleeve under the guise of film theory'.

The same outlet that had featured her as a gallery girl only a year before also reviewed the show, and favorably:

> Weatherford's 'Portrait of Orson Welles' seems like an oil on canvas [*sic*] distillation of notions such as lost fame and namedropping. Old Orson Welles, seemingly big as life, is delicately doodled over by invitation-nice inscriptions of famous leading ladies' signatures. A second panel of blinking targets and fading white letters comprises a ghostly sub-script. Another pair of paintings sets up and knocks down the association with women that also gives Jean-Luc Godard his aura. What's in a name? Weatherford shows that with the media-men the slightest association with the girls is important.[6]

Celebrating Weatherford's emergence, all of the paintings of disappearing females sold.[7]

Later that year, Weatherford was identified as part of a rising New York cohort – along with A. E. Bourodimos, John Currin, David Dupuis, Gail Fitzgerald, Sean Landers, Carl Ostendarp, Chris Pfister, Richard Phillips, Jack Risley, Fran Willing, and John Zinsser – dubbed 'the next generation' by Alexandra Anderson in *Smart*, a lifestyle magazine with aspirations in the vein of *Vanity Fair*. Accompanied by photographs taken by Lena Bertucci on East Houston Street that June, the feature detailed 'treacherous times for contemporary art': 'media-based and appropriated art has worn out most of its welcome'.[8] Anderson also lambasted 'limp remakes of conceptualism' and pointed to the spurious exhaustion of once faddish neo-geo. By contrast, she pointed to Weatherford and her peers as 'independent thinkers' who 'regard art history and theory as a vast warehouse of ideas without subscribing to received hierarchies. And they share an informed and intense seriousness about the purposes of art.'[9] Weatherford is quoted as saying, 'I want to politicize abstraction, to make something visually pleasurable that will prompt social and political associations.'[10] Blown up as a pull quote, the declaration appears next to her portrait and an image of her *Manon Lescaut*, 1989, which features fiery bands culminating in or emanating from a vital red hole, one of her many bullseyes from that year alluding to archetypes of whores with hearts of gold.

On the first Friday of the new decade, Weatherford was featured on the cover of the weekend arts section of the *New York Times*. Under the unfortunate headline 'Fresh, Hot and Headed for Fame', Roberta Smith selected Weatherford as one of the visual artists and performers who made a 'striking first impression in a debut', or 'achieved public awareness' after a period of anonymity.[11] The occasion was a solo show at her previous place of work, Diane Brown Gallery, where she showed more targets, including some newly conceived versions layered with flowers (fig.16). (Weatherford had eventually told Brown that she was an artist; after a studio visit, Brown had bought a piece and offered Weatherford the chance to participate in a group show, which was followed later by this solo outing.) Everything sold there, too, despite the wretched cast of the melodramatic titles, sourced from Puccini's *Madame Butterfly* and referencing the opera's protagonist, her child, and the setting, Nagasaki.

Weatherford's success story was not only touted by the *New York Times*, but claimed by her alma mater. In April 1990 the *Daily Princetonian* profiled her as a 'rising star'. The subhead puns that she 'targets sexism' in work described as mixing 'feminist themes with a postmodernist sensibility and operatic allusions'.[12] In this, the Princeton piece continued the reception of the targets as turned to 'feminist ends' that Smith had suggested of the 'boldly scaled targets [and] silk-screened images of peonies with ghosts of targets lurking among their papery petals'.[13] Smith praised Weatherford's use of color and also her 'determination to turn abstract painting into a crossover art form, infusing it with both feminist consciousness and references to the performing arts that are fraught with feminine stereotypes'.[14] Still, where Anderson celebrated ideological non-rigidity in the piece from *Smart* magazine, and the Princeton text followed suit (if by stressing the critique), Robert Mahoney – writing in *Arts Magazine* – posed instances of superfluity on this ground, grimly appraising Weatherford's paintings as mere illustrations for a structuring but absent text: 'This generational bookkeeping banks on a knowledge of art and world history: it may be too rigorous for some. Its feminist tone may preclude Weatherford from becoming what she clearly is becoming, the next Peter Halley.'[15]

Yet, as it had been in Weatherford's initial exercises with the pencil and compass, the target remained a pretext for the elaboration of principles internal to art's history and conventions. Representations rather than functional devices, the targets motivate what the critic Leo Steinberg described as 'a heuristic event' in the works of Jasper Johns. The crux for Steinberg was that Johns's paintings could be significant as subject or form, just not both simultaneously. Johns reconceived the picture plane, annulling transparency and repudiating perspectival depth, so that interiority is anticipated but never delivered. In Steinberg's account, pictures such as Johns's *The Drawer*, 1957, a monochrome canvas with a drawer embedded in its surface, embody 'a sense of desolate waiting'[16] – for the cabinet to be opened, say, or for a flag to be raised or a target to be shot at.

All of which is to contend that the specificity of Weatherford's references matters; but so does their status in and as painting. Sam Hunter understood this fact from the first, and he promoted Weatherford on these grounds in *Emerging Art 1990: Commodities Corporation Collection*, a show he curated at the New Jersey State Museum in Trenton in 1990, commending her for managing 'to tread most deftly the precarious line between polemic and formalist requirements'.[17] In another piece from the same year – written for *New Directions* at S. Bitter Larkin Gallery, New York, where he quotes Weatherford on *Vertigo* – he describes her work, contra Halley, as acting to 'subvert even her most didactic intentions'. Here is the relevant passage:

> She also manipulates conventional male/female symbols in a personal manner: the target refers at once to a traditional male preoccupation with shooting, but it also underscores women's role as the target of male fantasy, that strange and threatening 'other' which he must reduce to a relatively powerless status. The target is also formed of concentric circles (a traditionally female sign, as are her repeated use of blood-red colors). An increasing ease and mastery in large scale form recently combine with vibrant color interaction and nuanced surface to subvert even her most didactic intentions, however. Today her art clearly sustains her declared aim to 'make political art that can be beautiful'.[18]

Hunter's statement appeared in the exhibition's brochure printed alongside *La Traviata (Violetta)*, 1989 (fig.13), two targets in violet and cream mounted side by side

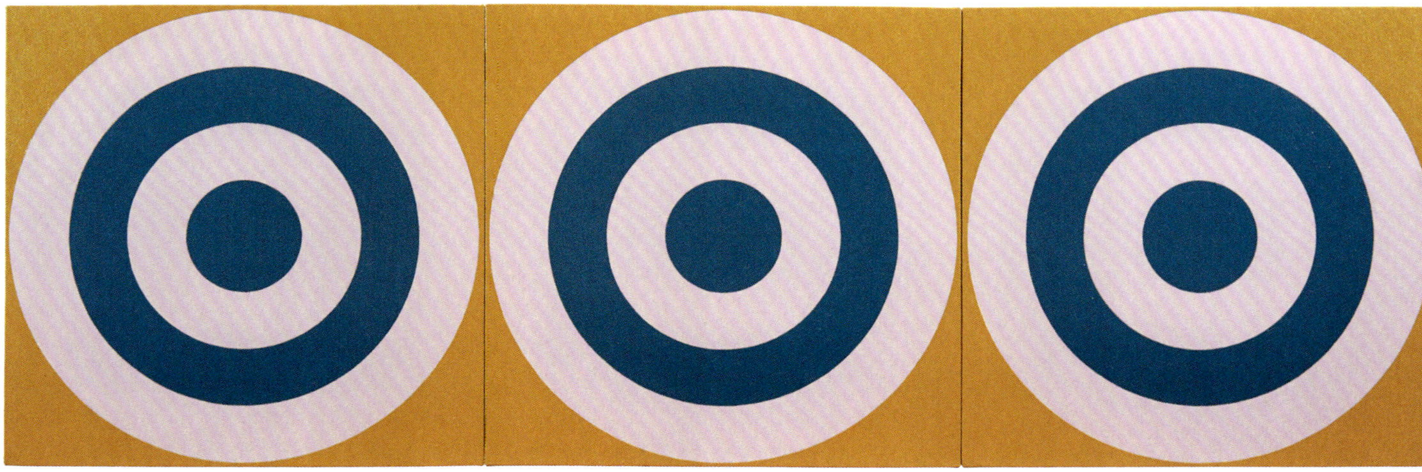

17. Three Years 1990

Oil on canvas
76.2 × 228.6 cm (30 × 90 in.)
Private Collection

with taffy-colored corners mixed from red and green. With this juxtaposition, one could not but note that the binary play Hunter conjures exists within both the namesake pairing of virgin and whore and the doubled motif: the pair are also breasts in the way that a conical shape for Eva Hesse is simultaneously exaggerated anatomy and abstract geometry. (Weatherford would extend this maneuver into the 1990s with her many variations of heads that also appear as buttes or phalli, and then into the 2000s with drawings and paintings of natural rock formations at land's end that might be illusionistic portals but that also, and perhaps most glaringly, expose gaping vaginal maws.)

By 1991 Weatherford was being contextualized within important group exhibitions including *Lyric: Uses of Beauty at the End of the Century* at White Columns, New York, curated by Bill Arning; the all-women group show *Plastic Fantastic Lover (object a)*, at BlumHelman Warehouse, New York (fig.21); and *Painting Culture* at fiction/nonfiction, New York, curated by Deborah Kass with Jose Freire.[19] The first was conceived as a zeitgeist show, playing up themes of symbolism and femininity. For *Lyric* and *Swan Lake Paintings*, a 1991 solo show at Galerie Marc Jancou, Zurich, Weatherford hyperbolized putatively feminine imagery, using black swans that she photographed at the Bronx Zoo with a telephoto lens purchased for the purpose, and also white swans from Central Park. Writing on one of these pieces at *Lyric*, K. K. Kozik noted of *Odette/Odile*, 1991 (fig.20): 'This print/painting features feathers wafting down the picture plane – a nostalgic, pretty image that takes a tragi-comic, even comedic turn when one recalls that the heroine of *Swan Lake* the piece references was a bird who was killed . . . and the feathers flew.'[20] Weatherford also took pictures of feathers, which she made into a five-foot screen; this became the basis for still other compositions, with a target put down first in paint, and then the feathers – photographic 'brushstrokes' – screened on top (fig.18). The feathers float in downy tufts, looking a lot like camouflage.

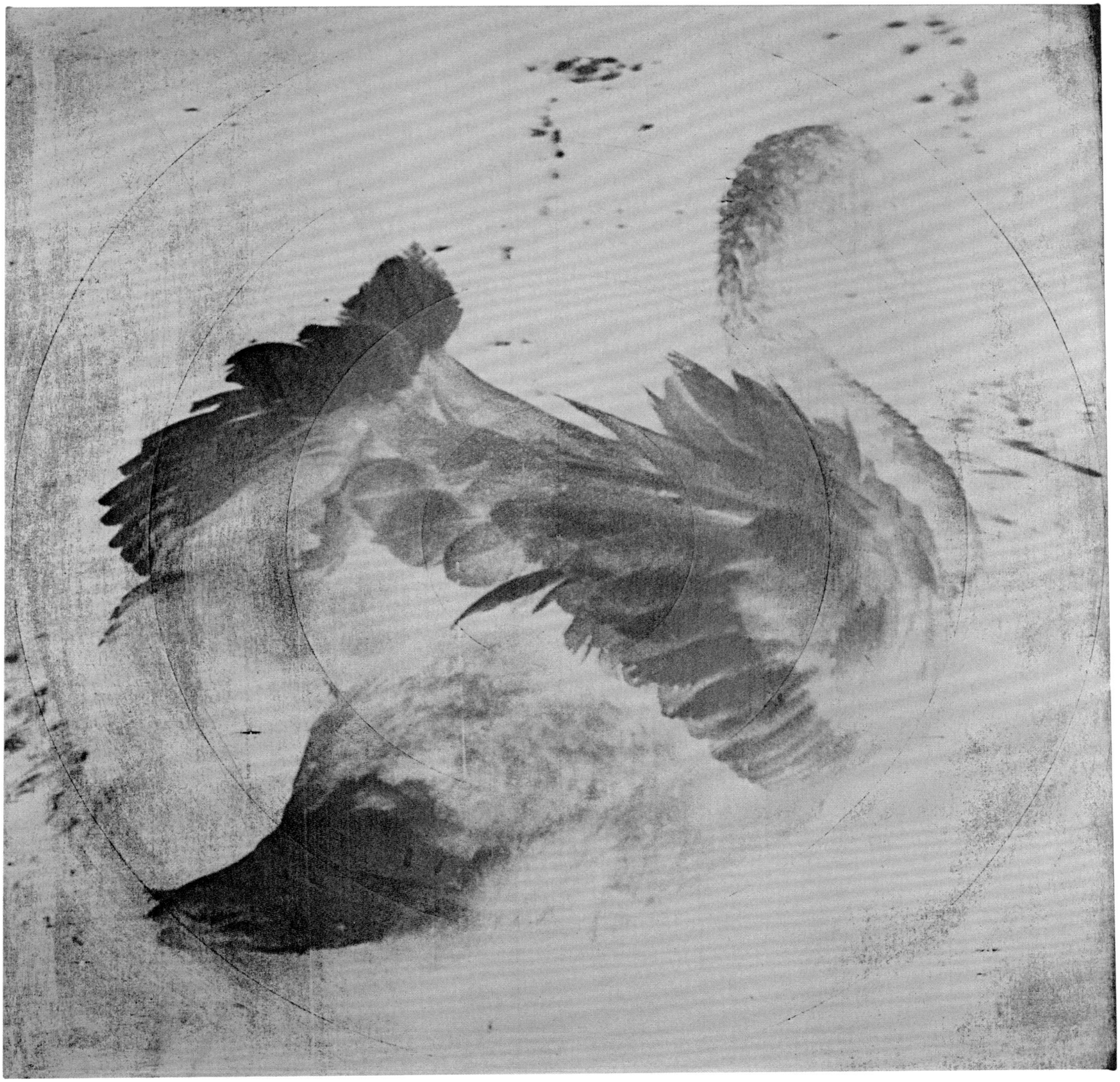

18. Odette 1990

Oil and ink on canvas
152.4 × 152.4 cm (60 × 60 in.)
Private Collection

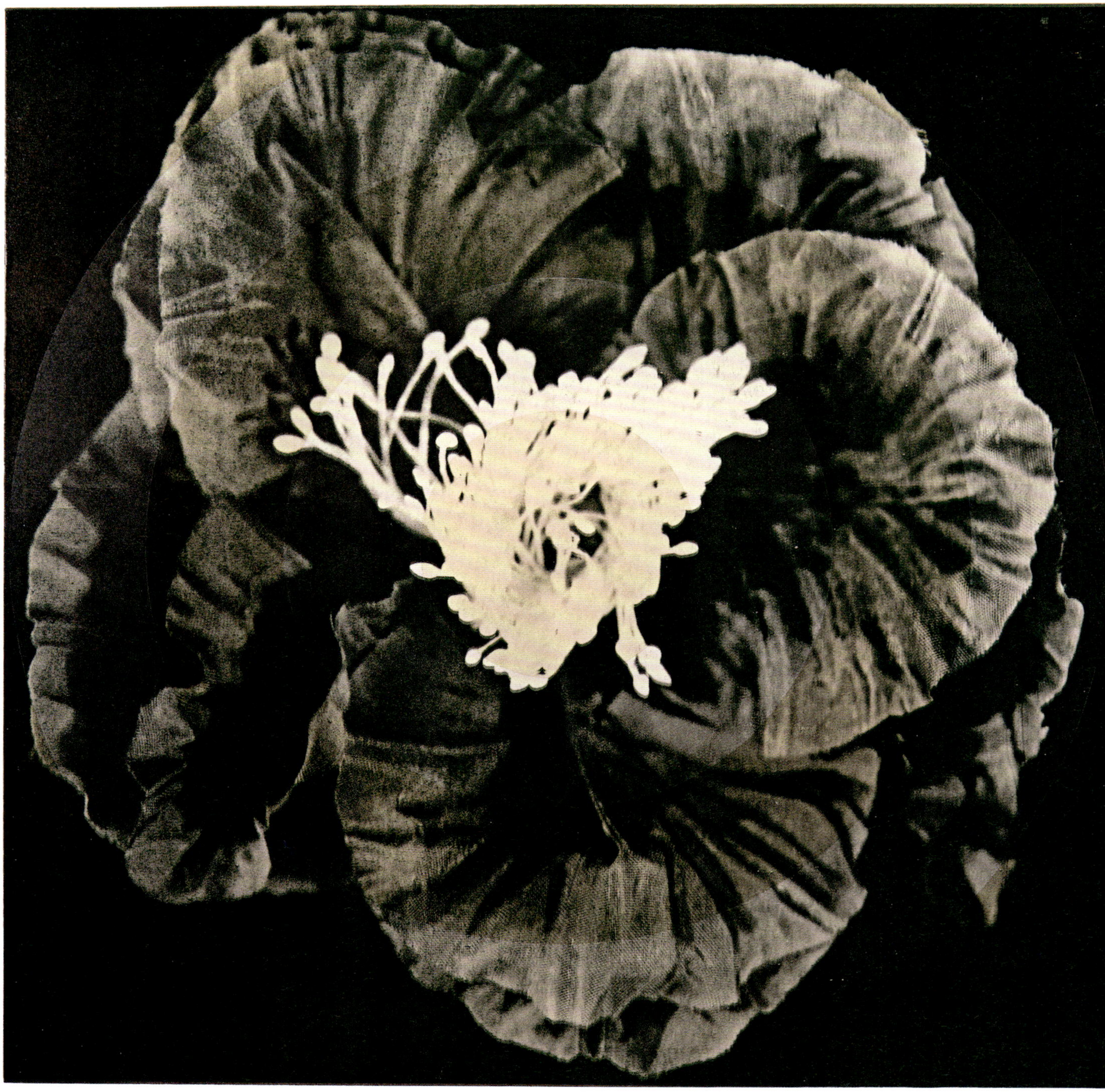

19. Cho Cho San 1989

Oil and ink on canvas
152.4 × 152.4 cm (60 × 60 in.)
Private Collection

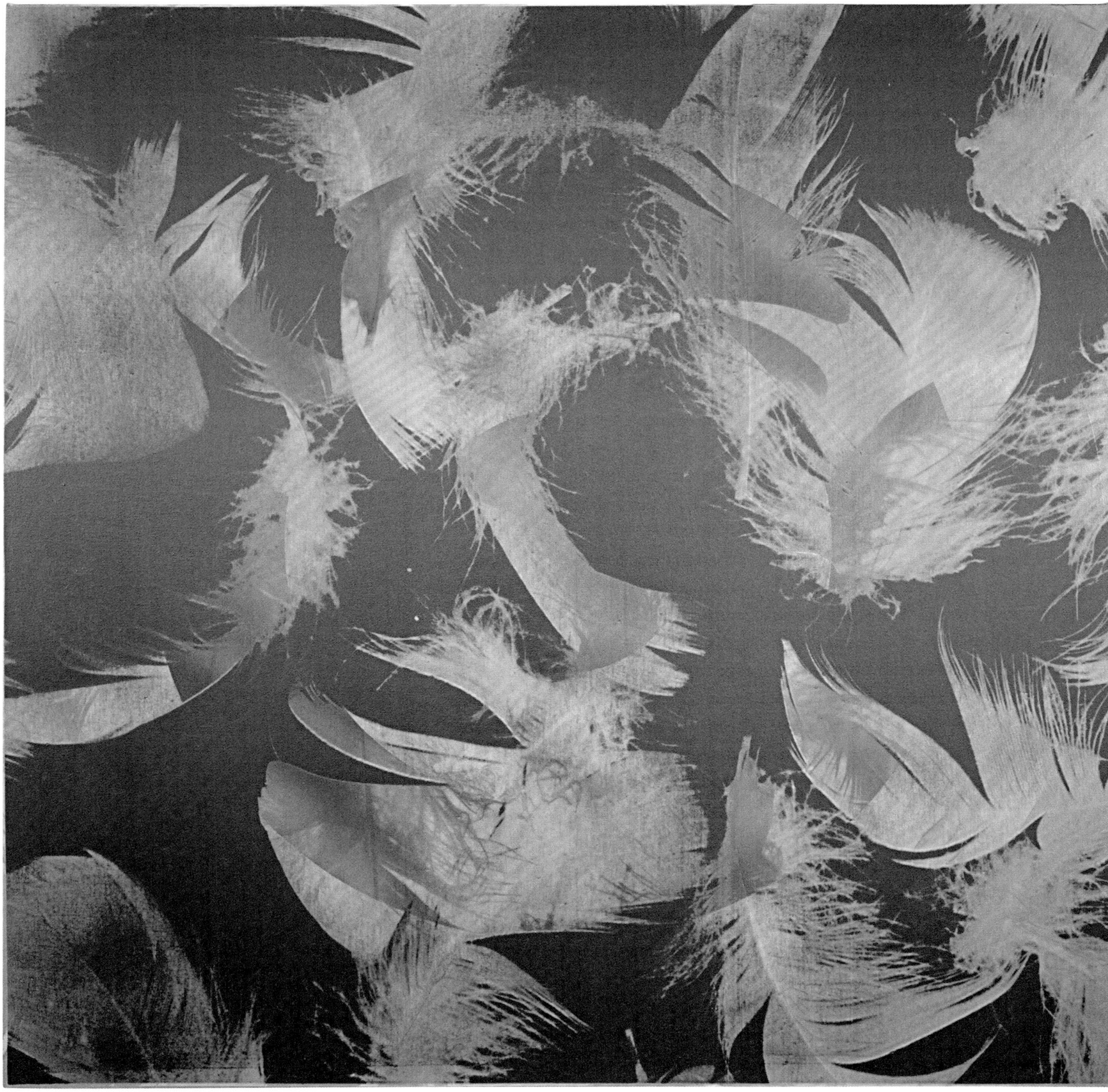

20. Odette/Odile 1990

Oil and ink on canvas
152.4 × 152.4 cm (60 × 60 in.)
Private Collection

Weatherford shortly realized that she could 'float' flowers as she had the feathers. Her friend Loring McAlpin (an artist and media producer, who was involved with ACT UP and was a founding member of Gran Fury) photographed African violets for her, and she layered these screened images over fields of color on raw canvas. The last target painting she made, *Violetta*, 1991, is a massive picture of double ovals at 183 × 335 centimeters. It was laid out using an ancient Greek drawing method with strings and wood lath. It shares its name with its sister painting, *Violetta*, 1991 (fig.22), a blue dyescape painted on one continuous canvas. The latter version of *Violetta* appeared in *Painting Culture* that fall, a group show of six painters (all women: Weatherford, Kathe Burkhart, Jane Hammond, Deborah Kass, Julia Wachtel, and Sue Williams). It yielded a range of responses. Steven Evans praised Weatherford's 'conceptual' painting 'based on a tragic opera' heroine for being 'subversive in a quiet way'.[21] In an article by John Zinsser about the moment's geometric painting and the 'increased attention paid to material concerns as well as to the emotional drive behind the work',[22] the author speaks favorably of Weatherford. Specifically, he writes that her 'reading of art history-as-text is an intentionally skewed misreading, calling into doubt the power structures that those images so readily recall'.[23]

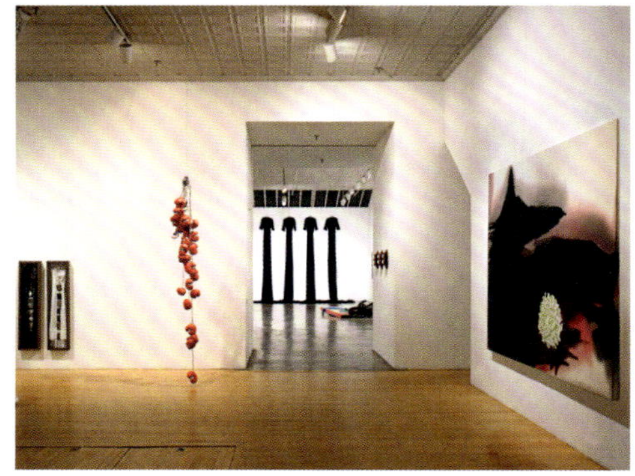

21. *Plastic Fantastic Lover (object a)*
BlumHelman Warehouse
New York
1991

In the *Village Voice*, Elizabeth Hess took a different tack, however, shaming her for appearing to want 'the privilege of inclusion into a men's club'.[24] (The extended passage reads: 'no one in "Painting Culture" (except maybe Weatherford, who paints flowers on fields of inky color) wants the privilege of inclusion into a men's club. These women are more interested in allowing their rage to give birth to new ideas. First of all, the masters must die.'[25]) Hess further lauded the rest of the group for resisting 'pretty pictures', framing Weatherford as an outlier in being 'the only abstract artist in the show' and also, relatedly, for abstaining from more caustic, accusatory articulation, which she regarded as potent exactly in proportion to the furiousness of its picturing.[26] Williams, an epitome, offered *Girl with Kitten*, 1991, a work with a tearful child holding a pussycat, both of which we see through a body become scenography: the spread legs of a hulking man, and none too subtly, his dangling balls and penis.

When an expanded version of *Painting Culture* traveled to the University of California at Irvine Fine Arts Gallery in 1992, Zan Dubin characterized it in the *Los Angeles Times* as 'one of a growing number of exhibits of funny, satiric or flat-out angry, confrontational feminist art'.[27] He wasn't wrong. It was also the supposed 'Year of the Woman', thanks to the election of a number of women to the US Senate. That autumn the art magazine *Tema Celeste* offered a special issue 'by and about women'. Suzanne Joelson and Andrea Scott affirmed that American society was arriving 'at a moment when gender politics are vital and topical, fierce and impassioned':

> In the United States, the recent Supreme Court revision of Roe v. Wade, the Clarence Thomas hearings, and the rape trials of William Kennedy Smith and Mike Tyson have renewed a sense of political urgency among women. In the

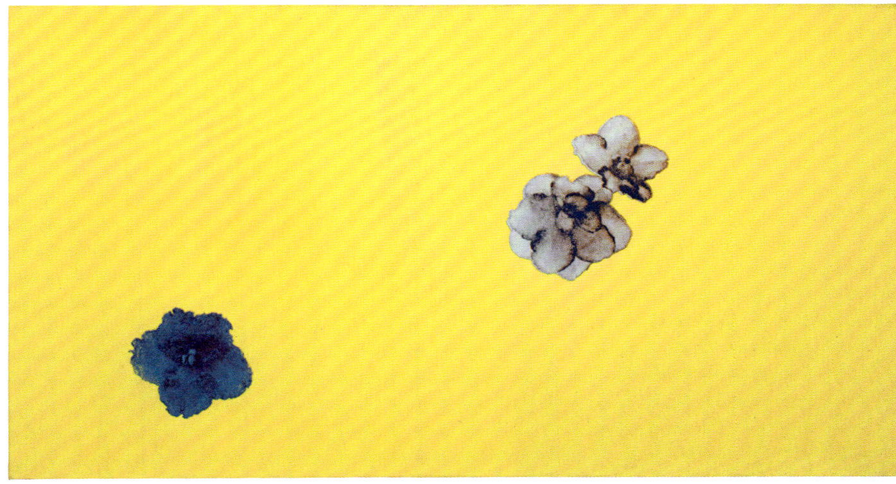

22. Violetta 1991

Acrylic, Flashe, and ink on canvas
99.1 × 182.9 cm (39 × 72 in.)
Collection of the artist

artworld the self-absorbed careerism of the '80s has faded along with the money that fueled the fantasy. It has been replaced by a call to action and reflection.[28]

Weatherford contributed a page titled 'Fleur du Mal'. Next to a reproduction of *Her Insomnia*, 1991 (fig.23), a large painting of rose stems extruding triangle thorns, she offered a set of caption-cum-prose poems, from which this selection comes:

> Her Paranoia
> The earthquake brought down our retaining wall and the backyard is poised to slide into our living room. I'm standing in the rubble, avoiding black widow spiders. Calling for Peter Pan.
>
> Her Delirium
> My bed is a bridge of thorns. It kindly supports the length of my shivering child flesh.
>
> Her Obsession
> My mother gave me a corner of the garden. Influenced by Wuthering Heights, I planted romantically: eight square feet of lavender, my own private heath. It bloomed like crazy. The little flowers were as blue as blue. Then . . . ladybugs. A few in the beginning, a trickle, enough to be wildly lucky. Then, hundreds. Swarms of scarlet locusts clinging to buds, to stalks, to leaves, turning the azure crop red. As red as red. As red as a fresh cut.[29]

These rubrics foretold a related show at BlumHelman Warehouse that Weatherford mounted a few months later, rather loosely based on the bestselling novel *I Never*

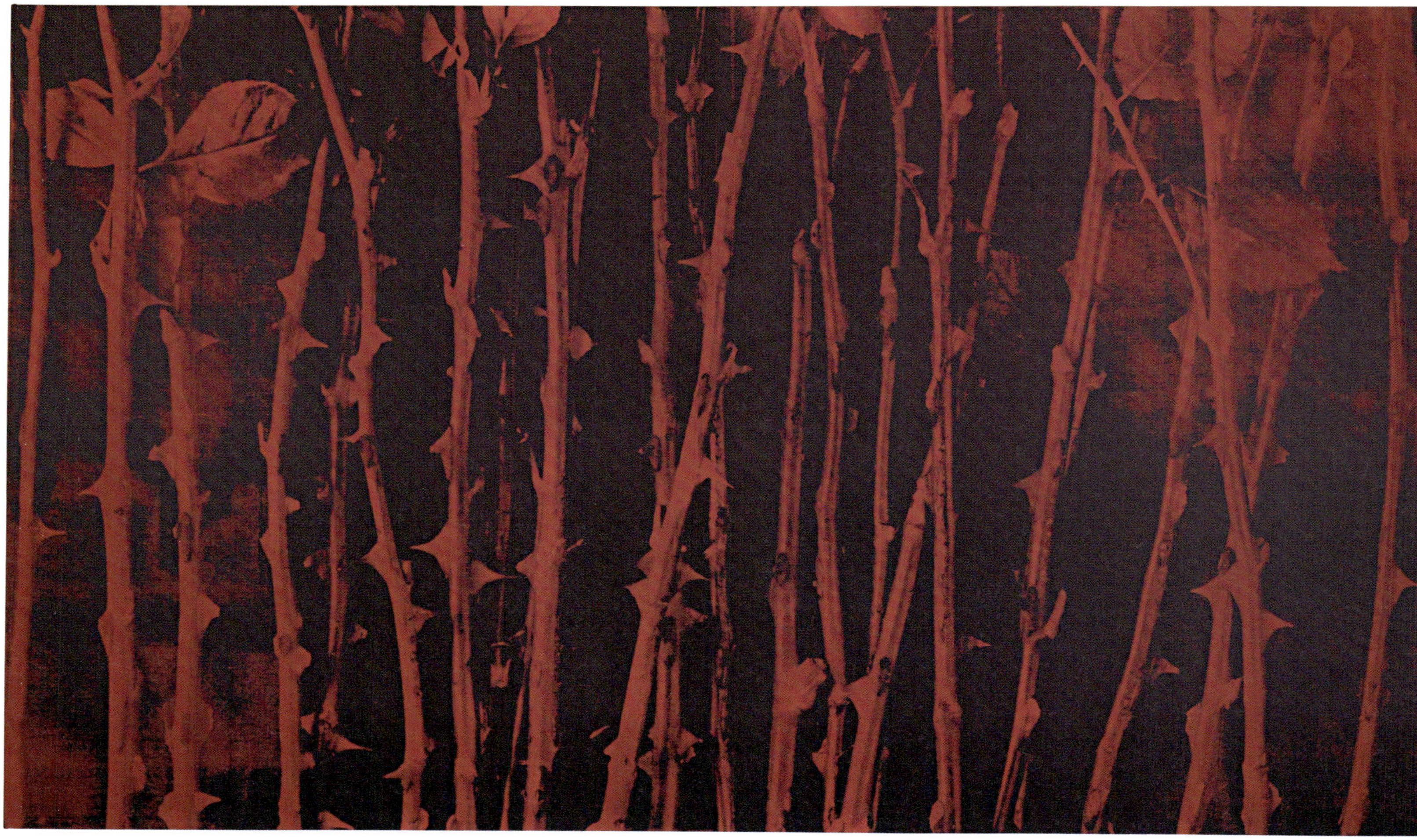

23. Her Insomnia 1991

Flashe and ink on canvas
182.9 × 304.8 cm (72 × 120 in.)
Museum of Contemporary Art San Diego

Promised You a Rose Garden, 1964 (fig.24), a semi-autobiographical fiction about schizophrenia by Joanne Greenberg (writing as Hannah Green). Weatherford showed large-scale paintings of parts of roses – either thorny stems or the flower – that took their titles from states of mind. Looking back, she pronounced that she saw no reason why 'you had to keep doing the same thing'. Indeed, after this show, Weatherford decided to stop working from external sources, taking a stance in opposition to many of her peers by more directly engaging with her own history and subjectivity. As she remembers it, the sudden realization from this time was to 'declare oneself author rather than reader' – something she justifiably claims as feeling 'ultra brave'. Arguably, an autobiographical if not authorial thread had been there all along in the many representative women who nevertheless – or precisely because of their status as ciphers responding to the conventional constraints of femininity with expressions of promiscuity or desires to let go – spoke so directly, if never exclusively, to Weatherford's experience.

Without pinning this departure from external photographic and literary sources on a single event, it does seem that a review by Ken Johnson in *Art in America* confirmed – if not precipitated – a shift in tactic. His writing on the installation at BlumHelman Warehouse exposed sexist clichés that recall the reception of Helen Frankenthaler's stains (they were the oozing menstrual blood to Jackson Pollock's seminal, focused ejaculations). Johnson cites the obvious precedents for Weatherford's work in a lead-footed way, seemingly assuming that their marshaling is called for rather than precluded by the remotivation of their intent. Weatherford's paintings, Johnson wrote, pose 'luminous staining à la Frankenthaler and Olitski, they present Warhol-esque silk-screened images of rose blossoms and thorny stems; and, in their conflation of an insane young woman's story with modernism's cool knowingness, they imply a feminist critique of recent history'.[30] Then Johnson shifts to meaning, using the works' titles to explain the thwarting of a 'strictly formalist reading of the paintings' since it seemed to him that 'psychological and narrative overtones kept impinging':

> In *Her Hallucination #69* [*sic*], a single rose blossom, pink with sickly green shadows, is starkly defined against a dark red expanse of staining that is consistent with Greenbergian optical space but also looks like a bed sheet on which someone has hemorrhaged; there's a suggestion of psychotic terror in the bloody wash and the psychedelically luminous flower. In *5 A.M.* [*sic*], four pale-green thorn branches stand out amidst a vast opalescent field of creamy pink which reads, in light of the title, as a frightfully transformed morning sky – an insomniac's nightmare.[31]

As Weatherford had put it already in the *Smart* spread in 1989: 'All these stories are part of the same big tragedy, the same social assumptions and mechanisms that deal with the undoing of women.'[32] Themes regarding the sociology of women and

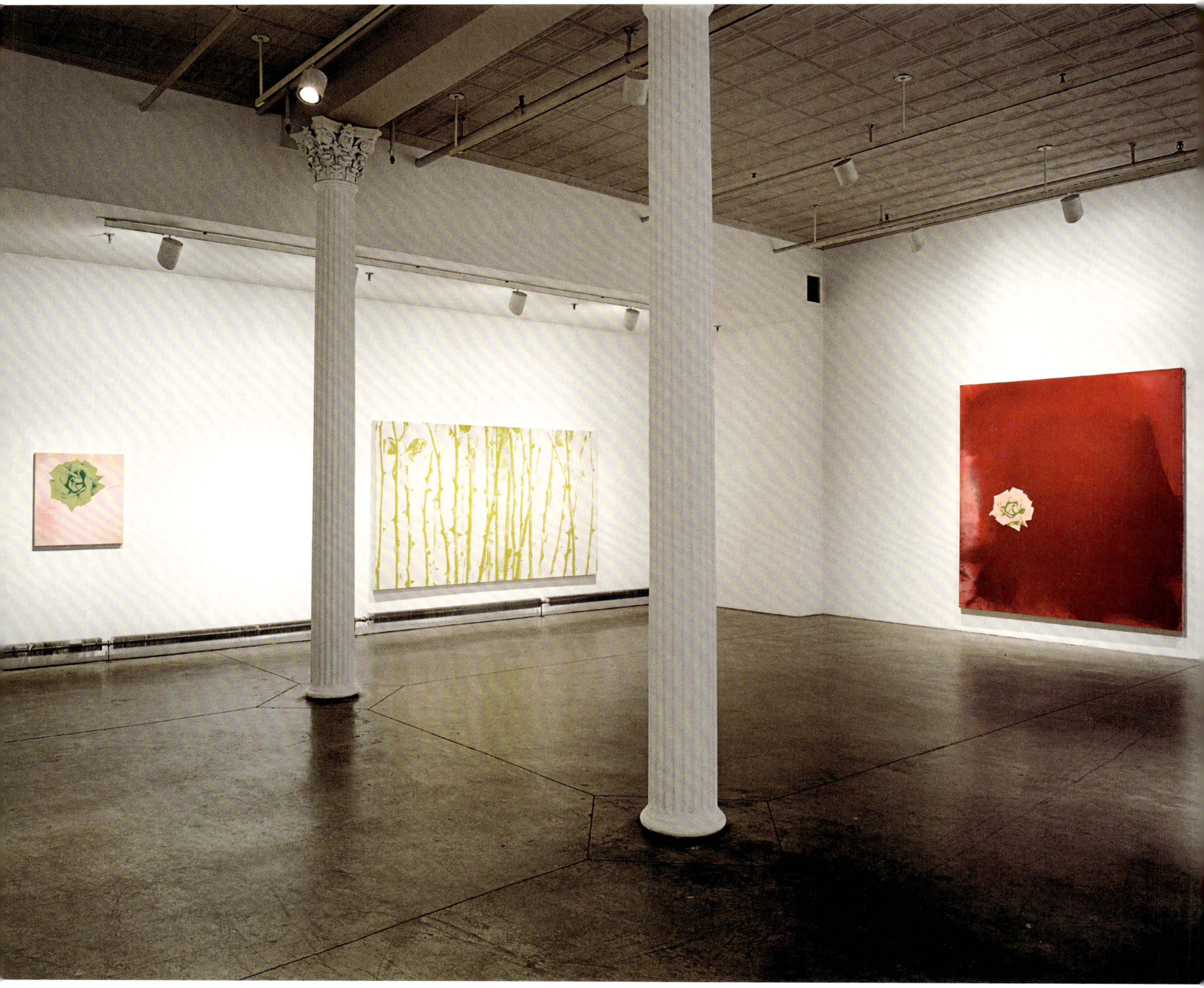

24. *I Never Promised You a Rose Garden*
BlumHelman Warehouse
New York
1992

madness obtained in the material and the conditions in which they gained meaning. This suggested yet another version of schizophrenia, wherein organisms come to resemble their environment, as Roger Caillois framed the issue of unintelligibility between figure and ground in his 1935 'Mimicry and Legendary Psychasthenia' (republished in *October* in 1984, where Weatherford first encountered it).[33] Her response was to make excessively, aggressively feminine work – massive in size, bedazzled with flowers configured like sex organs that could not be domesticated. Johnson may not have understood what she was after, but soon enough artists including Monique Prieto and Laura Owens did.

Within a year, feminism was being marketed in the guise of the 'bad girls' phenomenon, a moniker bestowed upon the likes of painters Cecily Brown and Sue Williams and trumpeted in exhibitions including *Bad Girls* at the Institute of Contemporary Arts, London, in 1993, and *Bad Girls* and *Bad Girls West*, respectively, at the New Museum, New York, and the Wight Gallery, University of California, Los Angeles, both in 1994. As Jan Avgikos lamented in *Artforum*, these shows traded on a 'girls just wanna have fun' mentality;[34] the problem for her was that this 'irreverent, anti-ideological, nondoctrinaire, nondidactic, unpolemical and thoroughly unladylike' work (this in the words of Marcia Tanner, the curator of *Bad Girls West*) 'not only trivializes work by women artists, but signals the death knell of a highly diversified movement that finds itself clumsily packaged and misunderstood all over again'.[35]

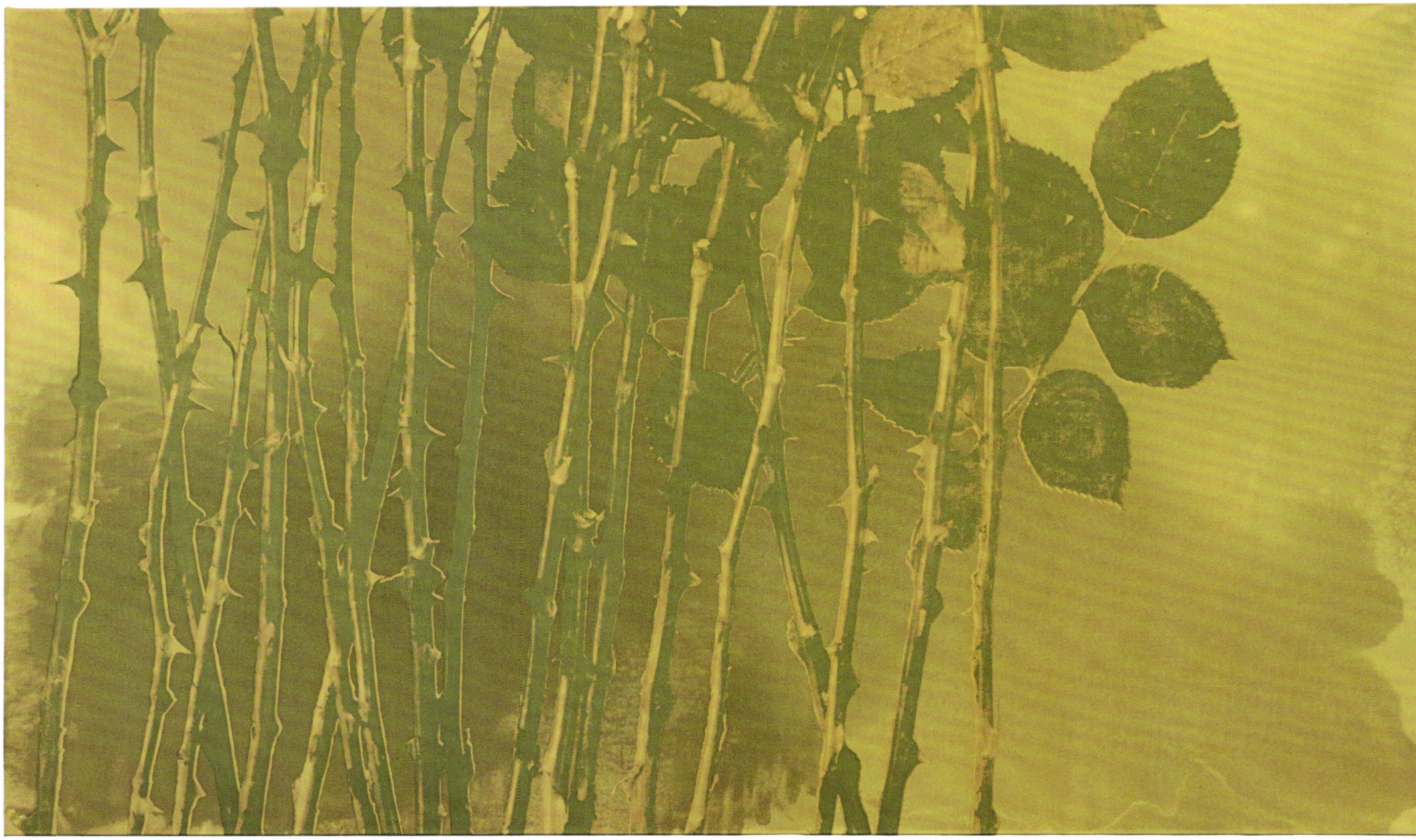

25. Emerald City 1992

Flashe, acrylic, and ink on canvas
182.9 × 304.8 cm (72 × 120 in.)
Collection of the artist

3 Stains and Starfish: The 1990s

Even as Weatherford cultivated 'political art', she maintained, as a correlate to the formal intentions discussed above, 'attention to surface and its control', as a reviewer noted at the time.[1] This focus was the common denominator that survived a change of style from the crisply delineated targets to the fanning, inky veils of the early stains, like *Third Riddle*, 1991. In this move – one not unrelated to her getting sober in 1992 – she exchanged an image of control, in the motif of the target, for one that pictorialized a process of assertion over recalcitrant material. This new imaging proved technically tricky to achieve, requiring Weatherford to juggle water tension, the subtle magnetic pull of the stretcher bars, and persistent calculations about how much sizing to wash out of the canvas. Although liquid acrylic emulsion can be diluted in water, it is hardly simple in practice to get intense stained color. In creating suffusions of pink, for example, she found that the red and white would separate. This complexity in particular necessitated Weatherford's working with the chemists at Golden Artist Colors to create something that they subsequently dubbed 'Weatherford white', a liquid white acrylic formulated to cling to other colors. Poured thinly, the specialty white was used to create the blushing rose pinks of *5:00 a.m.*, 1992. Poured without dilution, it would crack, an effect Weatherford later embraced with *Blue Night Moth*, 1995 (fig.35), and *My Dalí*, 1996 (fig.37).

As she began getting deeper into staining as a technique, Weatherford also began phasing out silk-screening from her works, a concession to expense and exhaustion of a technical mode, but also to make possible a different 'attention to surface' than the screen permitted. She started in 1992 to paste glued items – what she calls 'interruptions' to distinguish them from the stickers of the earlier checkerboard grids – onto the painted surface, first photocopies and photocopy transfers that artist Lecia Dole-Recio taught her to make around 1993 (when she was on break from the Rhode Island School of Design and worked for a short time as Weatherford's intern at her Fourteenth Street studio[2]), and then, in 1994, actual seashells and sponges. The painting thus became a ground for collage. The first giant violets riding on deliquescent stained-canvas beds (fig.27) were painted with Flashe and then silk-screened on top for added dimension; soon came chrysanthemums. Set against the picture plane, they hover in midair, but they also compromise the work's depth by fixing the surface as not just parallel to, but so forthrightly on, the physical plane where the space of illusion is simultaneously born and thwarted. This would be actualized differently in the methods thereafter, the pasting of discrete stuff to the surface. In all cases, though, Weatherford deftly conjured both the metaphoric window of painting operative since Leon Battista Alberti's foundational treatise and the modernist refusal of its promise of recessional space. Despite Clement Greenberg's theorizations that stains cancel interiority, being both on and of the flat surface, Weatherford demonstrated the stain's equal potential for penetration.

Yet the transparency fundamental to the Western pictorial tradition – the fictive realm that Zeuxis mastered by painting grapes so realistic that birds supposedly flocked to taste them – is also that of the sliding glass doors of her adolescent tract home in San Diego. An industry opportunistically sprang up alongside them to supply decorative stickers for the hazardous glazing, liable to being walked through when shut, so seamlessly and to such confounding effect did their wide panes integrate interior and beyond (especially in the Case Study Houses that were the progenitors of so much modernist-inspired domestic architecture throughout the region). In this surprising equivalence, Weatherford acknowledges what difference an orientation from the West Coast achieves, how it might reframe tenets of European origin recoded as orthodoxy in New York. Weatherford's 'stickers' are site-specific articulations of an expulsion from pictorial paradise, a strategy of blocking access to a pictorial beyond that she maintained from this point on: in her subsequent paintings of brick walls, vines, and rocks that blot the horizon, and finally in her most recent paintings with neon rods and electrical cords casting deep shadows, she likewise accomplishes the seduction of illusionism's promise precisely to refuse it.

The progression that Weatherford went through, from pasted paper to the painting as ground for collaged elements, happened alongside a diminishing of size after her BlumHelman Warehouse show. This shift owes something to her moving her practice in 1993 from her studio at Fourteenth Street and Ninth Avenue into her apartment, a product of escalating rents and changing circumstances that also saw the end of the sloshing stains for something tidier. Many works became small enough to hold in a hand or two, secular devotional objects that recall the precious interior world contained within the tight enclosure of a Joseph Cornell box. They 'got transcendental', as she puts it, under the influence, too, of Charles Burchfield and Arthur Dove, and especially Agnes Pelton, the painter who sought animating energy in the high desert, and who embraced numerology, astrology, and the presence of auras, which she represented in beaming spheres and ecstatic plumes of irradiating light.

The last works she made in the Fourteenth Street studio launched an extended group of lepidoptera made mostly from 1993 to 1995. (A few outliers came later, with *Blue Night Moth* also serving as a harbinger for the nocturnes that would become omnipresent in Weatherford's oeuvre, both as a subject itself and via the neon elements, a proxy for signage that comes on after dusk.) A folder that Weatherford saved preserves source images from this time, including pages from *American Horticulturist*, licensed photographic reproductions from the collections of the American Museum of Natural History, and other clippings, revealing models that she abstracted into more schematic saturations of near-monochromatic wings in the

26. Agnes Pelton
Translation 1931

Oil on canvas
50.8 × 61 cm (20 × 24 in.)
Courtesy Pace Gallery, New York

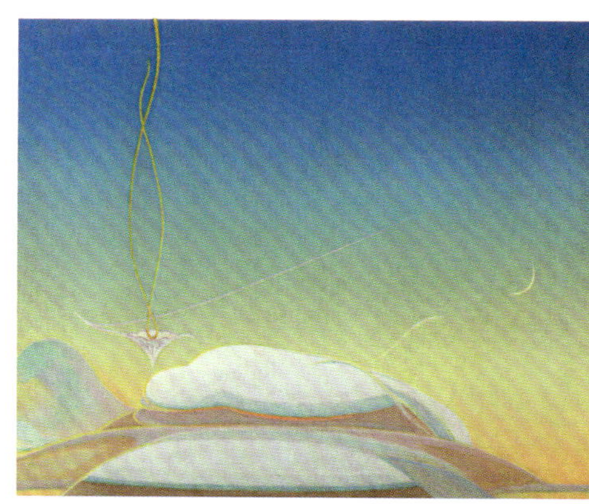

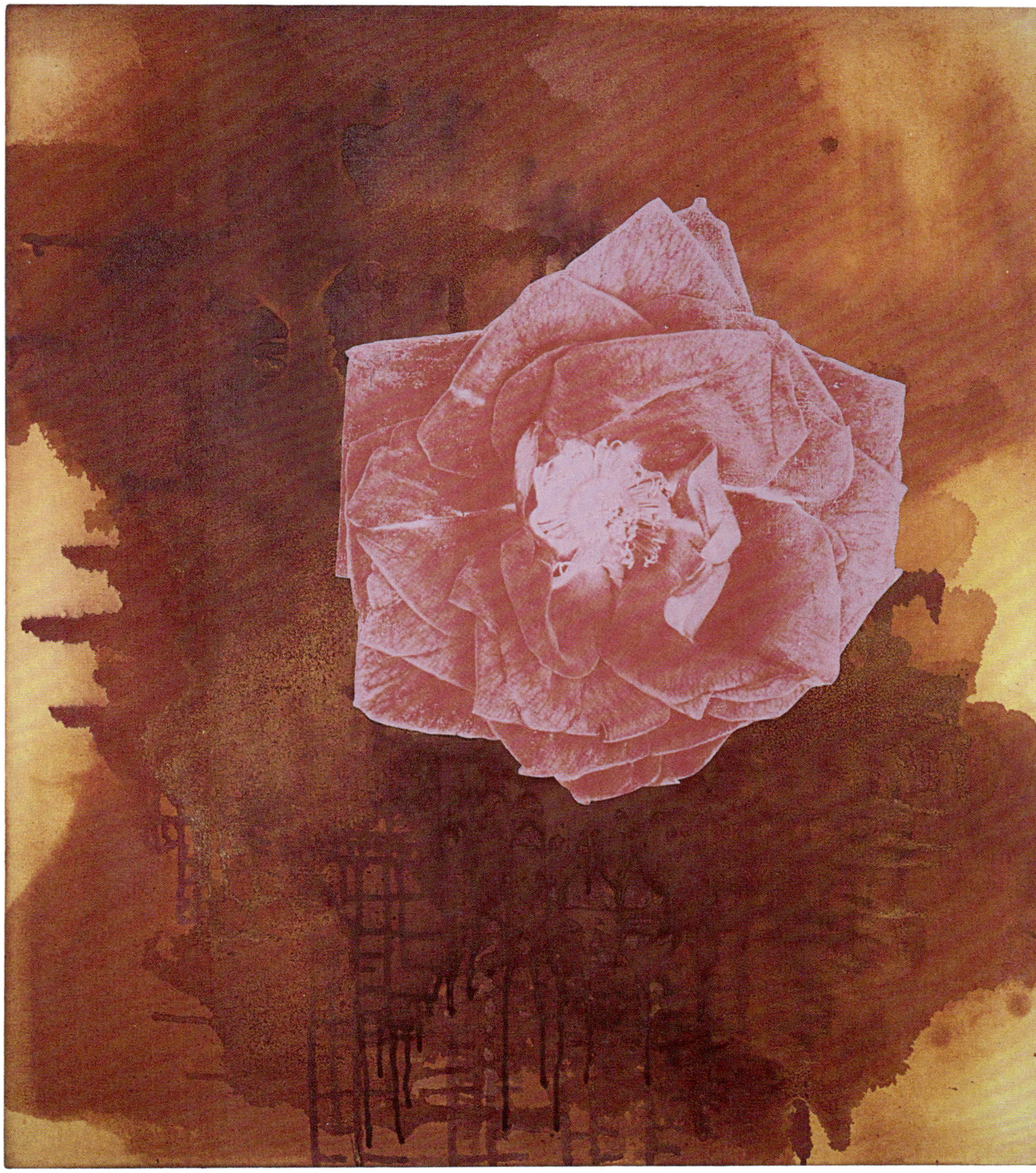

27. Blue Velvet 1992

Acrylic, Flashe, and ink on canvas
81.3 × 71.1 cm (32 × 28 in.)
Private Collection

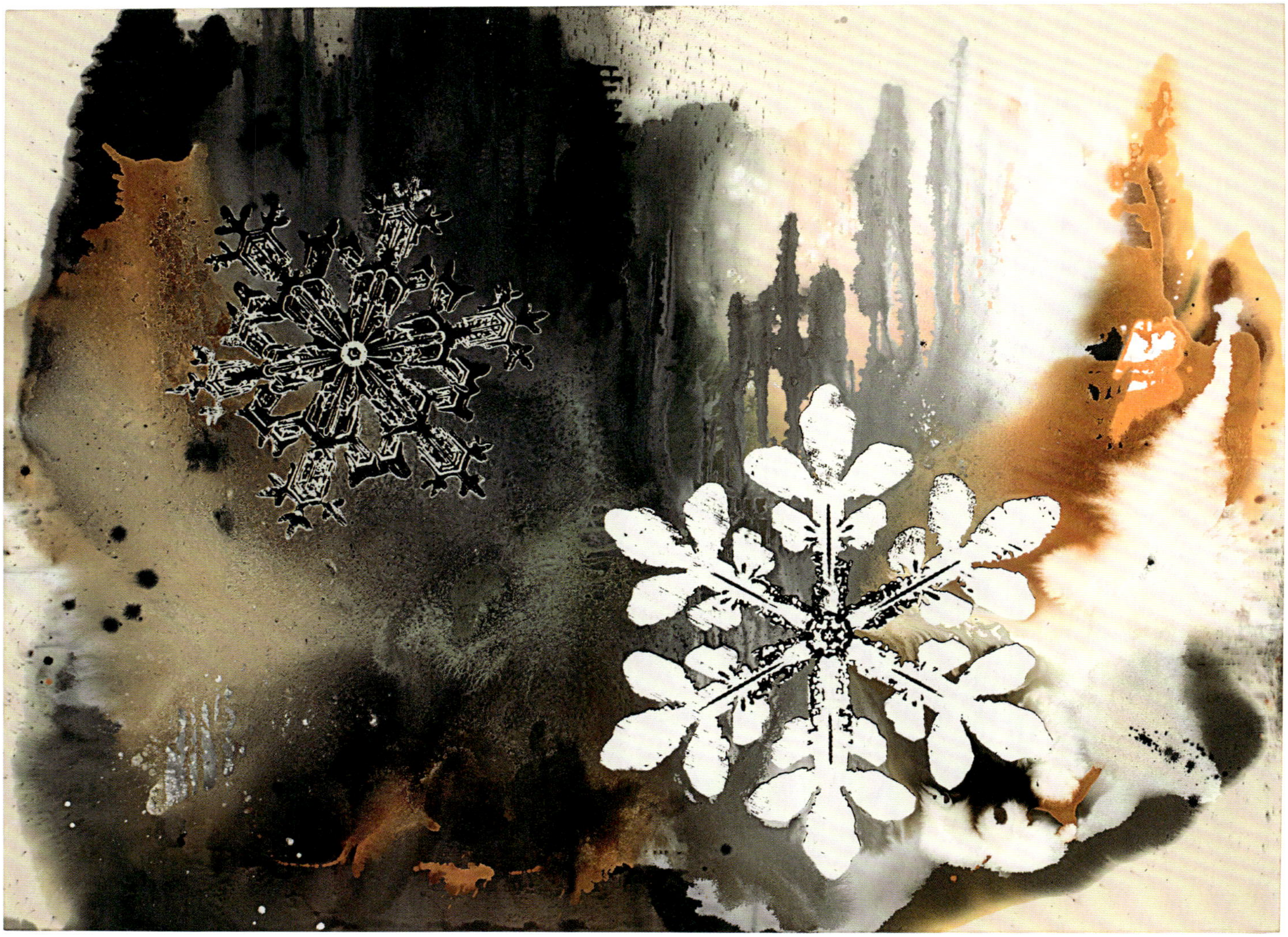

28. Snow 1992

Acrylic, screen print, and mica glass on canvas
182.9 × 243.8 cm (72 × 96 in.)
Collection of the artist

course of coaxing them into being. Some of the first daytime butterfly scenes, like *Earth*, 1993 (fig.30), a watercolor on paper with the creatures emerging only partly from the constituent medium, almost alchemically conjure representational acuity out of obdurate materiality.

Shown in great number at Galerie Ralph Wernicke's 1993 presentation at Unfair, Cologne (fig.29), an alternative to the Art Cologne fair held in a disused bank, the butterfly pieces were tacked up like naked specimens, curling at the edges as if to defy the fixed conditions of display, or flattened under glass. In Weatherford's recollection, people 'hated' them, failing to see beyond the superficial, fawning prettiness. She also remembers someone telling Wernicke that it looked like art that should be in a bank; his riposte: 'We are in a bank.' Audiences also found disconcerting the verses about the Coachella Valley and outer space that Weatherford scripted and interspersed among the butterflies on the walls, the small pieces of paper extending the reach of her newfound authorship in what remains the only time that she included her own writing within a show. The snippets of text in fact came from a short radio play, *Satellite Girl*, a meditation on memory that Weatherford wrote in 1992–3 and dismembered into sections, like this part of the opening with a mother and child gazing into the night:

> B[oy about seven years old]: What's that bright one? Is that Orion?
> M[other]: I don't think so . . . I don't think it's a star.
> Boy hums theme from *Twilight Zone* which makes the mother laugh.
> B: Mom! It's not moving mom. I think it's a satellite.
> M: I think so too.
> B: Who do you think shot it up there? The Pakistanis? The Republicans? What if it was some kind of top secret Republican spy thing? Do you think they'd try anything like that, I mean after Watergate and everything? Maybe since Nixon kicked it, they think maybe they can get away with some new shit![3]

29. Galerie Ralph Wernicke at
Unfair
Cologne
1993

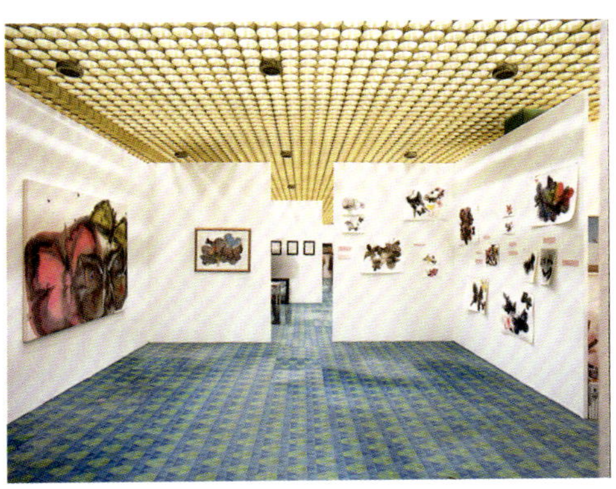

Weatherford's legend tells of Lila, who, in a devil's bargain with a scarab, traded immortality for living in space, 'relieved of hunger, fatigue, and response'.[4] Although the story is fantastical, Weatherford is present in the vivid details of Easter in San Diego and cars on the familiar mountain route from that city's coast to the inland Salton Sea. She also inhabits rather fully one character who sees snow for the first time when at school in the East, and in another, a version of her in the guise of a girl with a curvature of the spine that straightens in the absence of gravity, who 'gladly spun round to display in full noon light a sublime and powerful scar which traversed her spine originating high up between her shoulder blades . . . And now her deformity had been forgiven. She believed so – She knew so. She had uncurled like a fiddle fern to full length. Over five feet and eight inches tall.'[5]

After the reveal at Unfair, Weatherford disappeared the text, even as she made modest paintings preciously flecked with seashells as though they were concretions

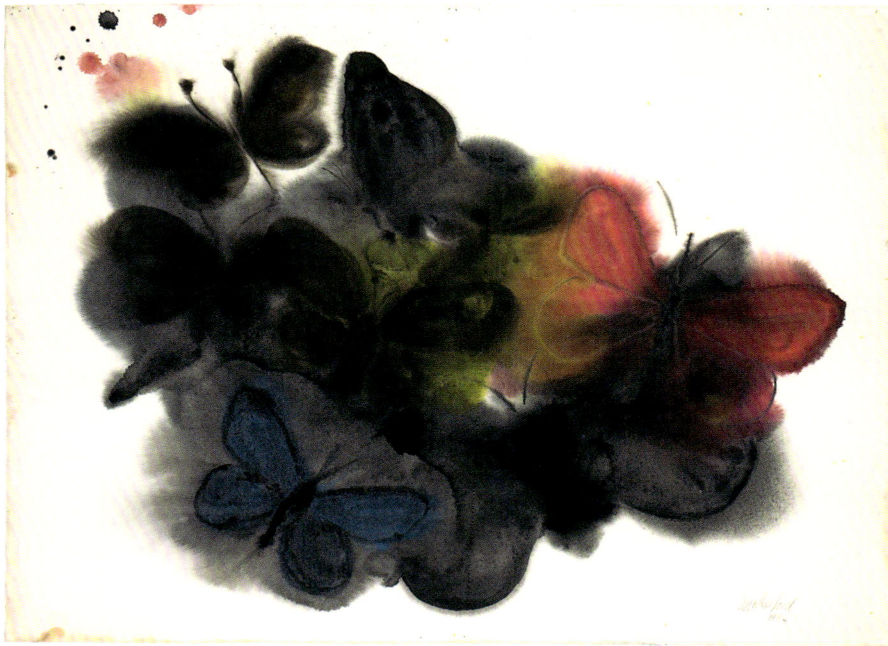

30. Earth 1993

Watercolor on paper
55.9 × 76.2 cm (22 × 30 in.)
Collection of the artist

of the play's descriptions. *The Ocean Is in the Sky*, 1994, was the first to commingle water and firmament, and takes its inspiration from this passage of Lila standing in the Pacific: 'She tried to memorize that moment, that afternoon, the sensation of standing beneath a pastel bow of heaven that bent to wrap the curve of the ocean-covered earth in a perfect, airless, and infinite kiss.'[6] So many more from the same year have sharks (also a gruesome plot point). Then there is the passage about Sunset Cliffs, a natural park on Point Loma's peninsula, near the former site of Lomaland (a pre-Ojai Theosophical community established by Katherine Tingley in 1900), which inadvertently laid out a program for future work:

> Out by the lighthouse, down by the Jesuit school, at the bottom of the cliffs is a secret beach. One would never know it was there. This beach is protected at both ends by great sandstone cliffs which extend into the sea creating lazy shimmering breaks with names like 'Pianos' and 'Abs'. The water is as turquoise as a heartbreak and the sand is as fine as sugar and strewn with piles of crisp auburn kelp. The shore break at the south end is decorated by tide pools which are inhabited by lavender sea anemones, tangerine starfish, purple limpets, and an occasional baby octopus.[7]

To read this alongside so many paintings of cliffs, shore breaks, and pools teeming with marine life from the mid- and later 1990s is to grasp a continuity of interest

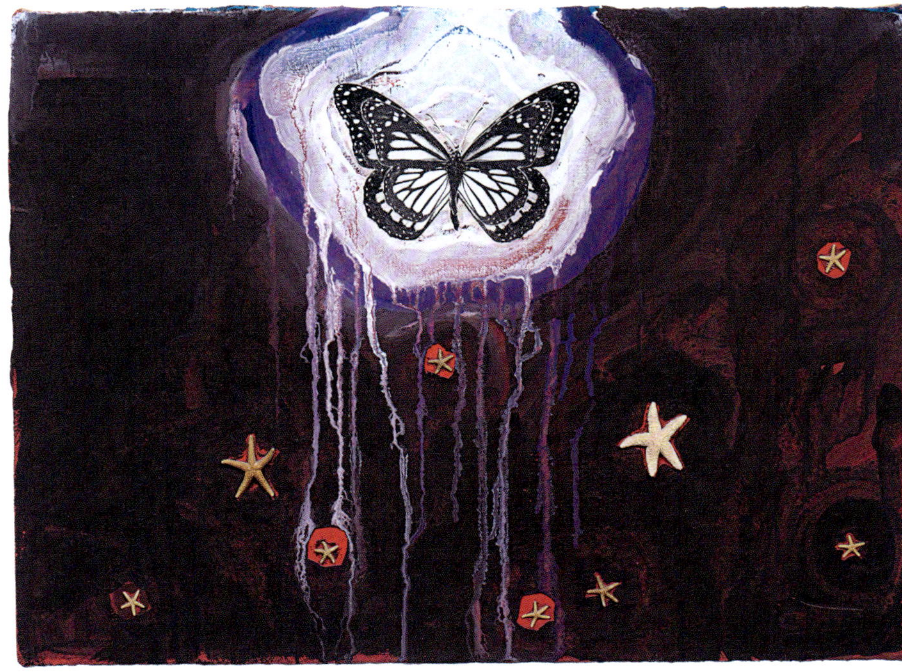

31. Deliverance 1994

Flashe, photocopy, and starfish on jute
45.7 × 61 cm (18 × 24 in.)
Collection of the artist

32. Little Night Scene 1994

Flashe, starfish, and flowers on linen
20.3 × 22.9 cm (8 × 9 in.)
Private Collection

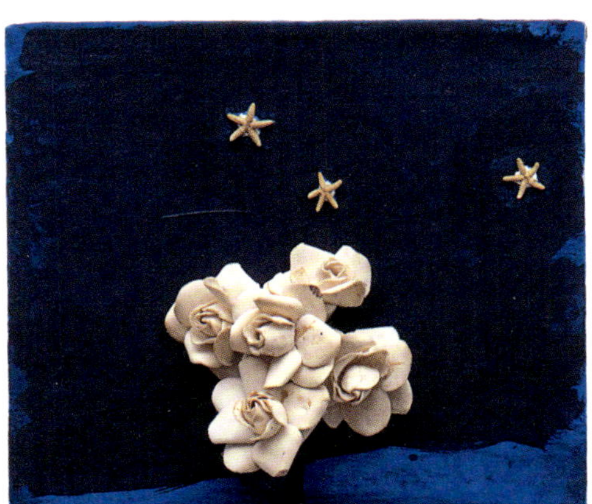

that would find a different articulation in those of sea caves from 2000 on. Still, as Weatherford began constructing a chronological sequence to her work in her own accounts of it, she stressed instead other aspects of her life, and other references. In one statement, she put the steps from the pasted flowers to the physical elements like this:

> I thought of them as stickers on a sliding glass door that stopped you from flying through, stopped you at the surface. Then my stains became giant butterflies and then the flowers became starfish. The starfish paintings came out of the Man Ray film *Emak Bakia*, which has a shot of the ocean rolling in, and then the camera turns upside-down, and the ocean rolls in over your head. So the first starfish painting I made was called *The Ocean Is in the Sky*. The stars at the bottom of the sea became stars in the sky. And in the back of my mind were a dozen shell mirrors I saw in Santa Cruz in 1968, leaning against a hedge on the grass outside the art department.[8]

In this telling, the Santa Cruz hippie context for the tactile sea elements represents something like a promise of freedom and licentiousness. But there were other determinants for her using collage – importantly the Watts Towers Arts Center, opened in 1970. It proposed yet another possibility, the formalization of community around structures encrusted with seashells, tile, and glass culled from soda bottles

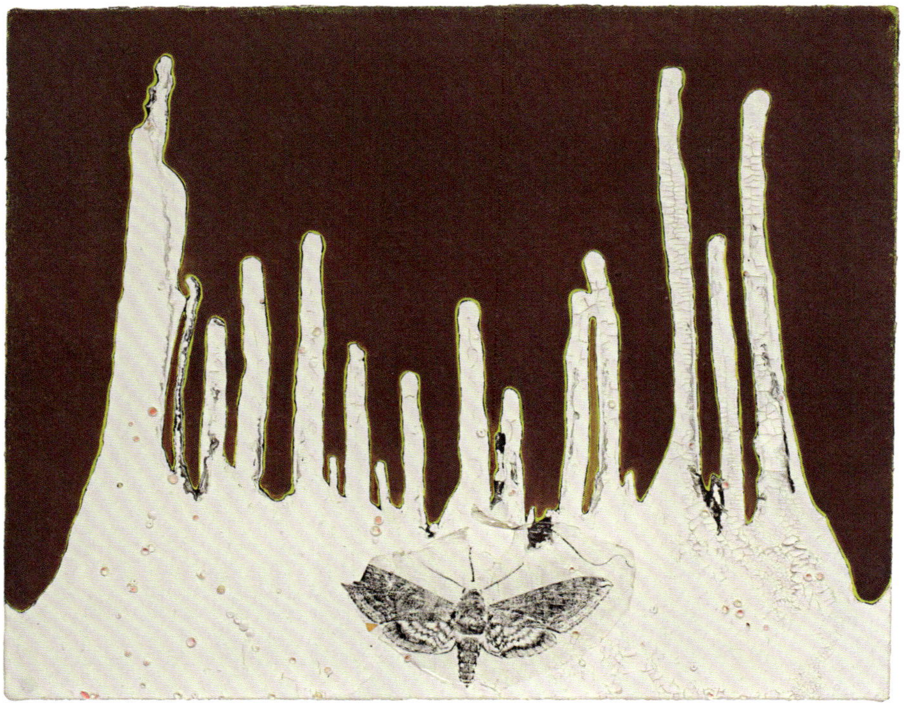

33. Sugar Mountain 1994

Photocopy transfer, acrylic, oil, and seashells on jute
61 × 76.2 cm (24 × 30 in.)
Collection of the artist

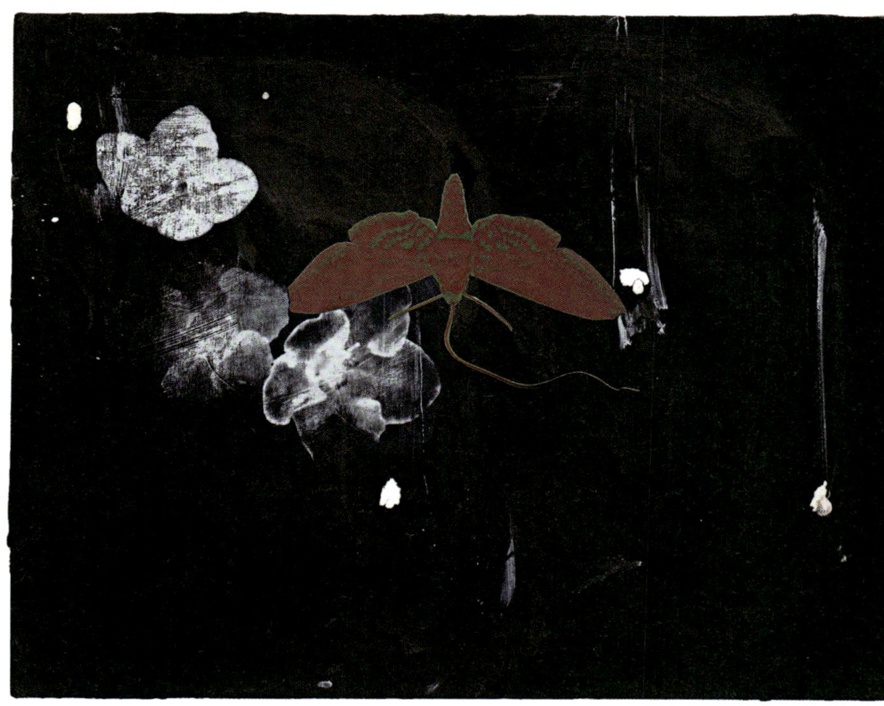

34. Scent 1995

Paper, screen print, seashells,
and molding paste on canvas
61 × 76.2 cm (24 × 30 in.)
Collection of the artist

35. Blue Night Moth 1995

Acrylic, snail shells, paper, and Flashe on canvas
22.9 × 33 cm (9 × 13 in.)
Collection of the artist

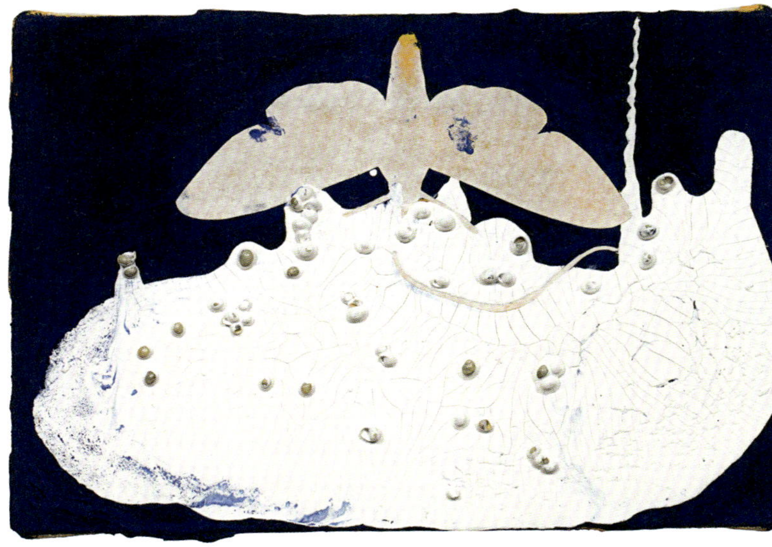

36. David Hammons
Higher Goals 1986

Mixed media
5 units, heights: 6–10.7 m (20–35 ft.)
Temporary installation, Cadman Plaza Park, New York, commissioned by Public Art Fund

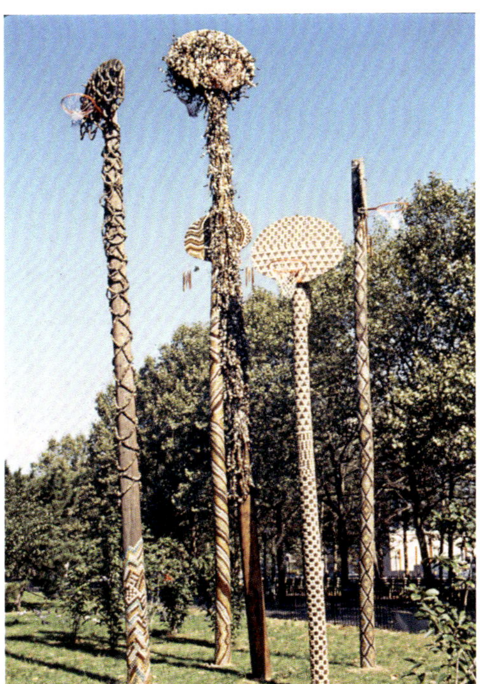

and cultural effluvia. (The towers' creator, Simon Rodia, himself was immortalized within the counterculture, standing next to Bob Dylan on the cover of the Beatles' 1967 album *Sgt. Pepper's Lonely Hearts Club Band* and appearing in *Shelter*, the *Whole Earth Catalog*–like sourcebook of organic architecture, edited by Lloyd Kahn, in 1973.) While living in Brooklyn after Princeton and the ISP, Weatherford also encountered on the way to and from the subway each day the work of David Hammons at Cadman Plaza Park. For *Higher Goals*, a temporary piece commissioned by Public Art Fund in 1986, he transmuted materials close at hand into sculptures – five telephone poles studded with bottle caps in diamond, spiral, and mesh patterns, each with a basketball backboard, hoop, and net mounted at the top – that hid in plain sight.[9]

Still closer to home, Weatherford recalls that when her father returned from military training, he studied painting with Dick Swift at Occidental College supported by the GI Bill. Because of these classes, he painted in Eagle Rock, in the hills above Los Angeles, making a particular oil that the wind knocked over into leaves. Unfazed, he hung it up at home, where his mother, Mary's grandmother, 'cleaned' the canvas by picking off each offending sprig. Weatherford learned of this story around the time she took up college, when she gave her grandmother a snail shell collage painting for her one hundredth birthday and her father warned her of the risk she courted.

Beyond starting to work with collage, Weatherford also shaped a gestalt-like form that might be a head, a landmass, or a phallus, an indecipherable region that extends into a citrus sky in *Missing Margaret*, 1995 (fig.41), and recurs in *Big Red Margaret Head*, 1997 (fig.42), and is notably named in these examples after the artist's sister, who lends the equivocal portrait a silhouette. In another series of repeating forms,

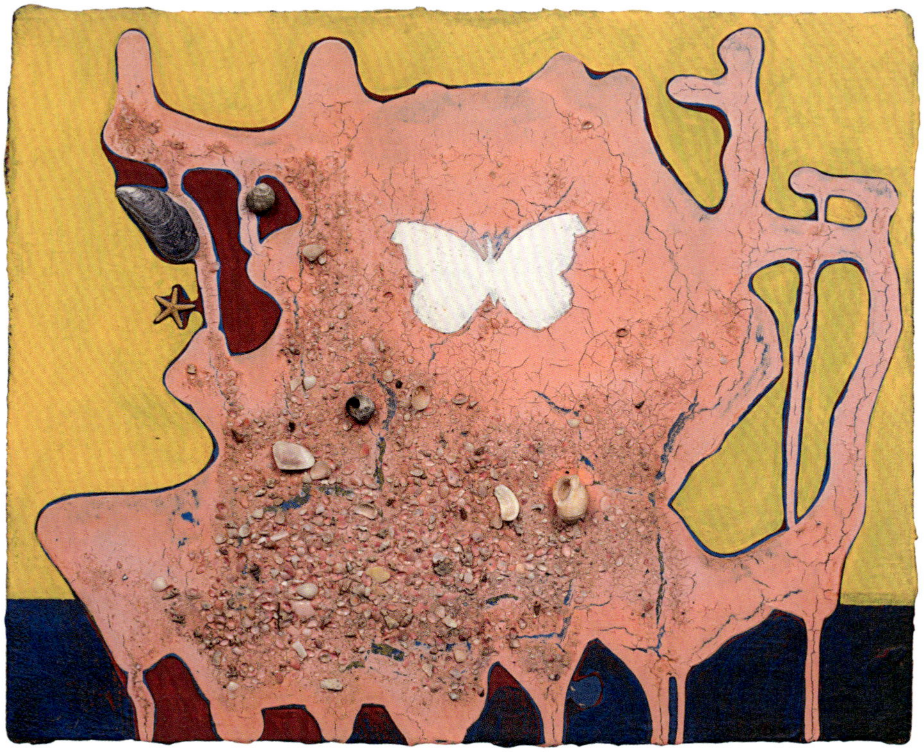

37. My Dalí 1996

Oil, seashells, starfish, and Flashe on jute
38.1 × 45.7 cm (15 × 18 in.)
Collection of the artist

Weatherford worked with the image of herself directly, using a studio self-portrait modeled after the sensual nineteenth-century cemetery sculptures of idealized, grief-stricken women collected in the photographs of David Robinson's *Saving Graces* (and characterized by Joyce Carol Oates as 'love objects of the previous century, icons of a church in which we no longer believe . . . embodiments of ritual mourning'[10]). She sits leaning forward, head in hands, like a riposte to Auguste Rodin's pensive visage of philosophy, her long hair hiding her face and the bodice of her disco dress pleated like a Greek chiton.

Weatherford affixed this image to many surfaces and there juxtaposed it with a seemingly infinite set of backdrops, sometimes decorated with collage elements and sometimes left flat: a composition with a black void is titled *Night*, 1996; one with two pink landscape-breasts is titled *Mountains*, 1996; another cleaved as a diptych of turquoise and marine is titled *Girl Menaced by Abstraction*, 1996 (fig.38). In a larger rendition, a silk-screened version of the photo is stamped on a goldenrod monochrome and titled *Any Cat Stevens Song*, 1996. This representation occurs again in *Cry Me a River*, 1996, where a pink bottom region reveals a cracked pool of water laced with little shells. *Girl Menaced by Early Work*, 1996, incorporates a diminutive version of a target painting looming above the figure as though it were a nefarious planet exerting an astrological influence.

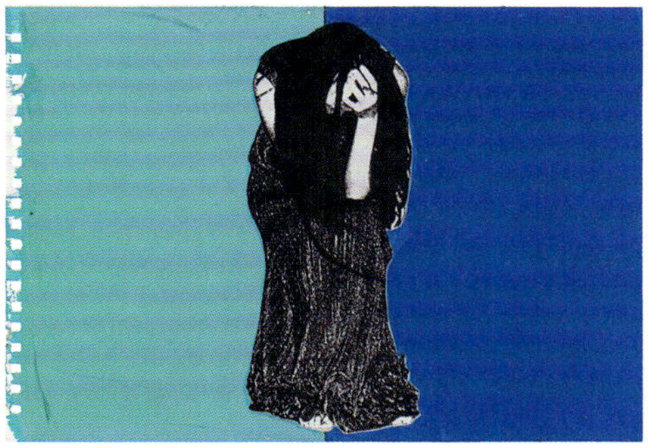

38. Girl Menaced by Abstraction 1996

Flashe and photocopy on paper
17.8 × 25.4 cm (7 × 10 in.)
Private Collection

39. *Easter*
Debs & Co.,
New York
1998

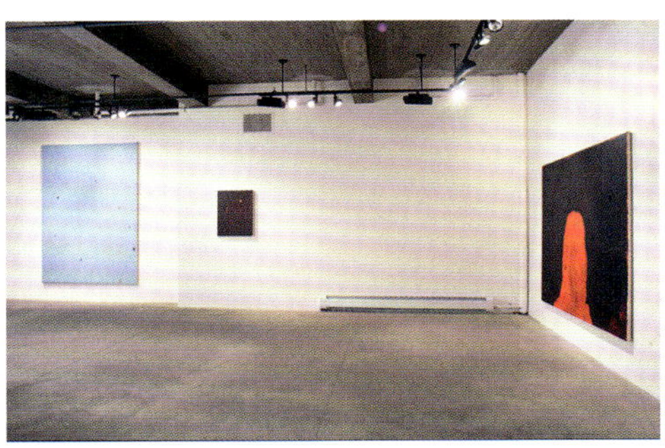

As her first solo show in New York following the pivotal 1992 exhibition at BlumHelman Warehouse, Weatherford presented *Easter* in March–April 1998 at Debs & Co (fig.39). She showed works from the years leading up to it, with *Big Red Margaret Head* as a crypto-landscape amid other, more obvious natural phenomena, such as *Change of Scene*, 1997, *liquid sky*, 1997, and *Heavy on Top*, 1998. As this grouping announced, Weatherford increasingly trained her attention on the mutable backgrounds (and jettisoned the head-in-hands woman who, for a time, had existed so comfortably within them). There is land and sea, presumably, but indeterminately so. Starfish, if anything, become characters. *Red, yellow, black*, 1997 (fig.45), cuts a horizontal band of red from yellow, a lone shell interrupting the latter swath as though its singular presence can bend space; two shells peer from the center of *Eyes in the Heat*, 1997 (fig.46). Nancy Princenthal described the show for *Art in America* as speaking of the 'seashore and the empyrean', in a positive reading that nonetheless analogized the work with 'nursery décor (Saint-Exupéry comes to mind), boardwalk tchotchkes and blameless lyricism'.[11] In *Coagula*, Janet Preston simply cheered on the artist in the amusing context of a 'New York Report Card': 'Mary Weatherford at Debs & Co. Welcome return of an ironic colorist. Grade A.'[12] (Comparably, Alice Neel at Cheim & Read got an A– for her 'vulnerable men in wacky suits'.[13])

In the catalogue accompanying the Debs & Co. show, a slender volume with an essay by Dale Peck and *Red, yellow, black* on its cover, the writer argues precisely against the irony Preston perceived. He avows that, unlike the 'art stars of the eighties . . . busy with their ironic refashionings of popular culture, Weatherford was consuming twentieth-century art with a voracious sexual appetite'. He has her 'castrat[ing]' Jasper Johns and Kenneth Noland and '[turning] phallic' Andy Warhol's soft open flowers, and also frames the titles from 1989–90 – *Violetta* (fig.22), *Camille* (fig.12), *Cho Cho San* (fig.19) – as a 'kind of enveloping exegetical context' without an actual female body.[14] Noting Weatherford's newfound independence from appropriated artistic and literary sources, he further describes an experience of 'release'. He gets to the crux of what this work in *Easter* proposes – and unknowingly what it portends for the work that will follow – in a passage I quote at some length for its perspicacity:

> Weatherford isn't out to attack anything; rather, she's trying to reclaim something, a myth perhaps, or something real, something which poets and philosophers and Parkay margarine have all called (Mother) Nature. But in a world where nature must be referred to in quotation marks, to wit, 'nature' or even 'the idea of nature', that referent has been stripped, not just of meaning, but of usefulness. If nature, as artists and critics have all along maintained, is just one more abstract construction, like gender, or race, or money, then why should art be limited to referring to just that one construction? Why not let it refer back to *all* abstract constructions? . . . *Easter* doesn't challenge the validity of such

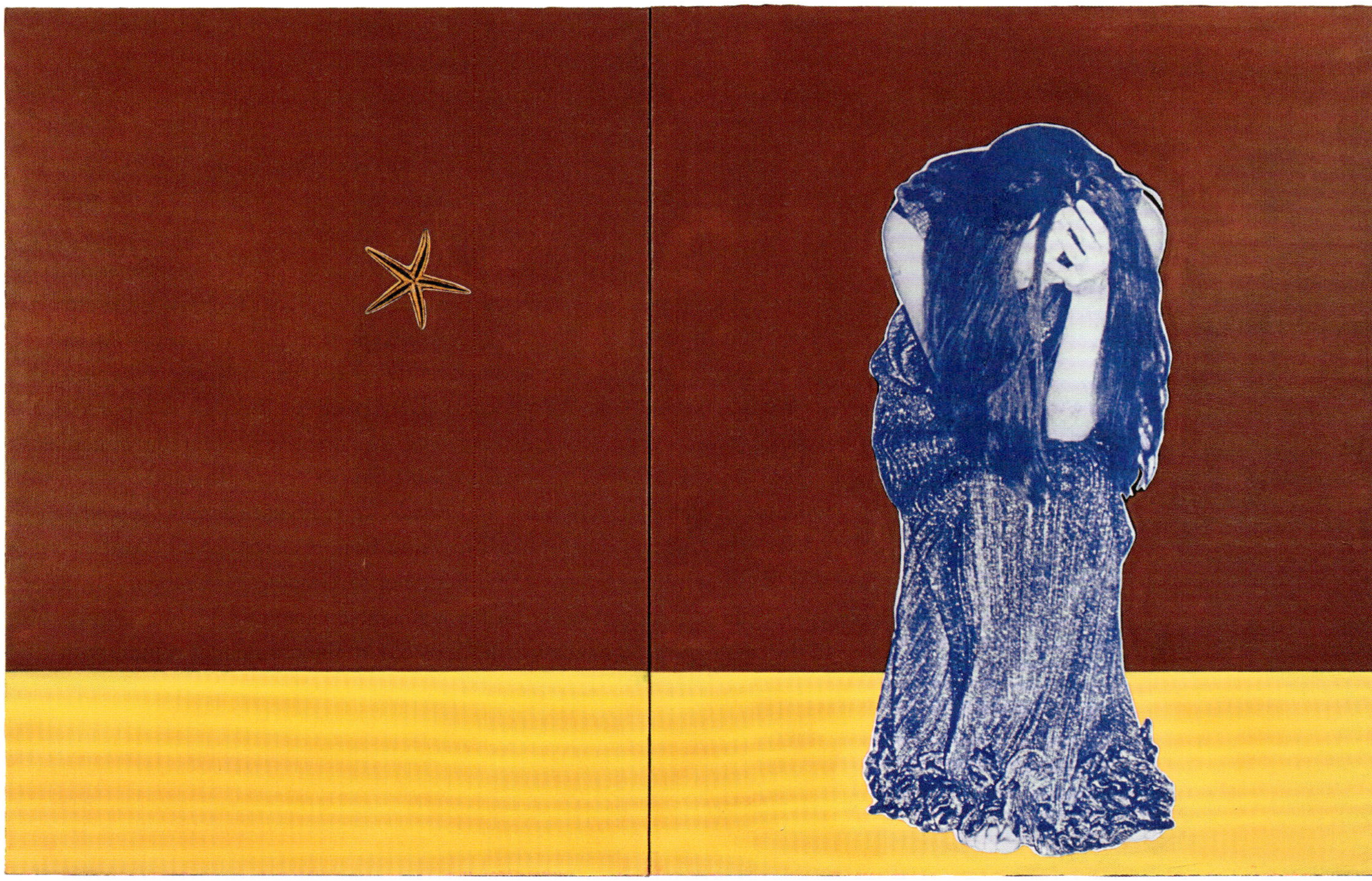

40. Girl Menaced by Starfish 1996

Oil, acrylic, photocopy, and vinyl on jute
Two parts, 152.4 × 233.7 cm (60 × 92 in.)
Collection of the artist

> an assertion outright; it only describes what it costs us. It reminds us, in the gentlest terms, that human beings long for nature . . . the desire to find a way to reintegrate humanity into nature without any quotation marks, which is, I feel, the journey Weatherford wants us to take from her horizons.[15]

It is uncanny, in this assessment, how Peck sensed a longing that would be so shortly fulfilled in Weatherford's return to California only a year later, and her subsequently taking up working on the sand, from direct observation of spray and tides, the light shifting overhead with the passage of the sun.

Later that year, Weatherford mounted another New York solo exhibition, at Thomas Korzelius Fine Art, which ran from November 1998 to January 1999. *Works on Paper* featured photographs of postcard size or smaller (many are 5 × 7.5 centimeters), developed on thick papers studded with tiny sand dollars that Weatherford glued on before applying the emulsion. (One of the twenty-four works included a starfish.) The press release suggested 'the detached state of mind required to comprehend a non-empirical, relativistic depiction of the real'.[16] As Barry Schwabsky wrote at the time, the 'irregular little disks' look like 'nail heads, that float around the women like stars'.[17] In some, visages of friends and her sister, Margaret – a writer and the inspiration for the topographic form of *Missing Margaret* and other works, as well as the editor of much of Weatherford's writing[18] – gaze at the viewer, the pasted objects in the scene, or each other, twinned, in plays of double exposure and slipped registers. Many sprout orbs. Weatherford also published with Margaret a collection of her 'prose miniatures' that relate to the sea:

> When the others ran down to the water, Terrence stayed near the bonfire with her feet in the cold, damp sand. The fog had come in, and the stars were gone. She felt so still that her forearms might or might not be touching the arms of her chair. There was the flush and sizzle of a wave. Afterwards, the sodapop fizz of a thin finger of salt water slipping the shore.[19]

Weatherford presented one related work at Dorsky Gallery, New York, in *Om*, curated by Joe Fyfe, which opened that February. *Supernatural*, 1998 (fig.47), features a sand dollar hovering at the midline above a mirror image of a dark-haired woman (photographer Dana Hoey, Weatherford's friend). The accompanying brochure went all in for claiming its symbolism of spiritual perception: 'The painting displays a portrait of someone meditating: staring at the third eye that is above and between two physical ones. The double image sets up a numerical progression, one (person), two (mind-body dualities), three (eyes). The sand dollars refer to the eternal ocean and the material world.'[20] Nobody mentioned the significance of the lone starfish in the Korzelius show, or its accumulating force in the companion pieces, its symbolism pointing to the vagina (as another of Man Ray's films, *L'étoile de mer*, 1928, makes abundantly clear) and also to its capacity for regeneration.

41. Missing Margaret 1995

Flashe and starfish on jute
53.3 × 68.6 cm (21 × 27 in.)
Collection of the artist

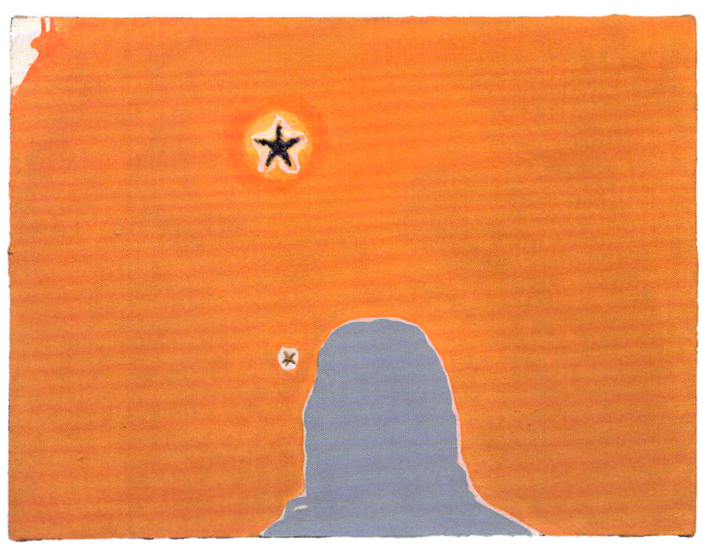

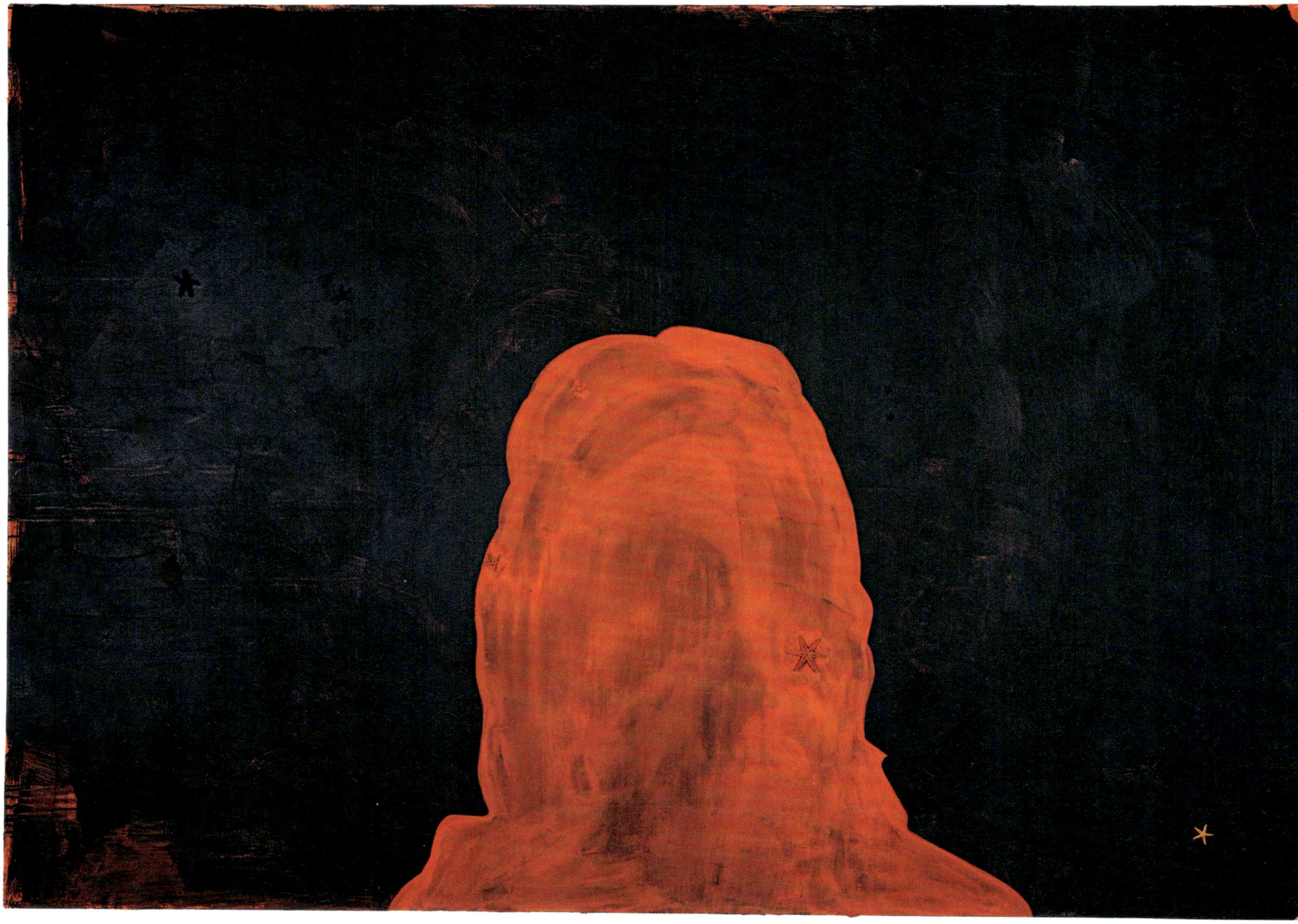

42. Big Red Margaret Head 1997

Acrylic, Flashe, and starfish on canvas
175.3 × 243.8 cm (69 × 96 in.)
Private Collection

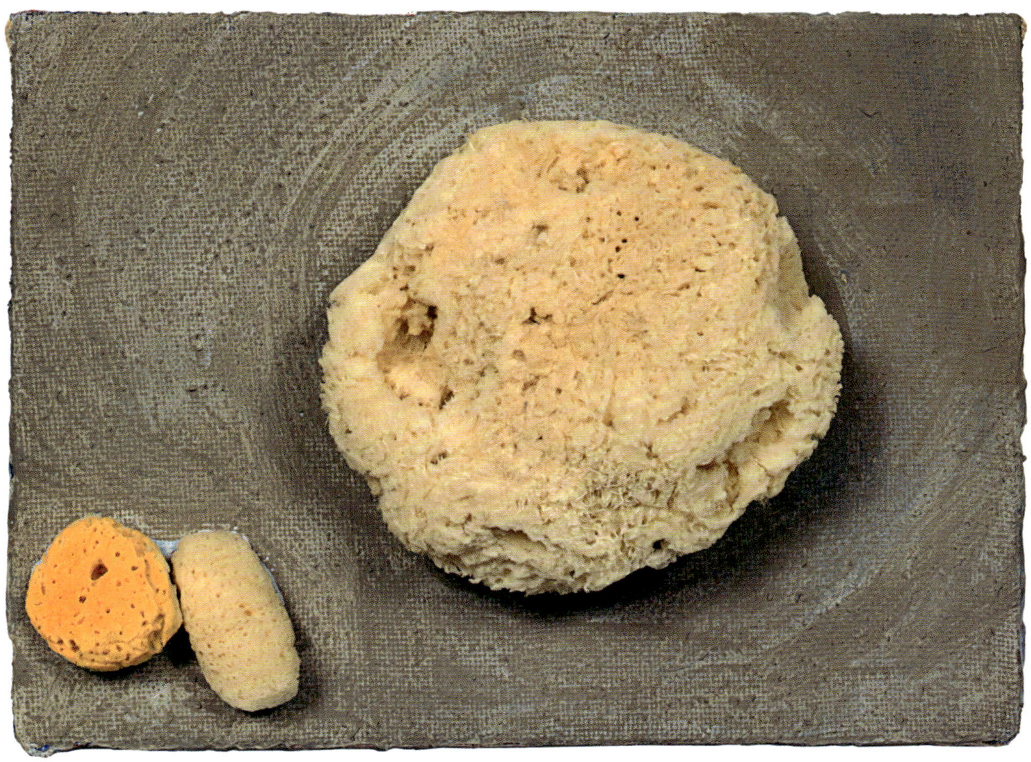

43. gravity 2000

Flashe and sponges on jute
22.9 × 30.5 cm (9 × 12 in.)
Collection of the artist

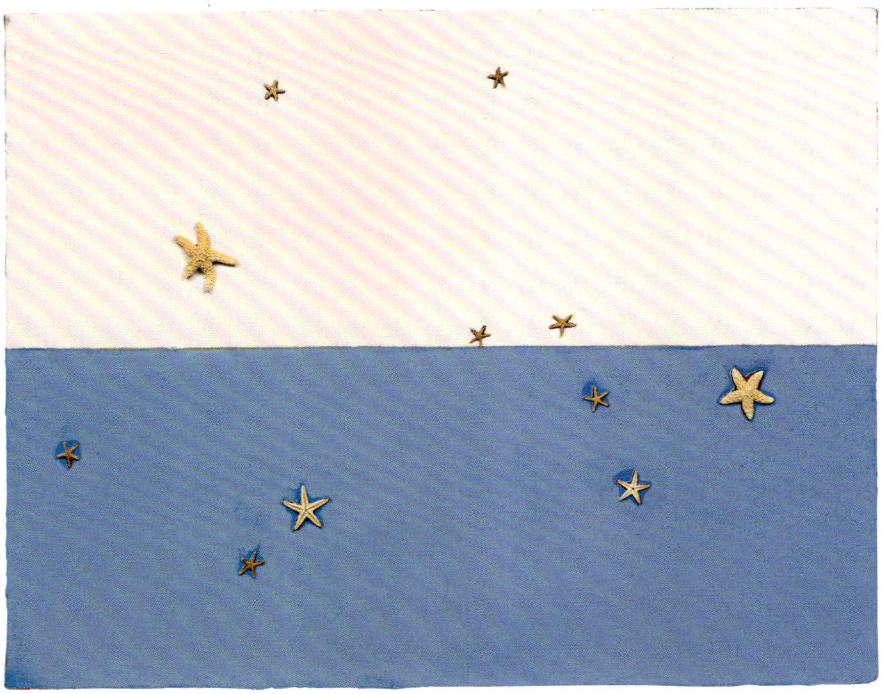

44. pink sky 1997

Oil, Flashe and starfish on jute
61 × 76.2 cm (24 × 30 in.)
Collection of the artist

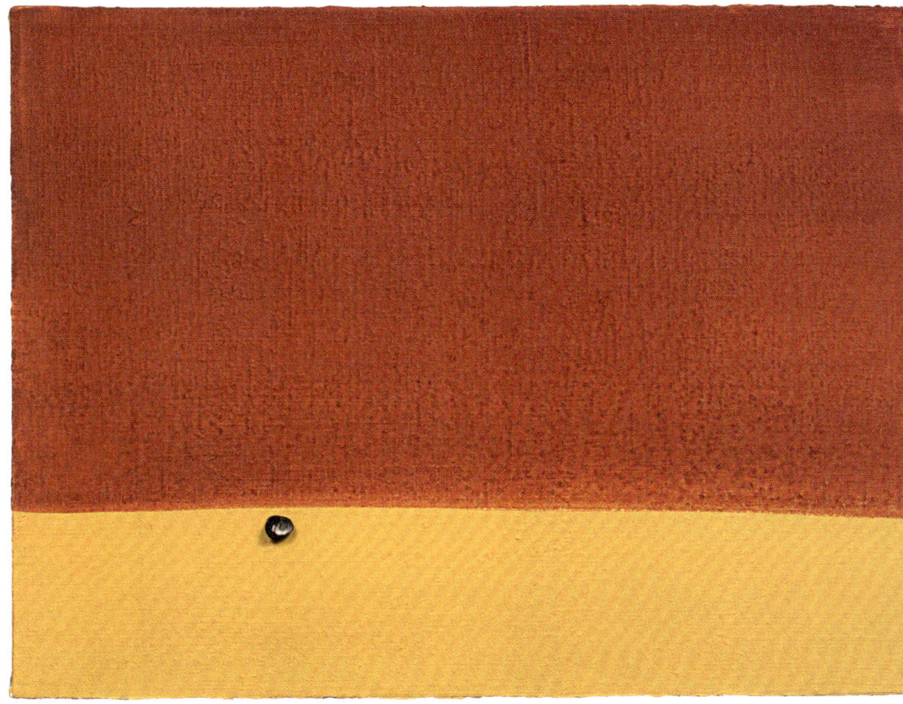

45. Red, yellow, black 1997

Flashe and snail shell on jute
45.7 × 55.9 cm (22 × 18 in.)
Collection of the artist

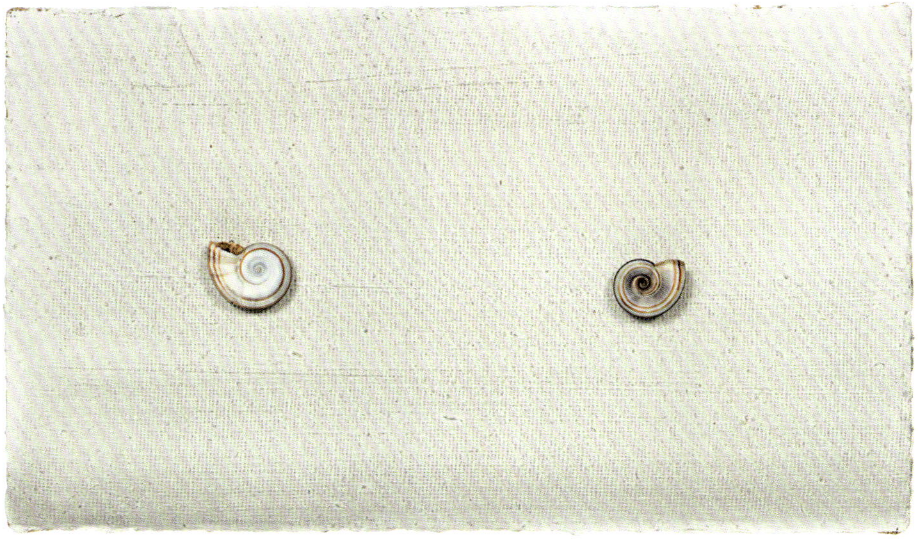

46. Eyes in the Heat 1997

Seashells and paint on jute
25.4 × 43.2 cm (10 × 17 in.)
Collection of the artist

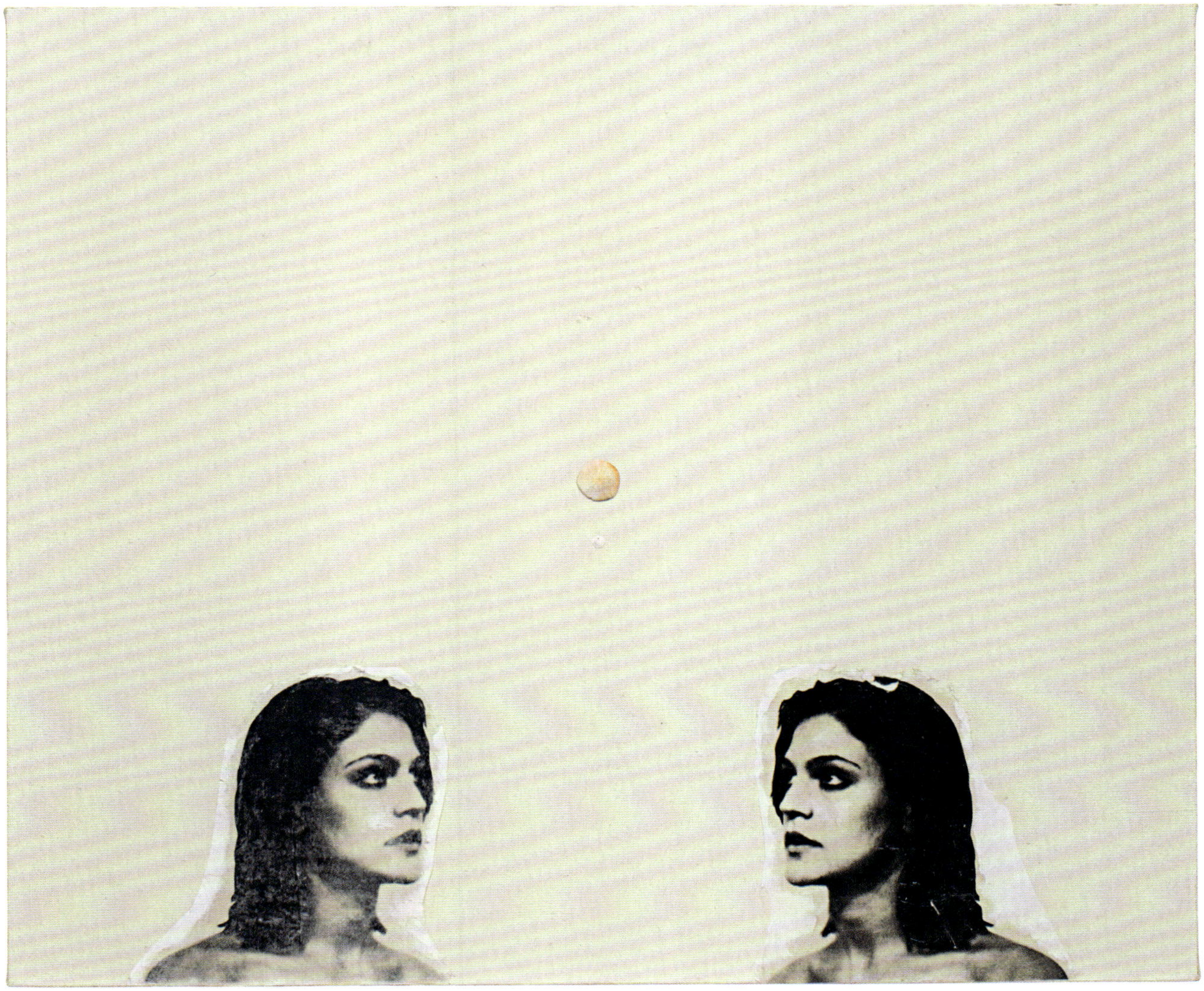

47. Supernatural 1998

Acrylic transfer and sand dollars on jute
86.4 × 101.6 cm (34 × 40 in.)
Collection of the artist

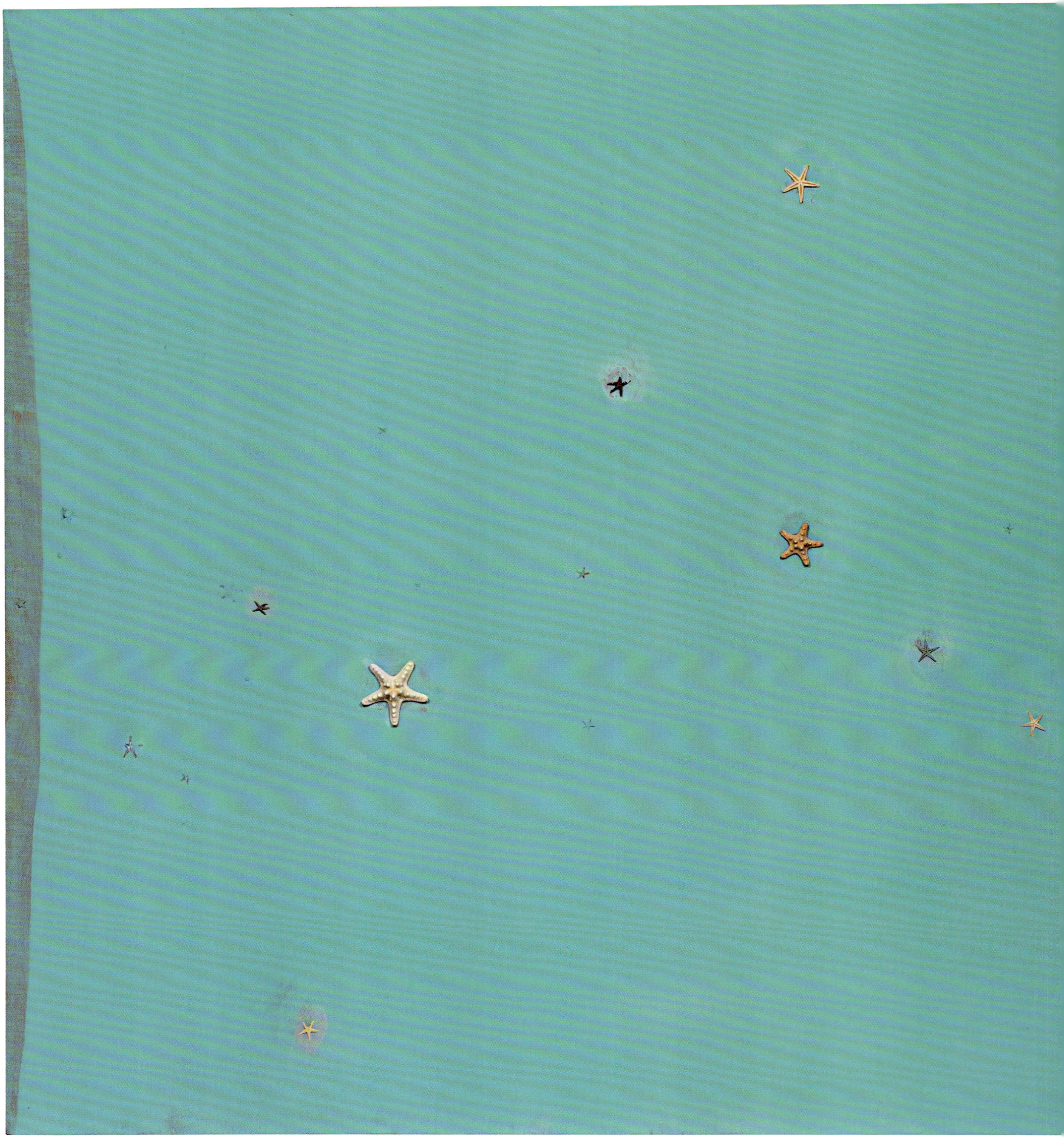

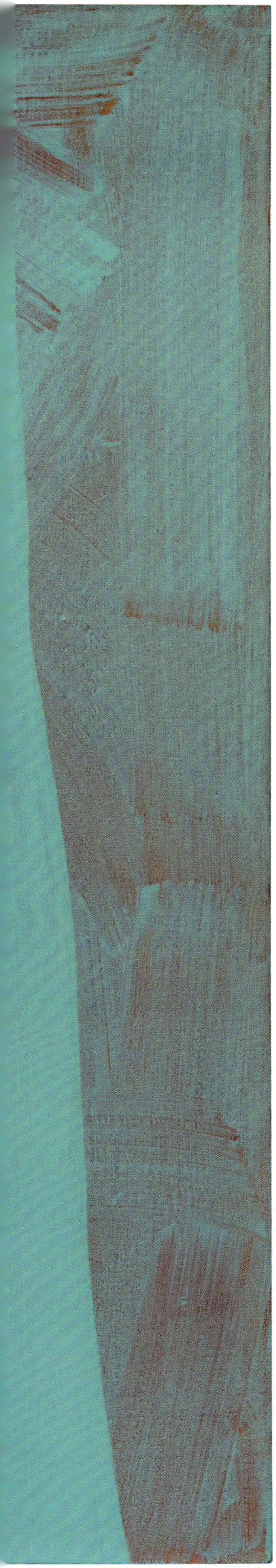

48. blue love 1999

Flashe and starfish on linen
175.3 × 200.7 cm (69 × 79 in.)
Collection of the artist

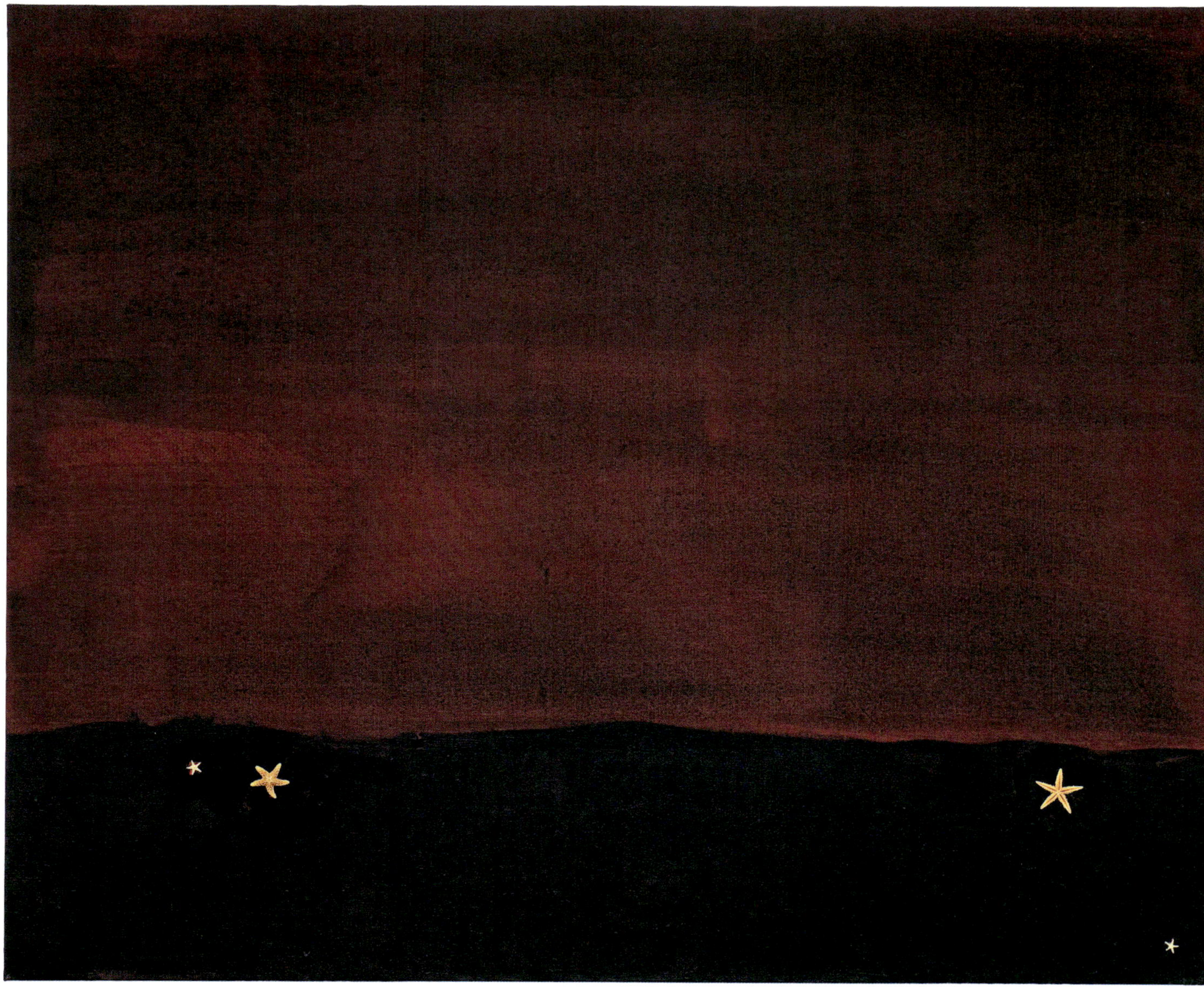

49. night scene 1999

Flashe and starfish on jute
139.7 × 167.6 cm (55 × 66 in.)
Collection of the artist

4 Rocks, Caves, Weeds, Vines: The 2000s

To suggest that Weatherford walked into an obliging rainbow-sherbet sunset when she returned to Los Angeles would be a gross mischaracterization. In the months before she left New York in late spring of 1999, she was robbed in a violent home invasion and her mother had a health emergency that took Weatherford back to San Diego. Perversely, these grave personal circumstances coincided with overwhelmingly positive reviews for the shows at Debs & Co. and Thomas Korzelius, making it a significant moment in New York, professionally speaking – particularly given that she hadn't really showed in the six years prior. Leaving with ambivalence but also out of necessity at this moment of validation felt irrevocable; Weatherford deadpans, acutely: 'The gates of New York slammed shut behind me.' When she arrived in Los Angeles, she started over.

That first year back, Weatherford took a class in botanical illustration at the Los Angeles Arboretum and Botanical Gardens near the San Gabriel Mountains in Arcadia. The first lessons involved demonstrations of how to mix color and how to use hue and value in the medium. The class progressed to cover flowers with leaves, ferns, orchids, and roots, with the syllabus's stated goals being to explore 'particular painting challenges, such as texture, white flowers, roots and bulbs as well as various plants in the same family'.[1] Another section dealt more with physical and surface patterning. In these studies, she employed source images of flowers, but she also worked from life, from flora at Descanso Gardens in La Cañada Flintridge, and later, for sketchbooks of her own beyond the class, at beaches in Malibu around Point Dume. Weatherford taught two watercolor classes at Otis College of Art and Design, and she also took a job at the Santa Monica Museum of Art as the finance manager.

During all of this, she settled into her art. She shared a studio with Sam Durant on York Boulevard in the Highland Park neighborhood. Within a year, she was participating in local group shows. In January 2000 she joined Carl Bronson, Dana Duff, Charles LaBelle, Paul McCarthy, Renée Petropoulos, Stephen Prina, Alexis Smith, Kevin Sullivan and Benjamin Weissman for *The Fashion Show* at George's gallery, Los Angeles. Her then-partner Dave Muller took pictures of her made up in red lipstick, modeling alongside Carla Denker and Kim Fisher a floral shift and a moiré blazer that Petropoulos had lent her for the modish cause. In 2001 Laura Owens curated Weatherford into a group show at Chicago Project Room, Los Angeles, with works by Michael Coughlan, Scott Reeder, and Ruth Root. It ended up in the pages of *Tema Celeste*, where it was touted as asking 'cheerfully . . . "old-fashioned" questions about painting's engagement with the messiness of material reality'.[2]

Exaggerating the smaller elements affixed to earlier paintings, she continued with encrustations disposed in clusters in *Shell Cloud* and *Sea wall*, and spaced out individual bits as punctuation amid broader planes of color in *Blue* and *Mirror Painting*, all 2000. She also introduced sponges in paintings from which the porous, organless masses (which in nature live attached to other surfaces) extend in bulbous efflorescence. In *heavy on top again* and *naked* (fig.50), both 2000, the sponges bulge outward so far that they cast deep and insistently present shadows that are recuperated definitively into the aesthetic. This exaggerated tactility embodies precariousness in *gravity*, 2000 (fig.43), where one engorged sponge is orbited by another, the first so large that it threatens to fall off, a suspension of imminent collapse.

Some of these sponge works ended up in a solo show back in New York, at Debs & Co. (fig.51), that opened in November 2000 with pieces that Weatherford completed in California. These included *absorbent*, 2000 (fig.52), a work that transposes the head of Margaret Weatherford (as from *Missing Margaret*) into a shrouded figure or a cavernous opening. This dual spatial reading of forms as both figure and ground is fundamental to the play of legibility and meaning that the works featuring caves would further foster; the sponges here also extend more aggressively Weatherford's 'stickers' into three dimensions. The shells and sponges alike thus were framed in the press release for the show as 'a continuation of her long interest in "attachment" and collage as carriers of meaning'.[3] An unnamed reviewer in the *New Yorker* read them as less melancholy than 'jokey attachments' but still offered a redemptive conclusion: 'Her best images aren't only faux-kitsch. They have a kind of resonant slightness, as if each contained a tiny pearl of embarrassed lyricism.'[4] In the New York context, Weatherford's frequent use of the shells, sand dollars, and starfish in the preceding years (the above-noted 'continuity') was ignored to better establish a narrative with a sudden geographic break. In *Time Out New York*, a critic wondered aloud if her use of 'sea-life details may or may not have been immediately related to Weatherford's move last year from New York to her native coastal California, but it's obvious . . . that she still combs the beaches and attaches what she finds there to canvases'.[5] (In fact she sourced the oceanic appliqués from farther-flung locales, Maine and Barbuda included, as well as shops in California.) Another writer similarly offered that 'Weatherford has moved from New York City to Southern California and . . . reinvented herself as a landscape painter . . . This is "California dreaming" seen through a downbeat New Yorker's jaundiced eyes.'[6]

Weatherford did double down on landscape painting. Her succeeding works from 2000 and 2001 include coastal scenes and cloudscapes, birds and rocks – and even, atypically, fugitive black cats. Most significantly, she began painting caves. Since 2000, when she first took up the cave as a subject, it has proved an enduring preoccupation, ranging in scale, medium, and appearance: from ink drawings with hatch marks and surging watercolor mixed with water from the Pacific, to studio paintings that transmute the results of phenomena observed outdoors into architectural masses of

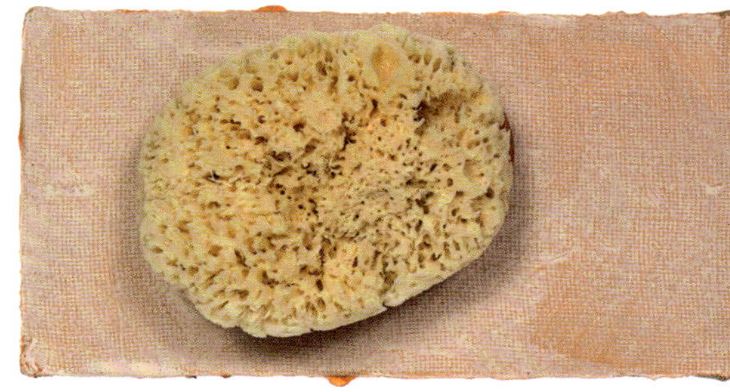

50. naked 2000

Flashe and sponge on jute
15.2 × 30.5 cm (6 × 12 in.)
Collection of the artist

51. *recent paintings*
Debs & Co.
New York
2000

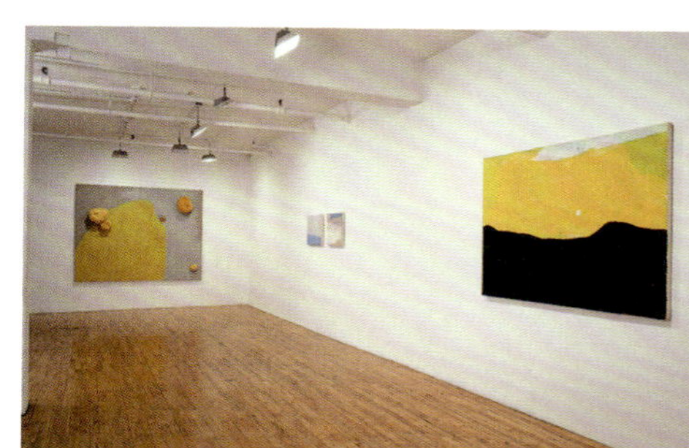

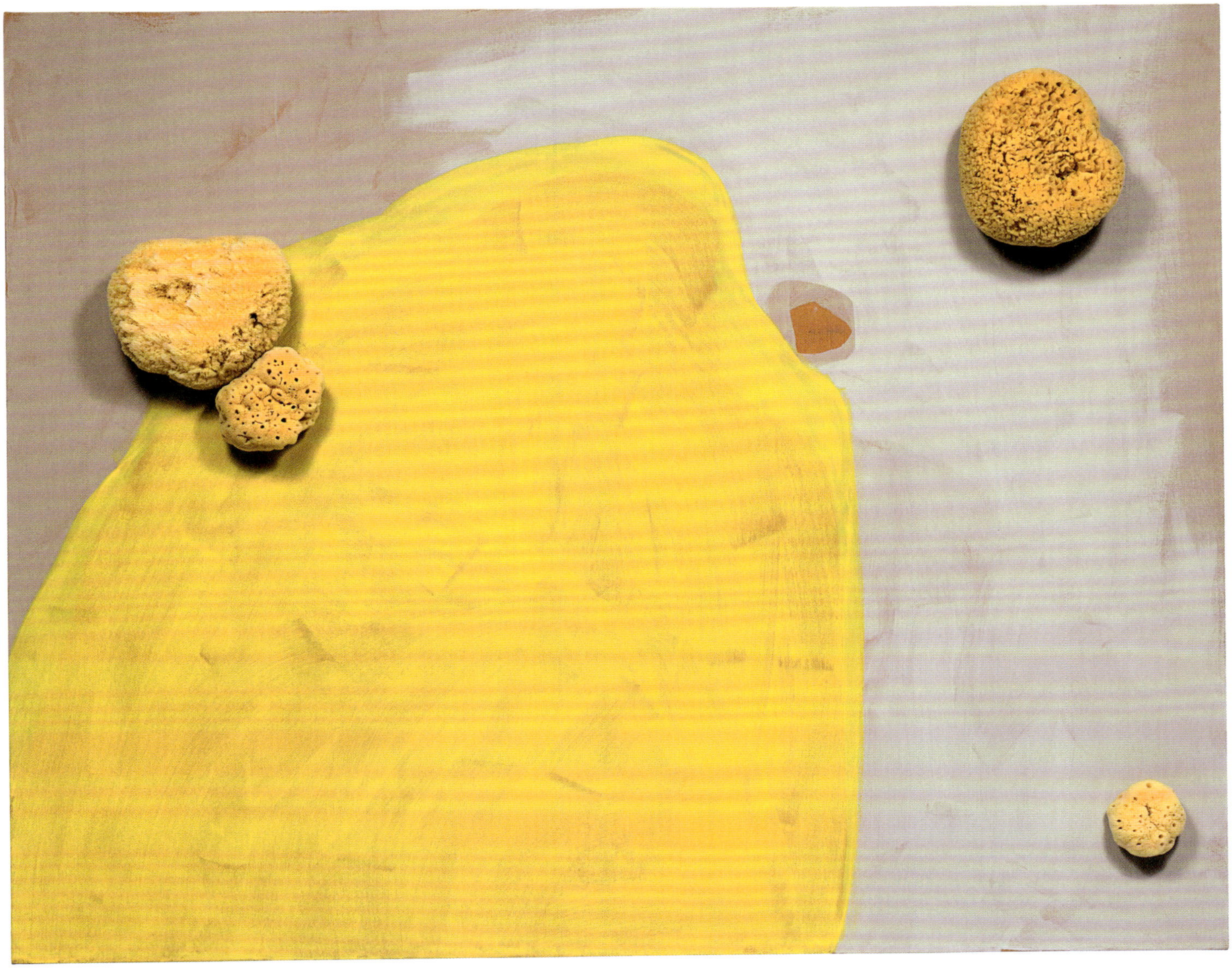

52. absorbent 2000

Flashe and sponges on canvas
167.6 × 208.3 cm (66 × 82 in.)
Collection of the artist

matte Flashe and then gossamer veils that become immersive environments, finally thrown into relief by the penumbral glow of neon.[7] Weatherford made the earliest of these works from the vantage of sheltering inside one, looking out with the grotto framing the view, as in *cave*, 2000 (fig.53), a small painting with an elongated cream oval set in an olive-brown enclosure, anticipating the use of sketching on site but, instead of empirical study, relying on the visceral recollection of the open ceiling and hollow wall of the San Diego sea cave at Sunset Cliffs that she had put in her radio play *Satellite Girl*.

The caves denote place but also organize representation. That they developed as Weatherford was simultaneously experimenting with meditations on the history of art and the conventions of picture making should not surprise. In *windowpane*, 2000, a sinuous line between a daffodil sky and a shadowy ridge could also be the margin between sand and night maritime, with both possibilities drawing on the residual illusionism of the image and title; in *bauhaus and the vanishing point*, 2001 (fig.54), orthogonals unify into a perspectival system made with seashells, crowned with a sequin demarcating deep space. *Cave*, 2000, in fact shares its structure of an emptied-out center with other, non-cave works of the period completed while Weatherford shared a studio with Sharon Lockhart; these include *junkhead alien*, 2001 (fig.56). *Moon*, 2001, a white circle dotted by a lilac-colored celestial body fitted within a black square frame, and *september*, 2001, with a cave-like outline establishing the parameters of the view beyond it, sky rosy and water a deep, hazy purple, admit landscape to be made as much as found. The cave's proscenium – a distended oval bisected by the edge of the canvas – could anyhow also become a shark (*Shark*, 2001), a man in profile (*the joker*, 2001), or a one-eyed monster (*Cyclops*, 2001). Even, or particularly, when it is straightened into right angles, as in *My Magritte*, 2002 (fig.57), space is ineluctably bound by the imposition of a framing edge.

From the first, the form of the cave in Weatherford's hands bespoke the mutability of givens within the parameters of a recursive set – an operation consistent with her earlier targets and mourners. In its infinite variations, the cave came to encourage evocations of weather – something like an Impressionist arresting of transitory phenomena – and also a version of locale that recalls a principal art-historical conversation about the way that climate allegedly fosters particular aesthetics in keeping with a region's environmental factors (the relation was famously causal for Johann Joachim Winckelmann, with Greece's mild climes nurturing, for him, the pinnacle of human achievement in art and male bodies). All of which is to say that the cave, while a part of nature, is also forthrightly framed for Weatherford within and by the aesthetic act, effectively redoubling it as a nominal subject. Of course, the cave is Plato's vehicle for allegorizing ignorance and truth as a critique of Athenian democracy, and a plea for philosophy – but also the setting for an origin fable of representation.

Seven years into working on the caves, Weatherford asked her father to write a text about them and various points of reference. In response, he offered 'Different Kinds

53. cave 2000

Flashe on canvas
30.5 × 22.9 cm (12 × 9 in.)
Private Collection

54. bauhaus and the vanishing point 2001

Flashe, seashells, and sequin on jute
22.9 × 30.5 cm (9 × 12 in.)
Collection of the artist

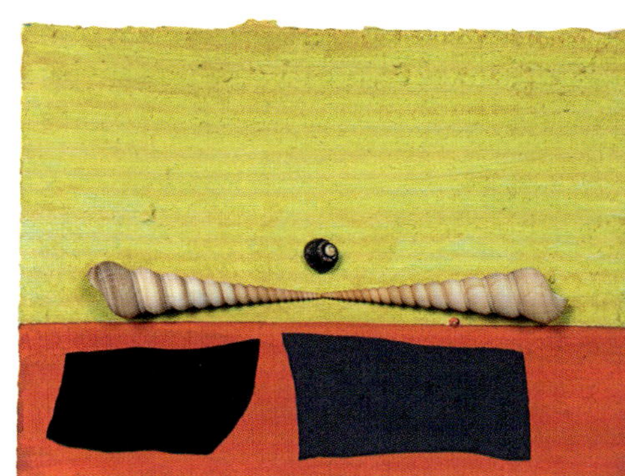

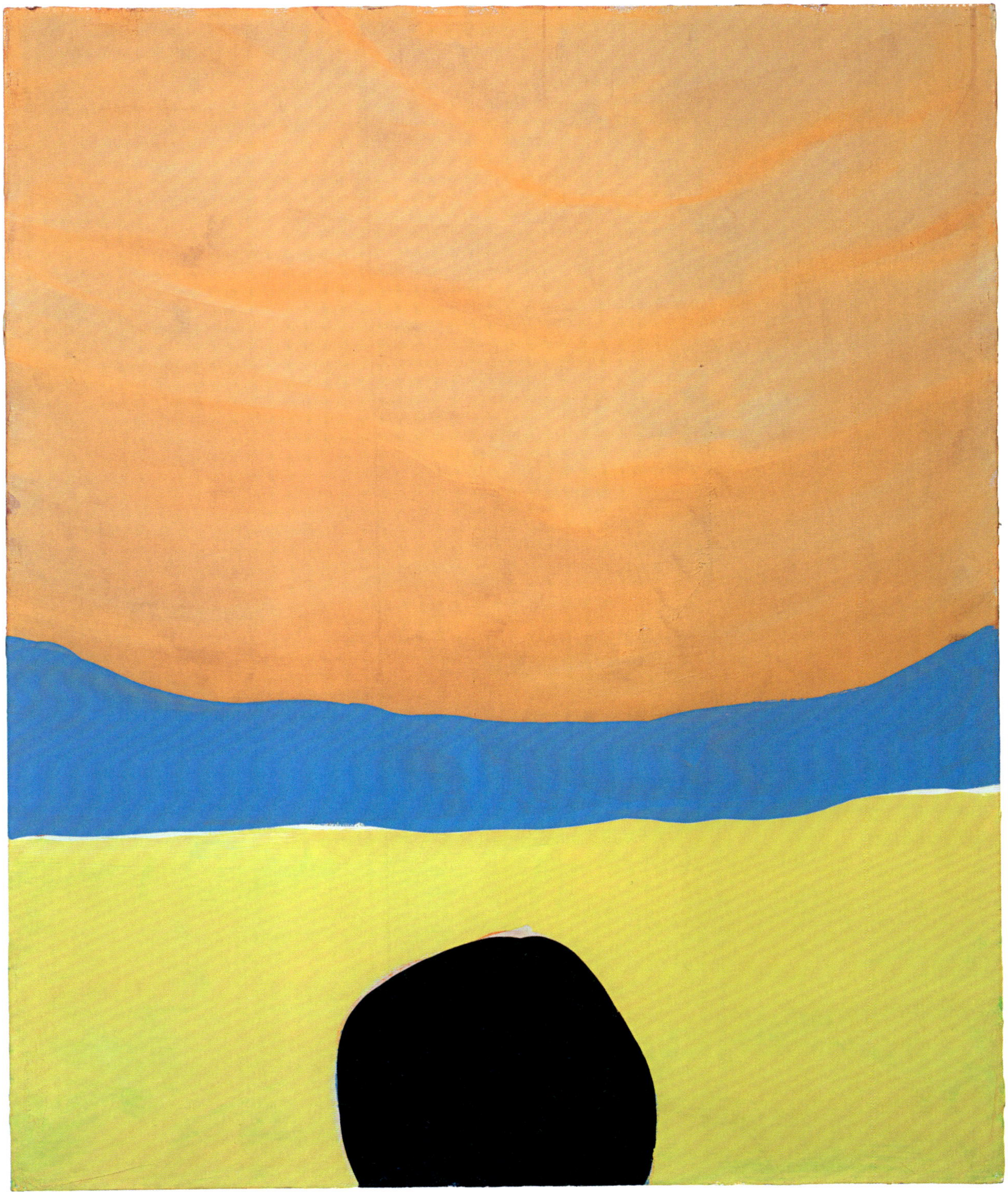

55. beach 2000

Flashe on canvas
152.4 × 124.5 cm (60 × 49 in.)
Collection of the artist

of Caves', 2007, a reflection in a tripartite structure: 'Paleolithic Ritual at Lascaux', 'Mythological Romance', and 'Classical Greek Philosophy'. The first section, about Lascaux, reads:

> Discovered by four teenagers in September 1940, these caves contain some of the earliest known art, dating from a time between 15,000 and 20,000 BC. The paintings show great bison-like beasts attacked by hunters. Animals are superbly executed, while hunters seem but pygmy stick-men. Paleo-anthropologists suggest that the caves and paintings were used as a numinous setting for total immersion in the minds and senses of candidates for adulthood. These prolonged rites invoked, encoded, and took possession of the very spirit of the animals (*anima*, spirit) to be found and stalked and killed and eaten. Thus rebegotten, the initiates squirmed unassisted through a 120 foot pitch-black exit passage barely two feet in diameter. One by one, they emerged into the earth-world above . . . reborn to exercise dominion over the beasts of the field.[8]

This story of a return from subterranean burrow into the living world above ground echoes sources from Persephone all the way to Alice in Wonderland, but it skews less to self-fulfillment (how Carl Jung would characterize such a passage to the restoration of ego after a period of psychic darkness) than ceremonial rite. It also resonates with the trope of the studio as cave from which the toiling artist emerges with work to exhibit.[9]

William Weatherford stresses the social dimension of the cave in the second section as well. He tenders it as a site of congregation and mutual beholding of realms 'vast and beautiful', as per Gimli in *The Lord of the Rings*, the character he cites in a passage culminating with the suggestion of a dream-world where 'towers bend and waver like weeds and corals in a grotto of the sea'.[10] In his third section, Weatherford quotes Plato's parable of the cave, wherein prisoners see only outlines thrown onto the wall they unendingly face. Weatherford ends by remarking on how liberation – possible only if one challenges 'inherited assumptions' and moves into the sun, where the outlines dissolve – is forgone by the refusal of action, a conclusion that constitutes something like a critique of word without deed. (He writes: 'The allegory's protagonist (Socrates?) does not try to drag the prisoners kicking and screaming into the light . . . However, he just couldn't stop talking about it.'[11]) 'Different Kinds of Caves' thereby retrospectively consolidated the varieties of intention manifest within what remained an ongoing engagement, with Mary Weatherford's mutability of process, appearance, and meaning signaled in the declarative as well as expressive title.

In the summer of 2004, three years after she made the last painting of the Sunset Cliffs cave, Weatherford went to Malibu for a friend's birthday party. She brought a sketchpad and recorded impressions of Point Dume, a fabled promontory that cascades into the Santa Monica Bay. It marks a hallowed area once populated by the Chumash, though it has more recently been used as the backdrop for Hollywood films (among illustrious examples, it appears in the final shot of *Planet of the Apes*, where Charlton Heston realizes he has been on earth all along). For Weatherford, it also rouses visions of 'Monet's pictures of the cliffs at Normandy and Picasso's massive bathers enjoying the seaside'.[12] After that initial visit, Weatherford returned frequently to draw the giant rock from the same vantage, from which she could move forward as though she was walking into a painting. Here, she illustrated the cliff with pencils and bamboo pens, using saltwater for solvent. These *plein-air* drawings led to studio paintings, with four from 2004 – *blue to blue* (fig.61), *the whiteness of the whale* (fig.62), *end of days*, and *of whales in paint; in teeth; in wood; in sheet; in stone; in mountains; in stars* – heralding a shift to larger-format meditations on geology, shadow, illusion, and presence when shown at Faure & Light Gallery, Santa Monica, in January 2005. Weatherford followed this process of transcription from direct encounter to studio production until 2012.

Where the first caves made geology into proscenium framings, in these and ensuing paintings from 2004 and 2005, Weatherford also painted rock formations with portals to an interior chamber as seen from afar, and then moved to closer-up views of the vestibule, by 2006 finding a wet cave and then a dry cave that made this process easier. The rock surfaces are continuous but also composed of discrete planes that shift what is available to sight, and from what vantage (figs 64, 65). Elsewhere, the solid mass of the rock serves as the foil for the colors developing within. This play of recession is notable in non-cave series from these years as well, which include brick walls (fig.70), thickets of weeds, and snares of vines (fig.69), the last of which she atypically painted from observation without sketches over a very long period. ('The vine paintings are made on site in my patio', Weatherford has written. 'I make them one at [a] time without reference material. They are the same size, grey palette, and nearly identical view into a tangle of ivy. The vine paintings are absolute residual evidence of perception, time, and physical translation – into the brain through the eye, and down my arm.'[13]) The vines were thus exceptions, a metaphoric record of tangled morass prompted by the American invasion of Iraq in March 2003, the beginning of the mangled war the United States euphemistically codenamed Operation Iraqi Freedom.

Everything Weatherford was doing then involved blockages – the walls and overgrowths, the rocks that loomed imposingly in the landscape as if physically in one's field of vision. Paintings including *town & country*, 2002, show brick walls erected to the painting's midline, the sky above; others like *moonrise*, 2004 (fig.70), extend the masonry to just shy of the top, where a full moon sits in the night sky. In both, a glimpse of the scenery beyond makes more emphatic the force of the impasse. Weatherford advanced these works as she was pursuing an MFA at Bard College's Milton Avery School of the Arts in upstate New York.

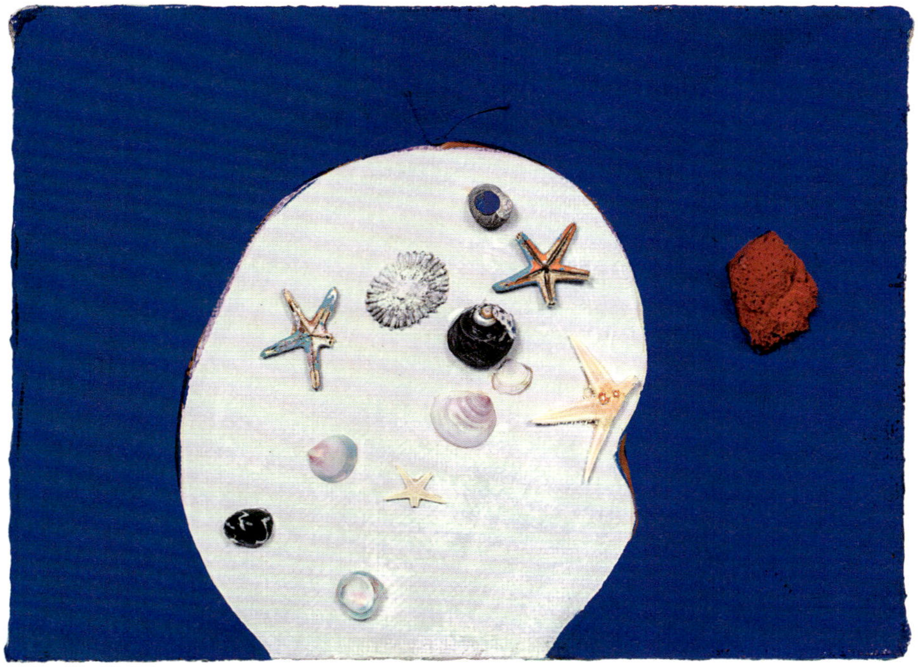

56. junkhead alien 2001

Starfish, seashells, sponge, and Flashe on jute
22.9 × 30.5 cm (9 × 12 in.)
Collection of the artist

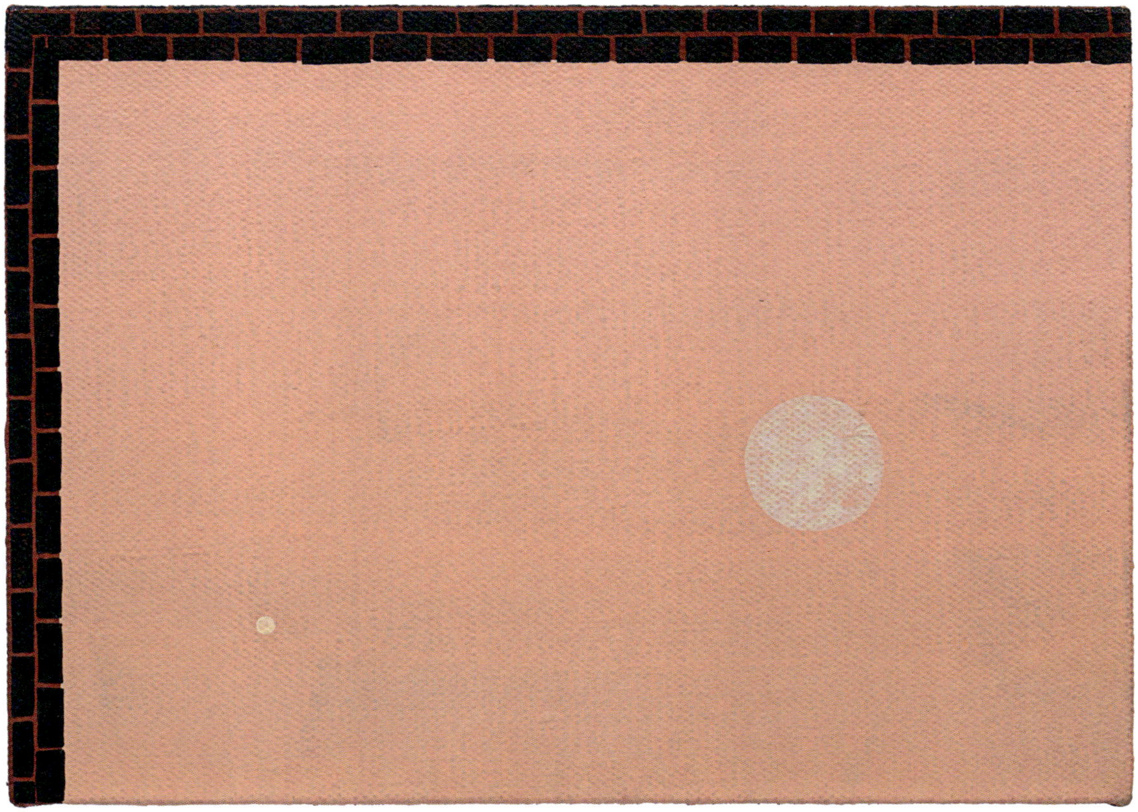

57. My Magritte 2002

Flashe on linen
27.9 × 38.1 cm (11 × 15 in.)
Collection of the artist

A low-residency program, Bard allowed her to continue living in California as she worked with Amy Sillman and Stephen Westfall, who ran the painting section. (Weatherford had applied and been accepted in 1995 but did not end up attending until 2003.) She completed her degree in 2006, showing Point Dume paintings (including *Egyptology* and *bather*) and laced vines as her thesis show.

Weatherford explained the relationship of these bodies of work to one another as follows, in an undated artist's statement:

> The themes of my work are the big ones: mortality and morality. The visual cues are day/night, seen/unseen, above/below, inside/outside. Sub-themes are painting, abstraction, representation, paint.
>
> In 2003, after fifteen years of abstraction, I started drawing from life. I read that Hodler made his great Symbolist paintings of Lake Geneva from 1,000 drawings he made at the lake. Now I make drawings on site and use all of these drawings as source material for the painting.
>
> Recent images are a thicket of **weeds**, a cliff and outcropping of **rocks**, **caves**, and a tangle of **vines**. All *essential* subjects, all pursued in series.[14]

In all these series, she explicitly thematized blindness, from the aforementioned Cyclops to Oedipus wandering unseeing. In the caves in particular, she also referred rather directly to Christian theology, and again (as she had with *5:00 a.m.*) to Mary Magdalene standing before the empty tomb.

After Bard, Weatherford moved her studio to San Luis Obispo, on the remote Central Coast of California. She sought out natural formations with rushing water, but settled on a dry sea cave at the north end of Pismo Beach, which remained a touchstone even as she went back to her Los Angeles base after about a year. As she began the works on this sea cave, which she would make public the next year, she premiered other Point Dume paintings at Sister in Los Angeles in 2006, in what was her first solo show in the city (fig.59). She exhibited *night painting, bather, Western Mystery* (fig.64), *american transcendental*, and *mountain*, all 2005. In the press release she authored, Weatherford describes herself as an 'unreliable narrator' in that she 'interprets her working drawings' such that each changes: 'A pyramid appears on the horizon; boulders are rearranged; the beach disappears. Some pictorial elements are repeated, others are dropped.'[15] In a review, Amra Brooks described the subjective creation of nature in the studio as an intercession that registers 'different emotional and physical qualities . . . as the original image gets farther away from the truth. Sometimes elements are left out, and at other times they are added, making each image a subjective interpretation of a California landscape. Similar to the ideas of the Impressionists, these paintings seem to express all the intricacies found in a moment.'[16]

In *Paintings of a Cave*, the ensuing presentation at Sister in 2007, for which William Weatherford authored the cave text, Weatherford exhibited works based on the sea

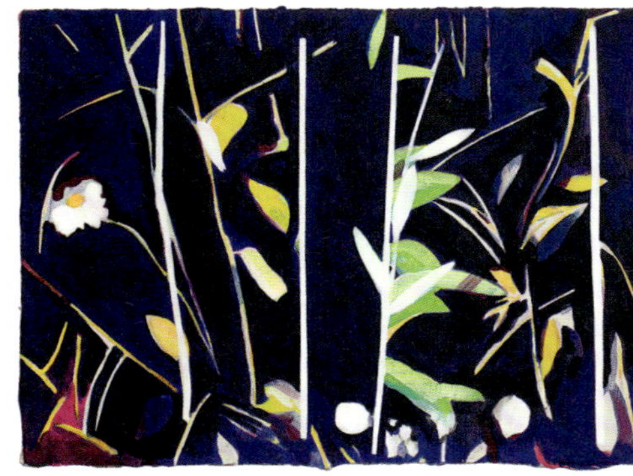

58. weed painting (blue) 2003

Flashe on jute
30.5 × 40.6 cm (12 × 16 in.)
Collection of the artist

59. *New Paintings*
Sister
Los Angeles
2006

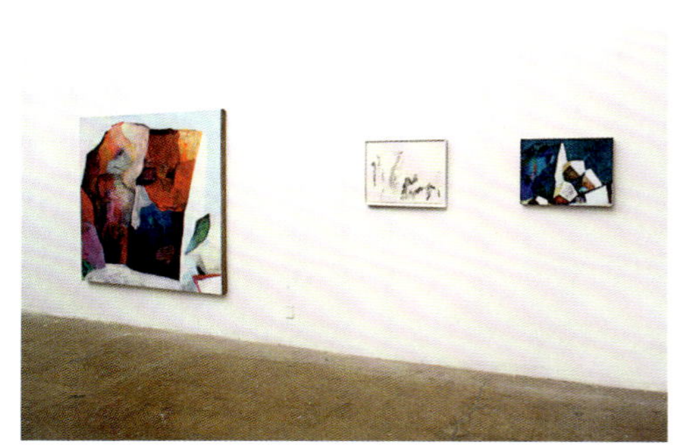

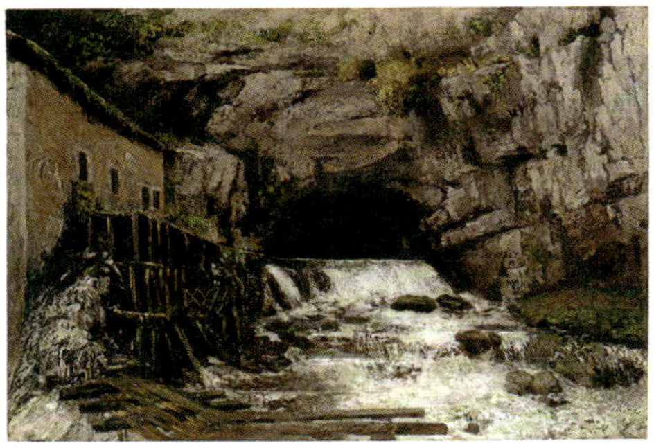

60. Gustave Courbet
The Source of the Loue 1864

Oil on canvas
99.7 × 142.2 cm (39¼ × 56 in.)
Metropolitan Museum of Art, New York

cave at Pismo Beach, a small formation that she loved for its compactness, entrapped within a giant aperture that bares internal contours as sunlight moves across it; it didn't hurt, either, that it so astonishingly evokes Gustave Courbet's *The Source of the Loue*, 1864 (fig.60). She showed *equus* and *the spiritual in art*, both 2006, together with others, such as *heat and shadow*, 2007. *El Dorado*, 2007 (fig.68), is another standout in this group, a painting with the entrance to the cave seemingly punched into the flat picture plane, promising the existence of something that it will never disclose. Even in its monumental stasis, with colors subtly asserting themselves out of the inchoate darkness it suggests a changeable aspect that was registered also in dozens of monoprints Weatherford made this year, all titled *Cave at Pismo*. Many are black and white, but others shade to concentrated lapis blues or lusciously synthetic pastels.

A conversation with artists Kathryn Andrews and Julian Hoeber had convinced Weatherford to amplify the watercolors into paintings that preserved the effect and spontaneity of the ink drawings, to achieve something like a large-scale watercolor that kept the looseness and iterability of the improvisatory act of seeing and knowing through making. She did. She used the background of the painting as though it were the incipient blankness of a watercolor page. These looser caves were a solution to problems of figure and ground in that they flipped from one to the other in a perfect gestalt of legibility. She later showed the newly spare *green cave*, *red cave*, and *black cave*, all 2006, at the Orange County Museum of Art's *California Biennial 2008*, curated by Lauri Firstenberg.

The biennial opened a few days before two other simultaneous shows: Weatherford exhibited vine paintings at Sister and collages with starfish and brick walls for a companion installation at Cottage Home, Los Angeles (fig.71), which opened the same night (October 11, 2008). New caves from the Pismo spot continued apace, ultimately in the vein of those on view in the California Biennial. If anything, Weatherford intensified her work on them amid these various modes of retrospection: her father's text and the paired presentations that made visible ongoing concerns from the previous decade. Considering the two venues together in a *Los Angeles Times* review, Christopher Knight noted the return to established series over the temporal bracket represented. He assented: 'It's easy to see why. The modest repertoire is surprisingly compelling, like a quirky set of self-imposed limitations that demands continual reinvention.'[17] Importantly, too, in Knight's claiming of multiple references (Jackson Pollock, J. M. W. Turner, Jasper Johns, Vincent van Gogh) in but a few expedient words of short-format prose, this piece affirmed Weatherford's capacious knowledge of art history and established a precedent of source-hunting for her iconographic or stylistic cues as the basis for critical engagement with her painting.

Works on paper continued also, and not merely as a means to another end. Weatherford showed one such group of ink-on-watercolor-paper caves a couple of

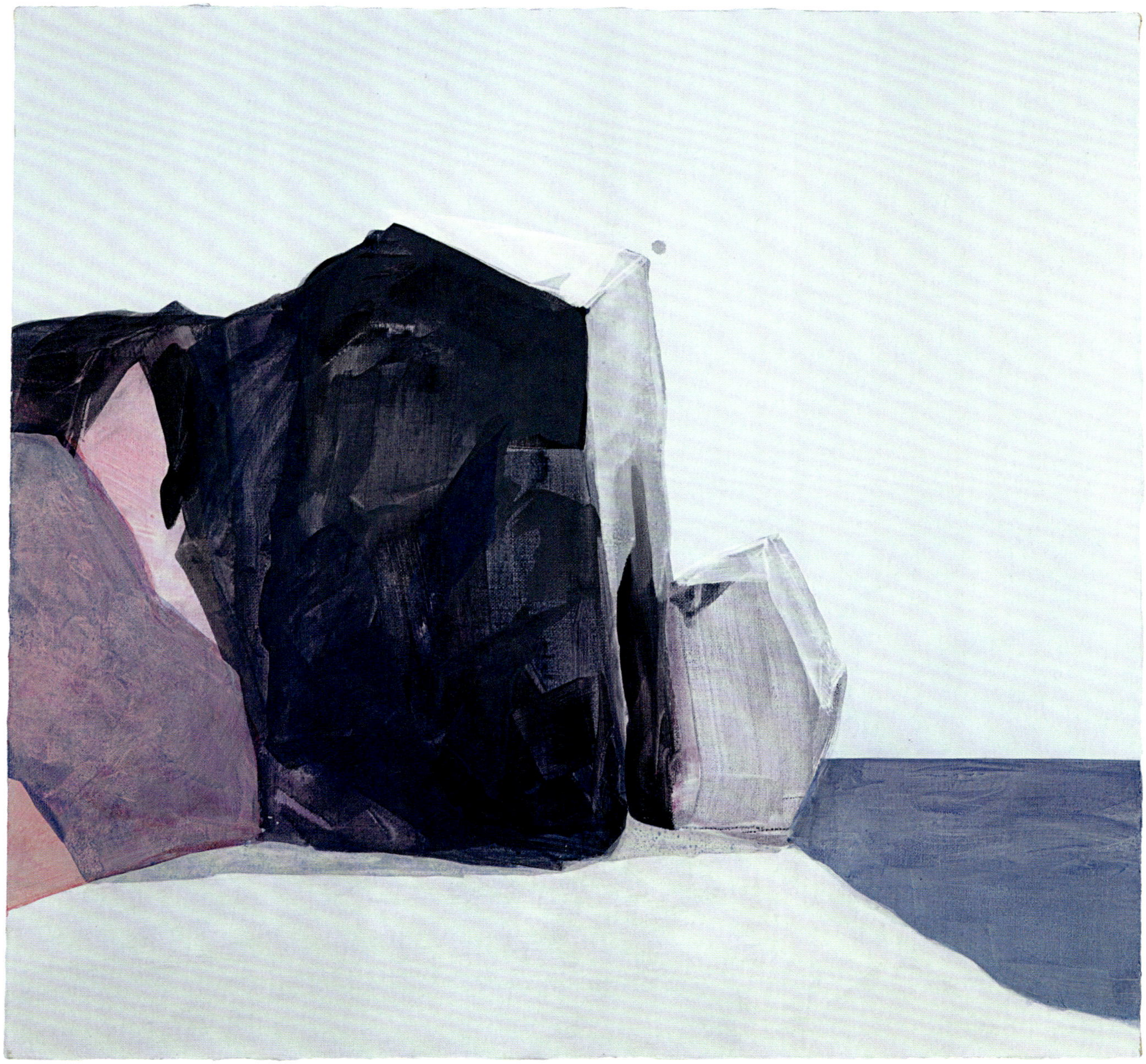

61. blue to blue 2004

Flashe on jute
101.6 × 106.7 cm (40 × 42 in.)
Private Collection

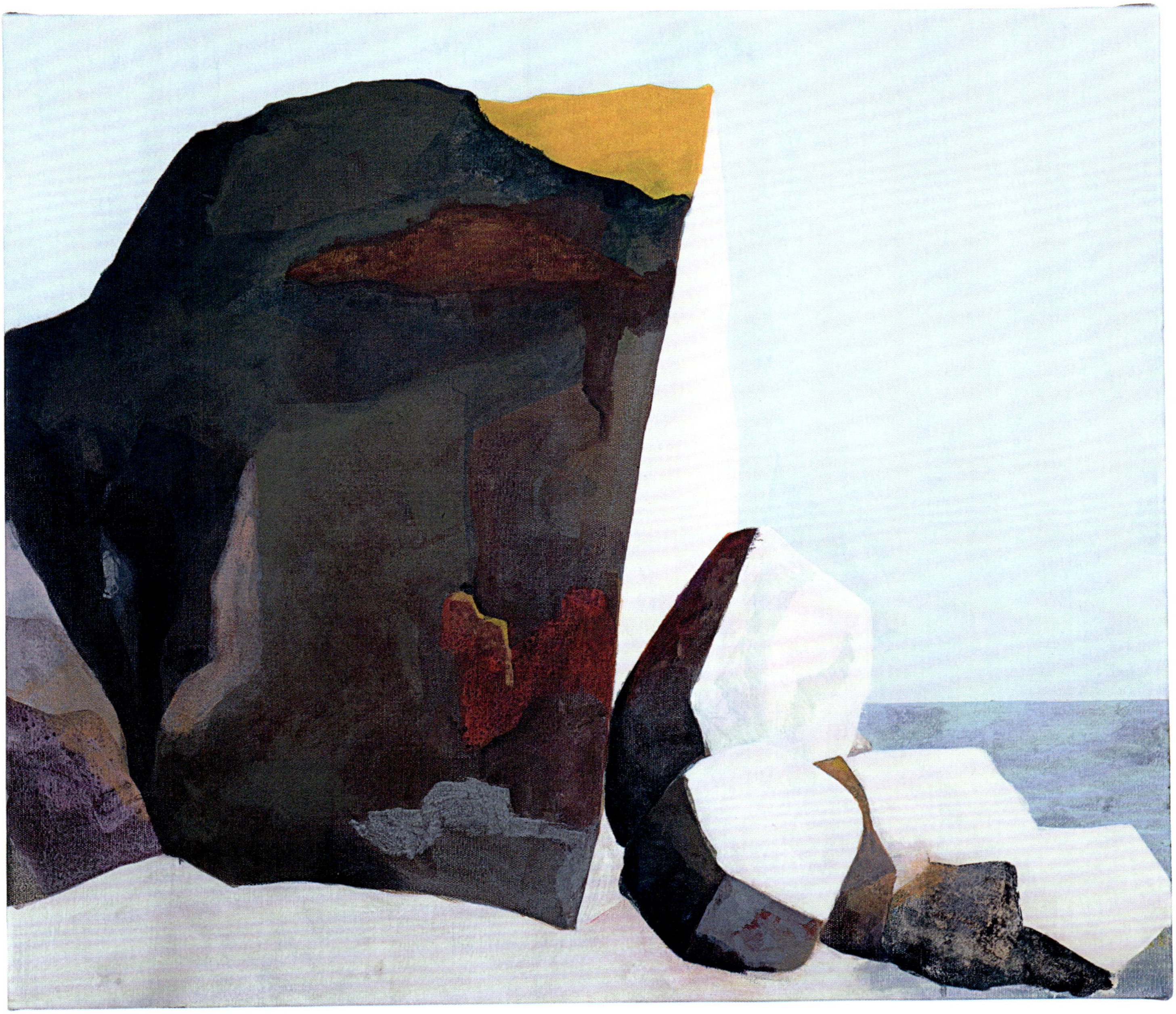

62. the whiteness of the whale 2004

Flashe on linen
106.7 × 121.9 cm (42 × 48 in.)
Private Collection

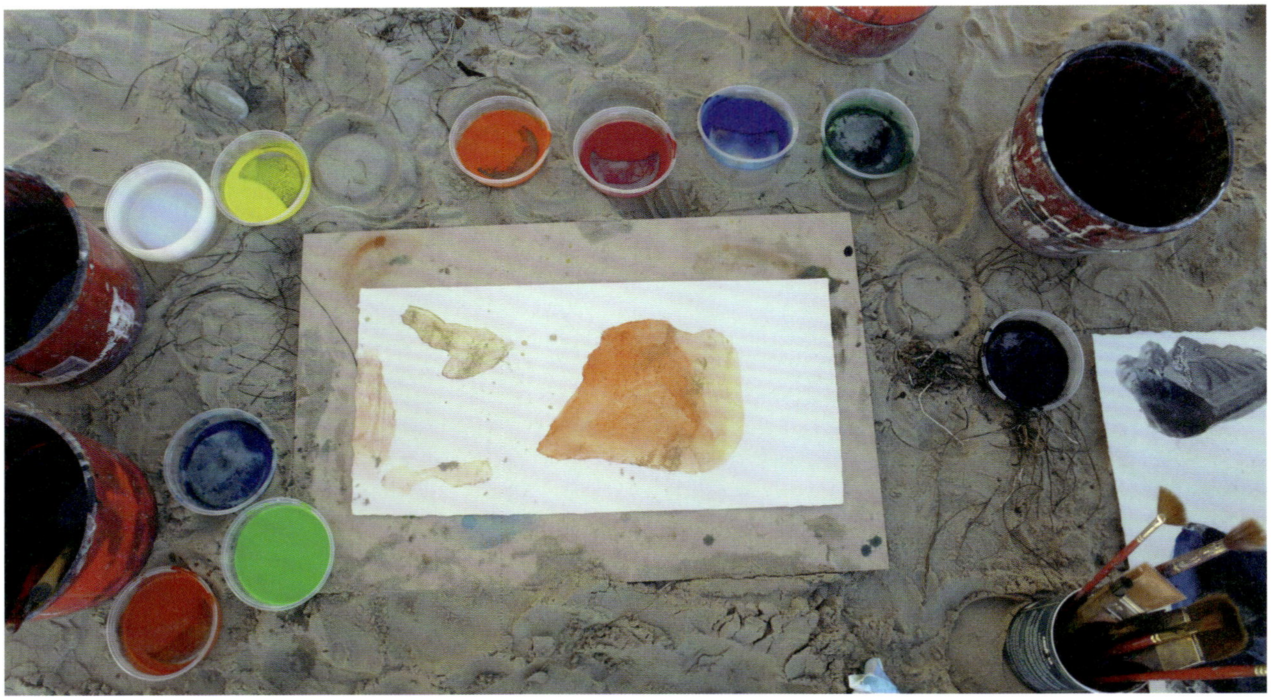

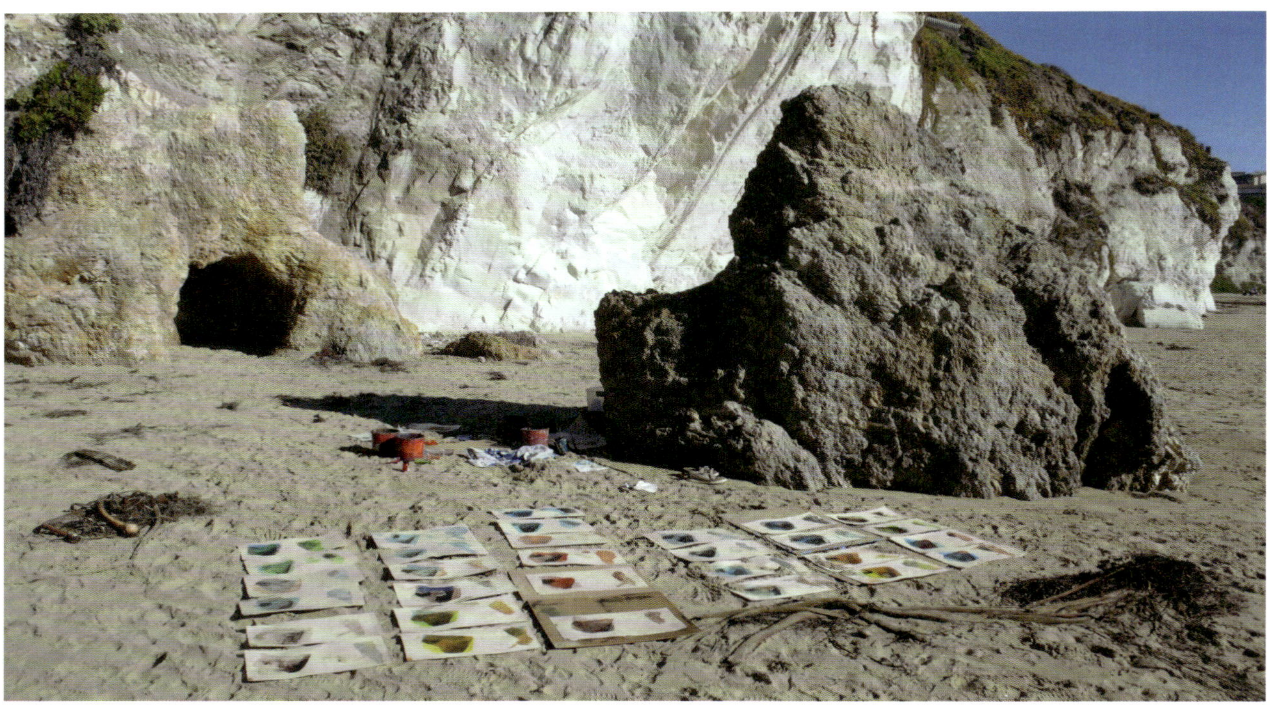

63. Works in progress, Pismo Beach, 2010

years later, in 2010 at John Tevis Gallery, Paris. The press release notes that the Pismo Beach works

> have their origins in Gustave Courbet's paintings of the source of the Loue. Weatherford's caves reverse the expected figure/ground relationship: her voids are ink and the solids are the white of the paper. At first glance, Weatherford's images might depict a head, a rock, or simply an abstract blob. The naming of the works (all works are entitled *cave*) compels the viewer to see them anew. In effect, language turns the images inside out, as in Edgar Rubin's perceptual gimmick, popularized by Duchamp, where one sees either a vase or two opposing faces.[18]

Before this – and likely accounting for Weatherford's conceptual framing of the works on paper in the above press release, which she authored with Tevis – she made clear the stakes of the void and its invitation to meaning in an interview with Alex Israel:

> AI: When I first saw your work, I wondered whether the joke was on you or on me. I wasn't sure if you were consciously borrowing from the [Georgia] O'Keeffe calendar and the Laguna Beach Festival of Arts. But over time I realized that the paintings are quite dark.
> MW: They're all about mortality.
> AI: It's not just the reference to time, tides, and erosion that's dark. There's another kind of heaviness to the images. The biennial paintings are deceptively thin. There's darkness, a kind of anxiety, to your thin veils of paint.
> MW: Morris Louis's veil paintings are my all-time favorites. Some look like an American Airlines ad, and some are the saddest paintings I've ever seen.
> AI: And they're sublime in the Burkean sense. There's an element of terror in Louis's paintings and in your biennial paintings. They're so elemental, I can see exactly how you made them, and I know exactly how to pull them apart. And that's the scary part: I can imagine peeling back one veil of color at a time, and ultimately I'm left with nothing.[19]

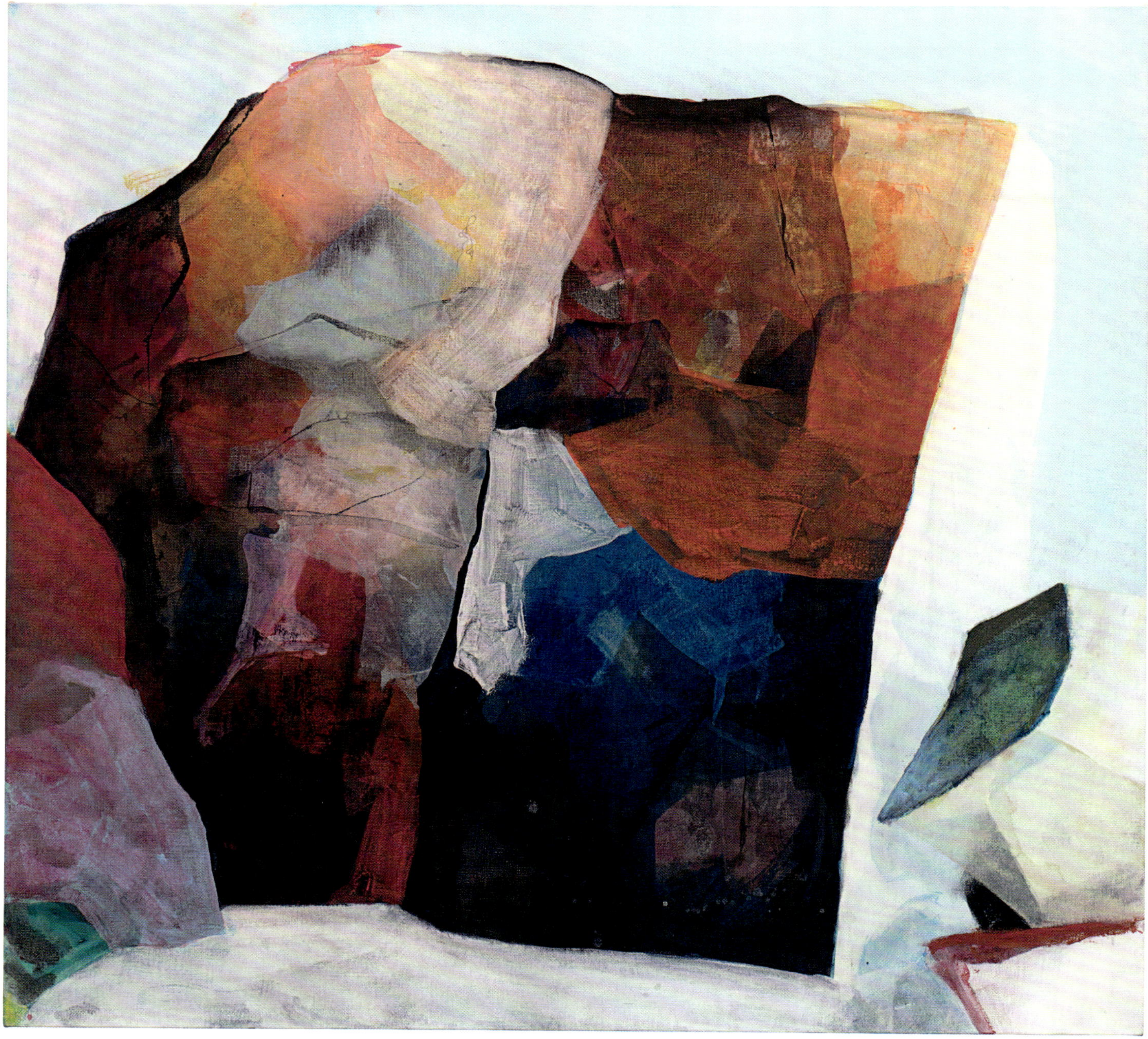

64. Western Mystery 2005

Flashe on linen
162.6 × 177.8 cm (64 × 70 in.)
Private Collection

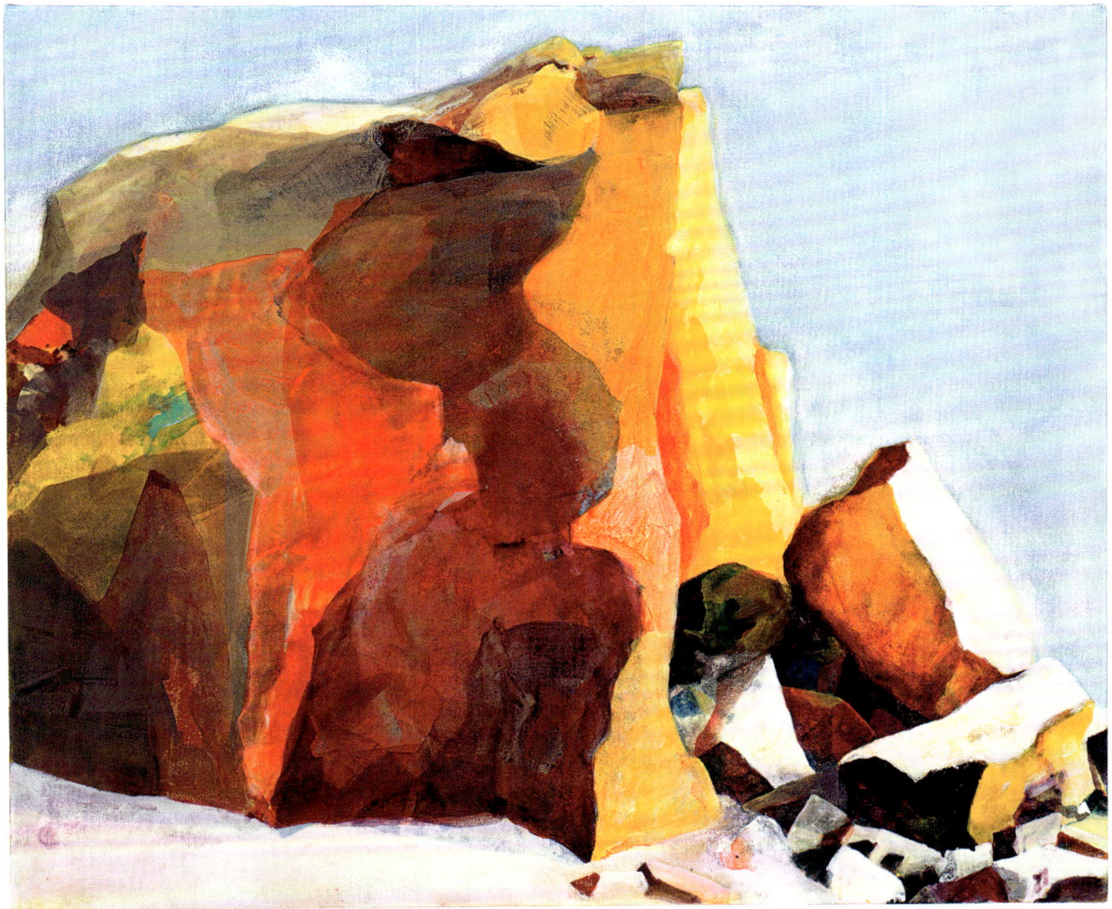

65. after Hodler 2006

Flashe on linen
91.4 × 111.8 cm (36 × 44 in.)
Private Collection

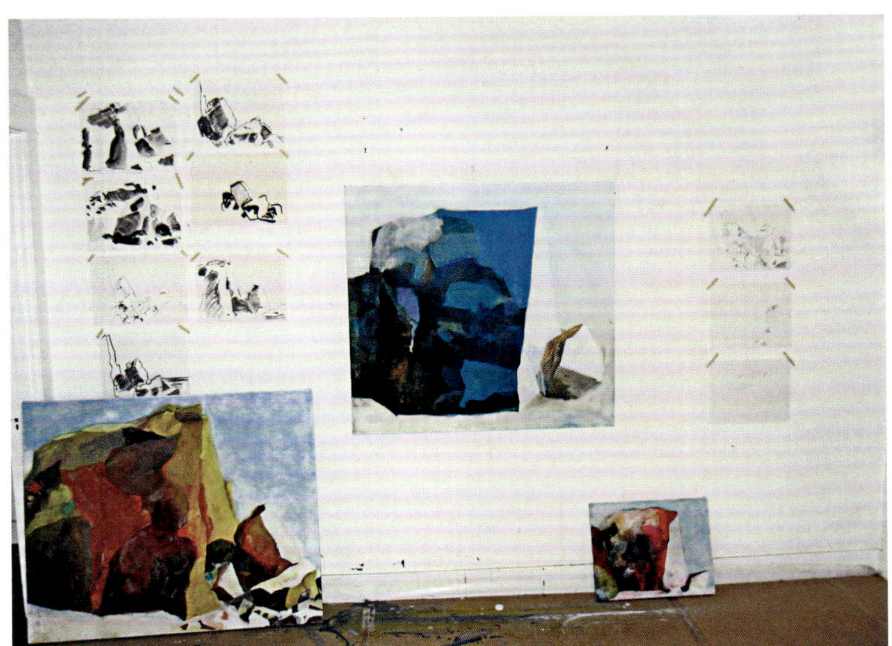

66. Weatherford's living room studio, Los Angeles, 2006

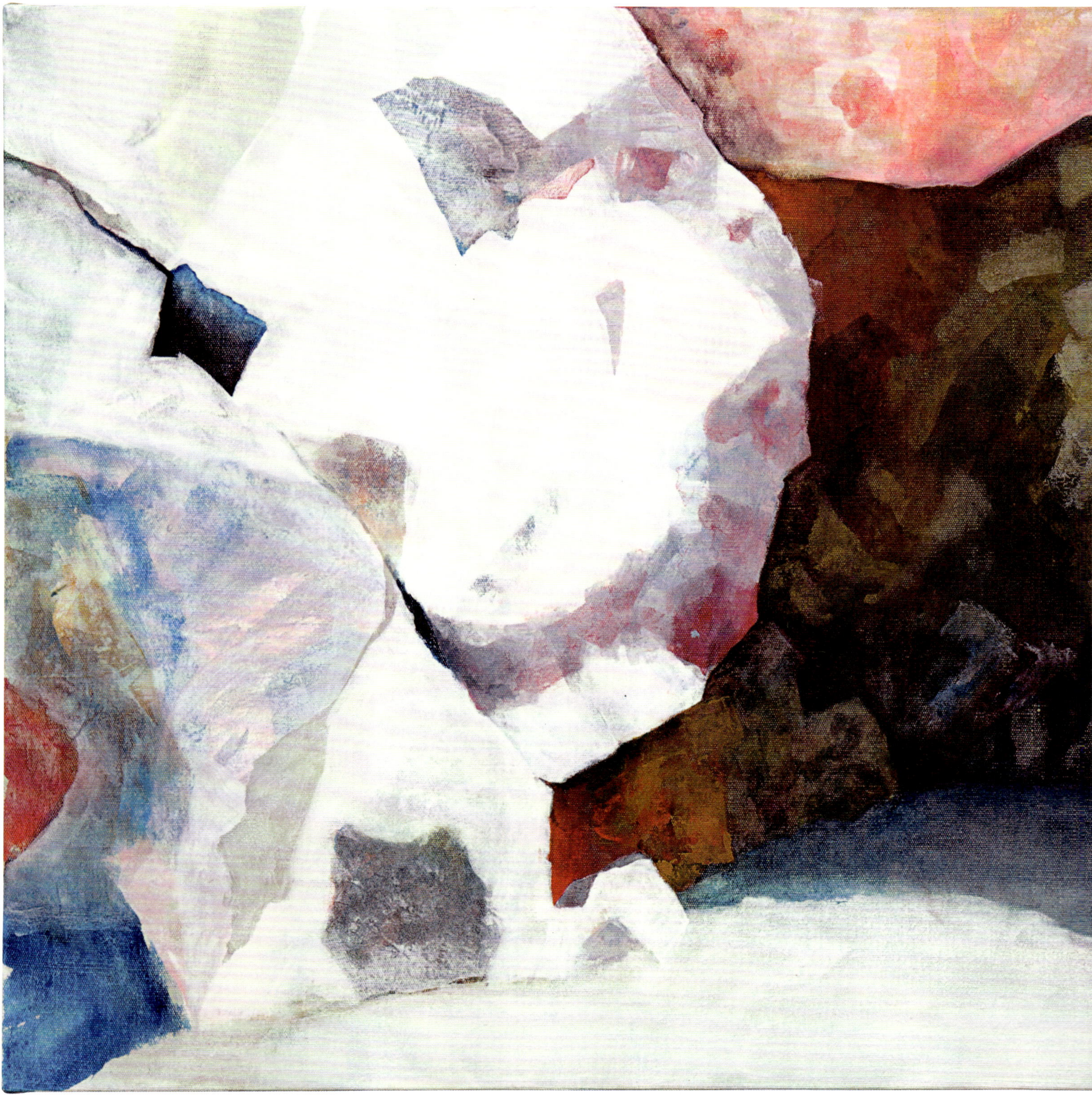

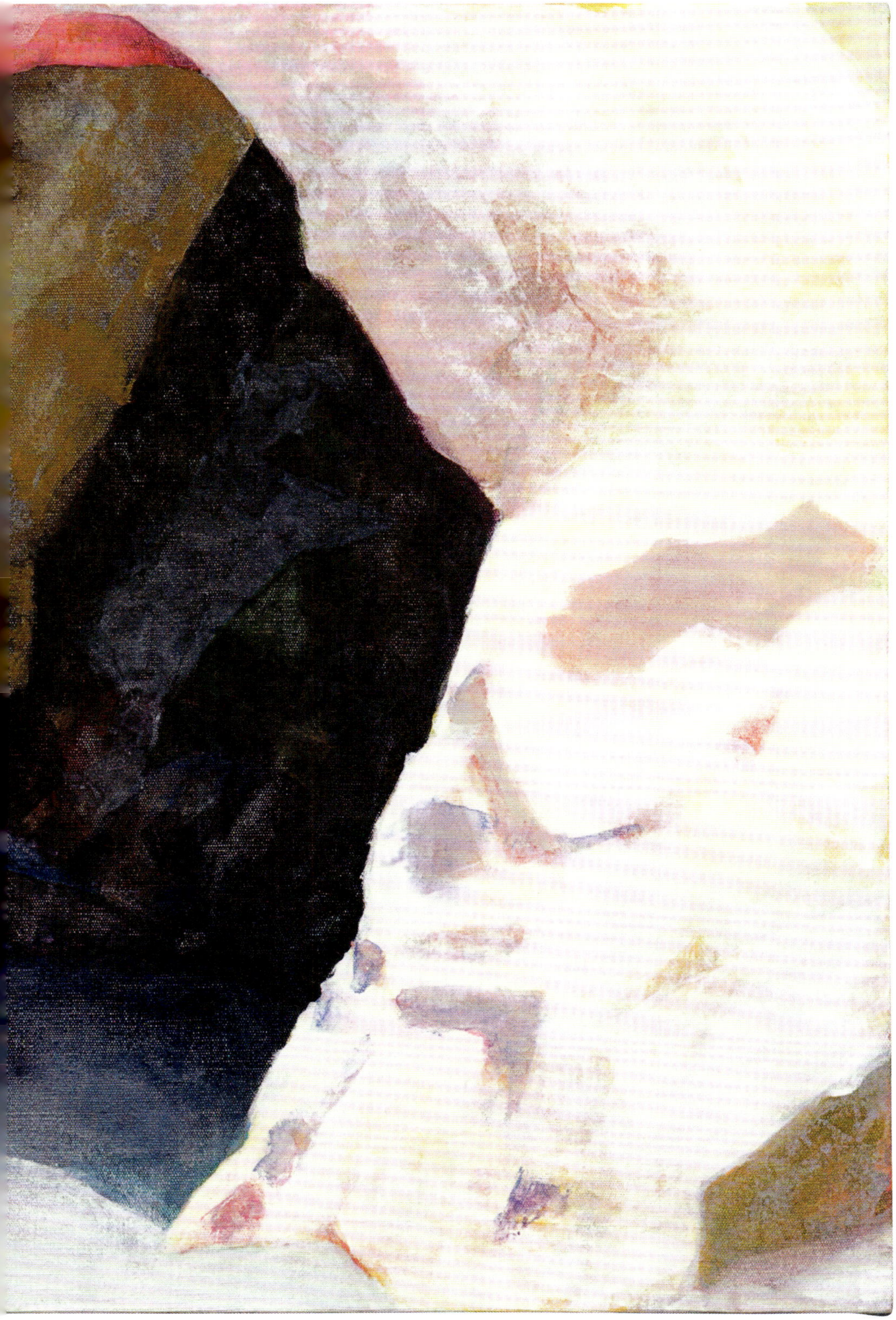

67. after Ensor 2006

Flashe on linen
104.1 × 177.8 cm (41 × 70 in.)
Private Collection

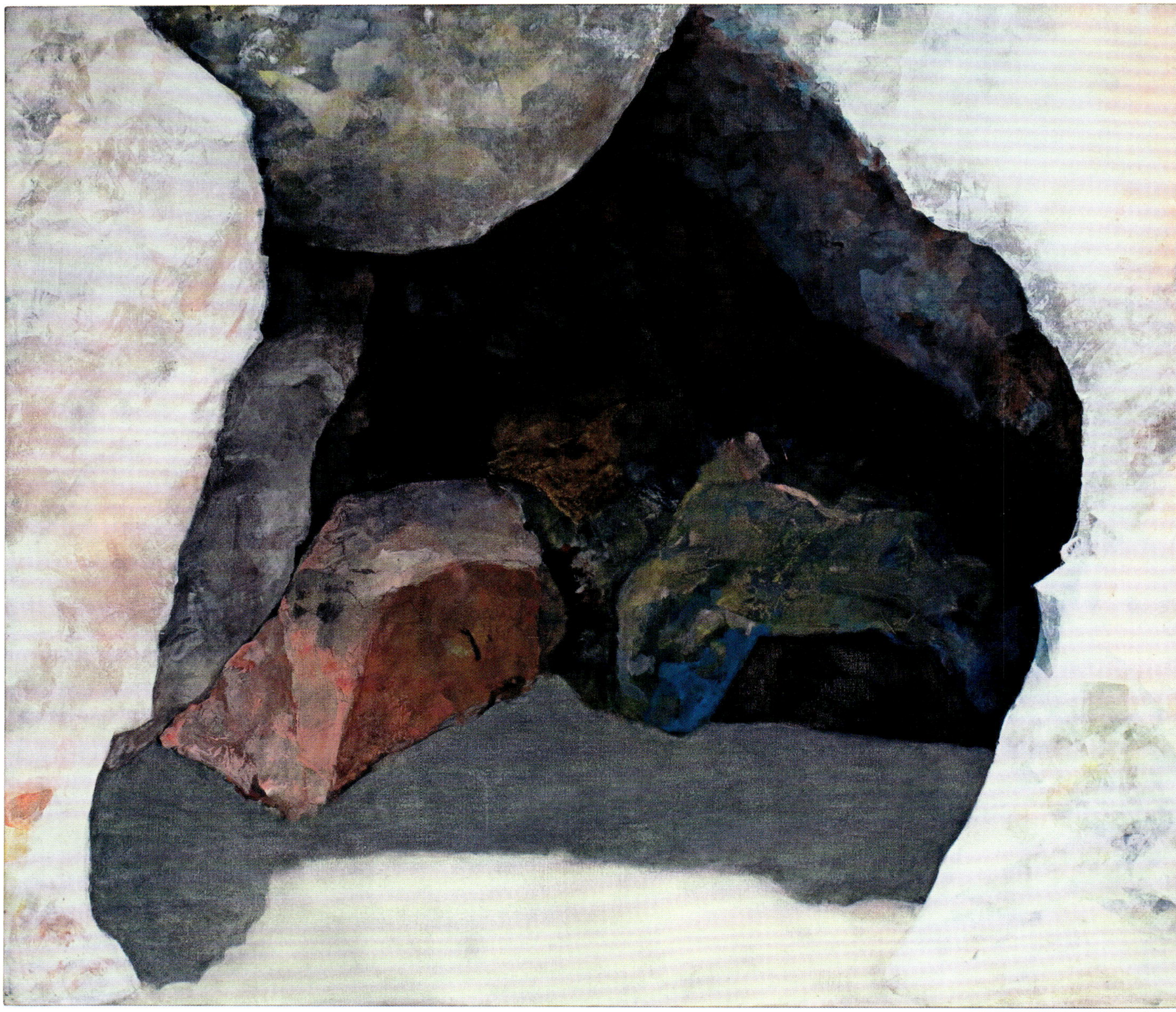

68. El Dorado 2007

Flashe on linen
172.7 × 198.1 cm (68 × 78 in.)
Private Collection

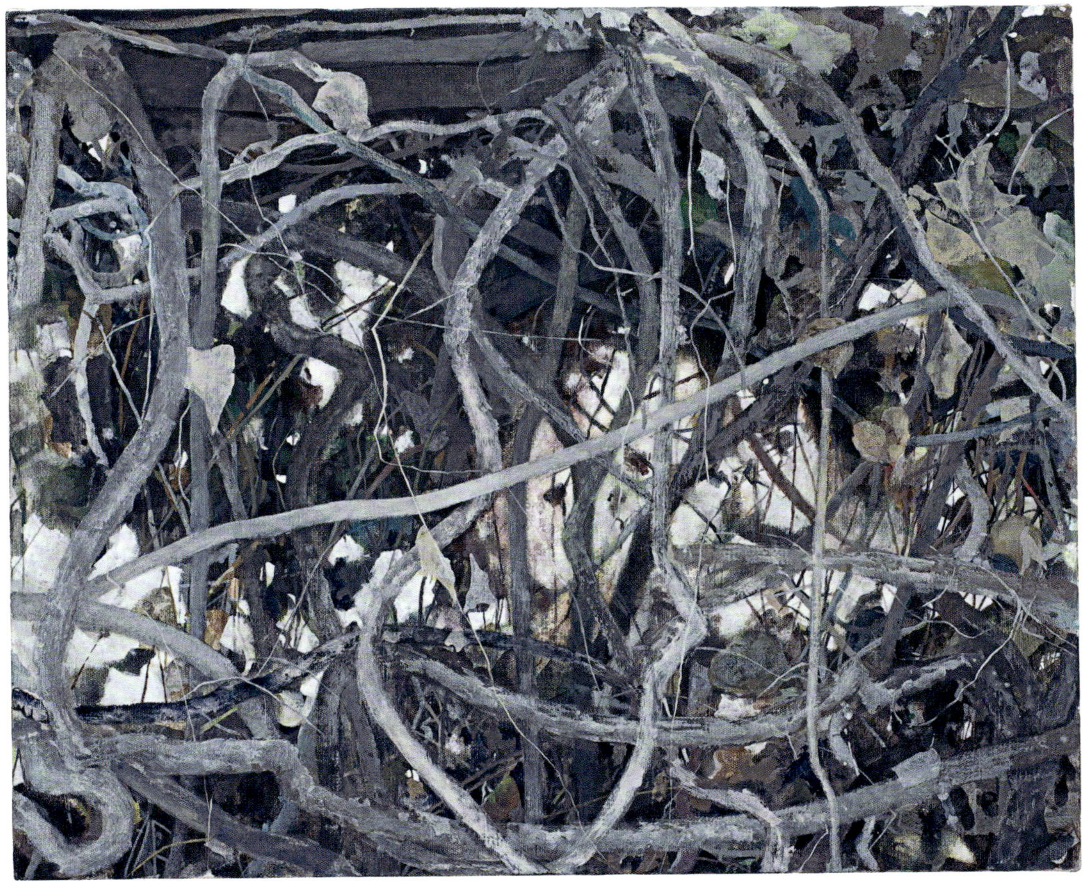

69. vines 2007

Flashe on linen
94 × 111.8 cm (37 × 44 in.)
Private Collection

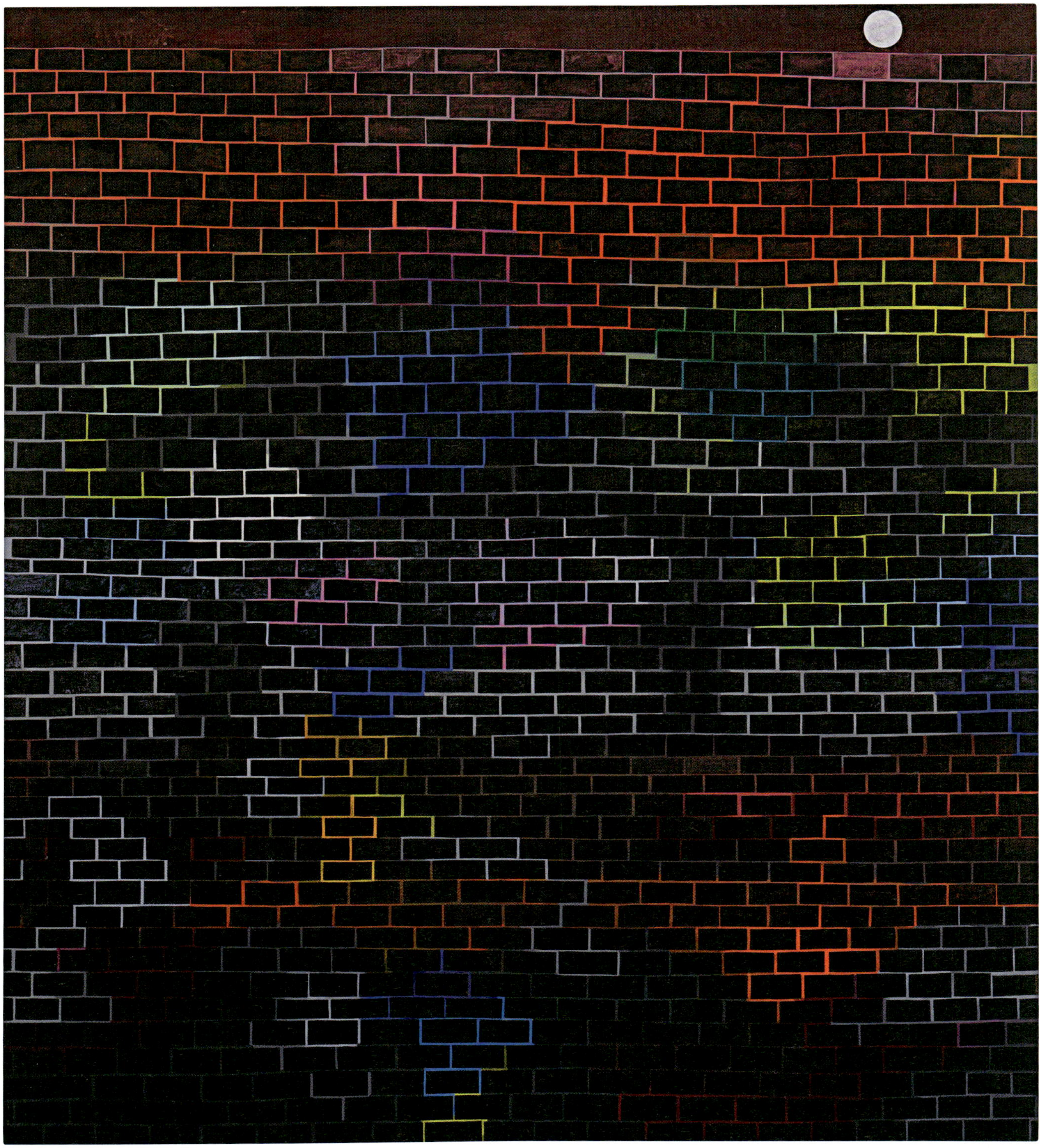

70. moonrise 2004

Flashe on canvas
167.6 × 147.3 cm (66 × 58 in.)
Collection of the artist

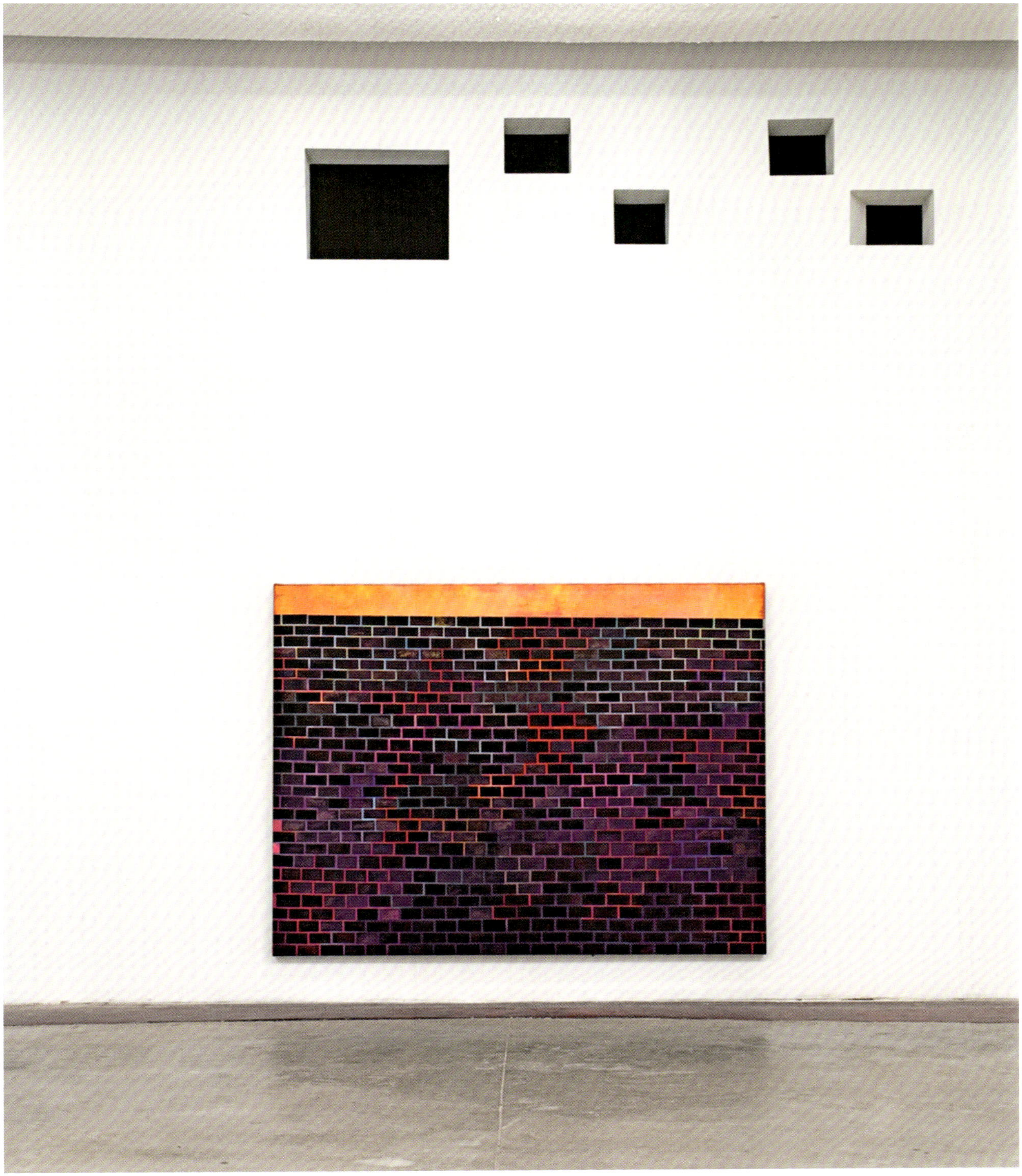

71. Brooklyn 2008

Flashe on linen
198.1 × 254 cm (78 × 100 in.)
Collection of the artist

Installation view
Bricks Walls and Sea Life
Cottage Home
Los Angeles
2008

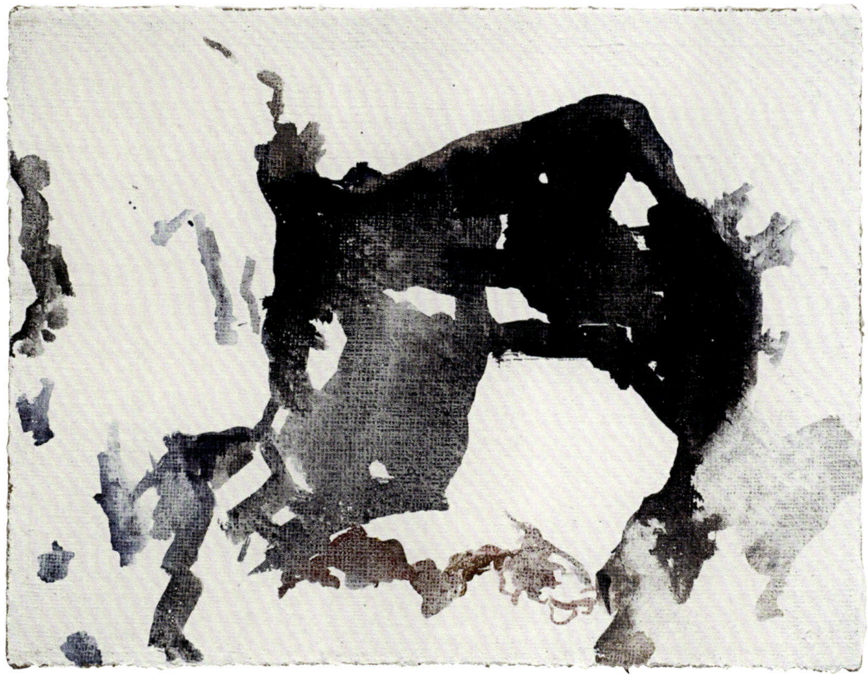

72. January Cave 2008

Flashe on jute
40.6 × 50.8 cm (16 × 20 in.)
Collection of the artist

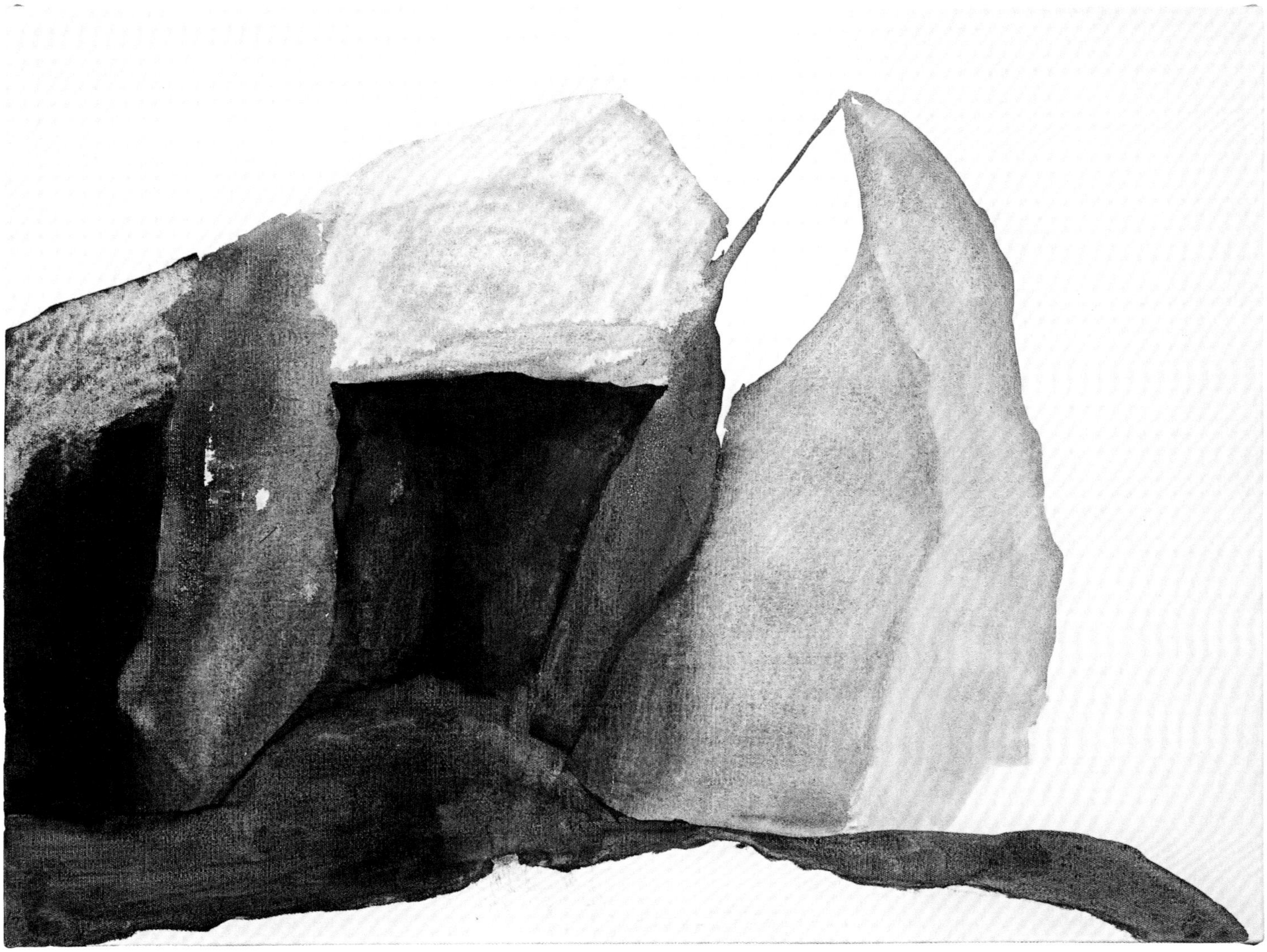

73. black cave 2008

Flashe on linen
101.6 × 132.1 cm (40 × 52 in.)
Collection of the artist

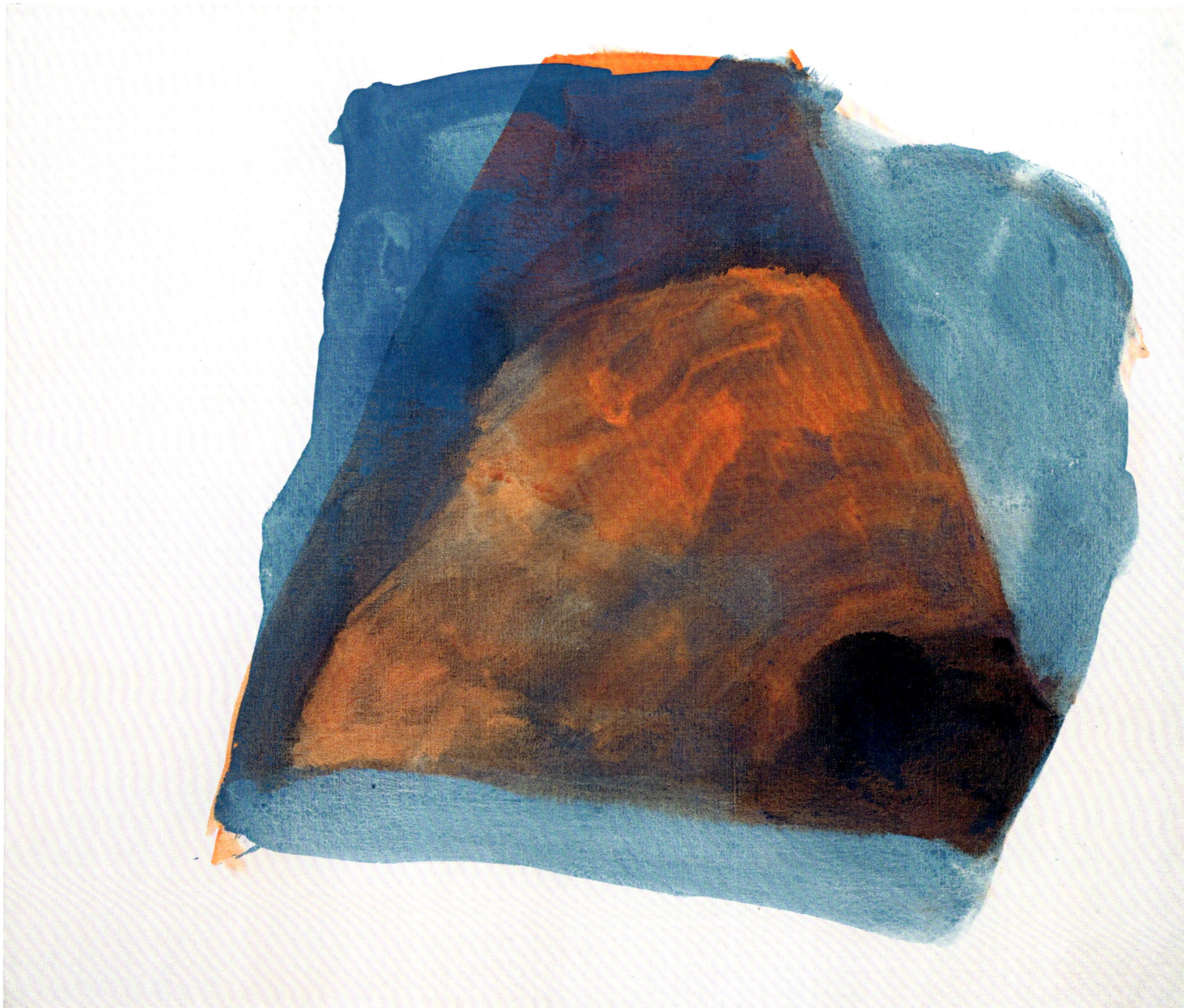

74. blue and coral cave 2011

Flashe on linen
147.3 × 167.6 cm (58 × 66 in.)
Private Collection

5 Atmospheres and Lights: The 2010s

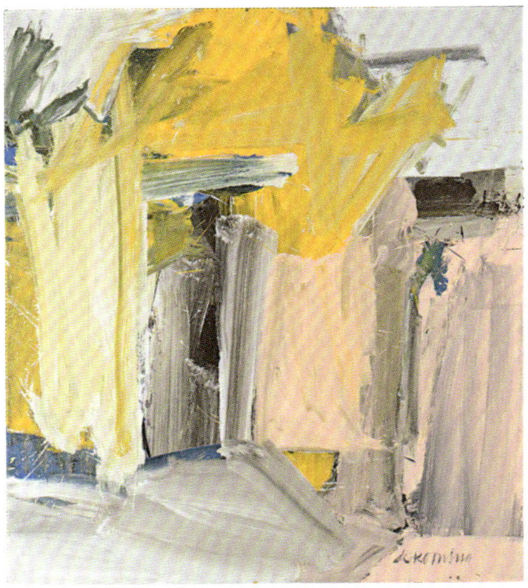

75. Willem de Kooning
Door to the River 1960

Oil on linen
203.5 × 178.1 cm (80⅛ × 70⅛ in.)
Whitney Museum of American Art, New York
Purchase with funds from the Friends of the Whitney Museum of American Art 60.63

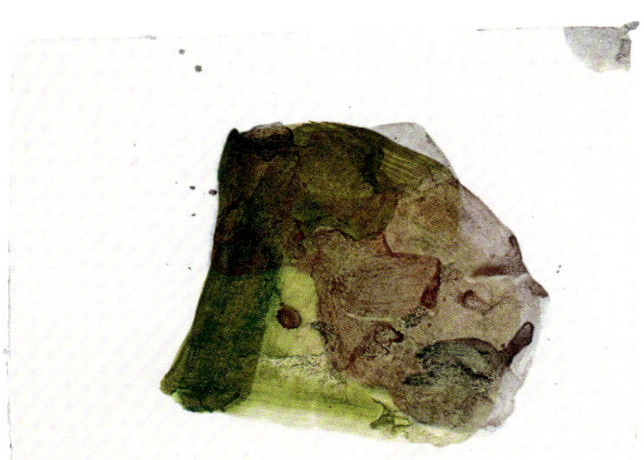

76. cave 2011

Shellac ink on Gampi Torinoko paper
38.1 × 50.8 cm (15 × 20 in.)
Private Collection

When scaled up from the page, Weatherford's caves become diaphanous, terrifying not for their flimsiness but rather for their overture to a dismantling that might be coeval with the viewing subject's undoing. This quality of terror further recalls what Weatherford's father compelled her to see as existential dread in Vincent van Gogh's *Wheat Field with Crows*, and what was more widely characterized in pop-psychology discourse of the period (incarnated by Werner Erhard and his lifestyle engineering, in which he spoke of peeling back the layers of consciousness like an onion until emptiness remained). In any case, the possibility of undoing adheres in her caves through the potent regression into the void: an orifice-like incursion redolent of the bullseye, flower, and starfish. Weatherford makes of the antimonumental, burrowing cave a feminist opportunity, putting the absence of sex at the picture's core. The conflation of hollow and female anatomy is one that painters from Gustave Courbet to Willem de Kooning have tended, with the latter's *Door to the River*, 1960, where pinky-peach tones organize into a carnal portal, serving as a reminder of the long-standing analogy. (None too subtly, in 'The Renaissance and Order', a talk he delivered at Studio 35 in New York in 1949, de Kooning avowed, 'Flesh is the reason why oil paint was invented.'[1])

Courbet comparably exploited this oscillation between landscape and woman in his 'depictions of caves and grottoes and certain overtly erotic paintings of female nudes centered on the vagina', as Michael Fried summarizes, invoking *The Origin of the World*, 1866, a painting that affords a permissive view of the genitals and abdomen of a naked model.[2] However – and to the point of Weatherford's candid appropriations of *The Source of the Loue* – Fried also argues that, simultaneous to their spatial enclosure (to which Courbet was 'regressively' drawn), the caverns also issue forth 'water coursing outward'.[3] He does not characterize this series of multidirectional thrusts in and out of the picture through the movement of water and the stable orthogonal lines of the rocks that steadfastly usher it in more graphically sexual terms, but the point is clear enough, as is the subjectivity of Fried's 'painter-beholder'. In symptomatic response to the womb, Fried – in the interpretive guise of Courbet – resupplies the phallus. He poses that the parrying movement merges the viewer with the painting; Courbet not only established but also experienced the absorption that is also, and importantly for Weatherford, an 'eclipse of visuality'.[4] As Weatherford seems to have understood, the possession of painting undoes distance, and she pulled this off on her terms.

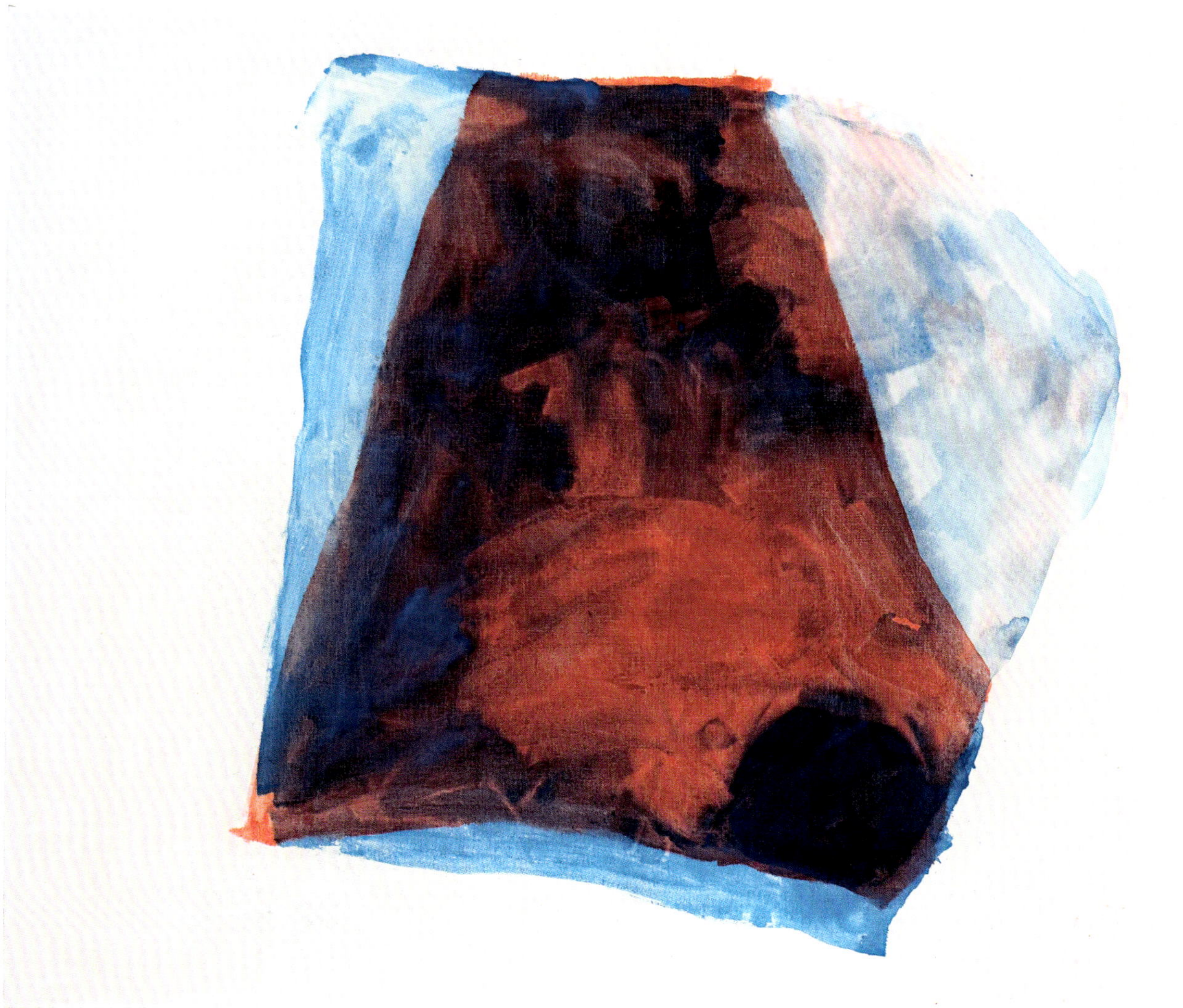

77. red cave 2011

Flashe on linen
200.7 × 231.1 cm (79 × 91 in.)
Private Collection

78. Delilah 2012

Flashe on linen
200.7 × 266.7 cm (79 × 105 in.)
Private Collection

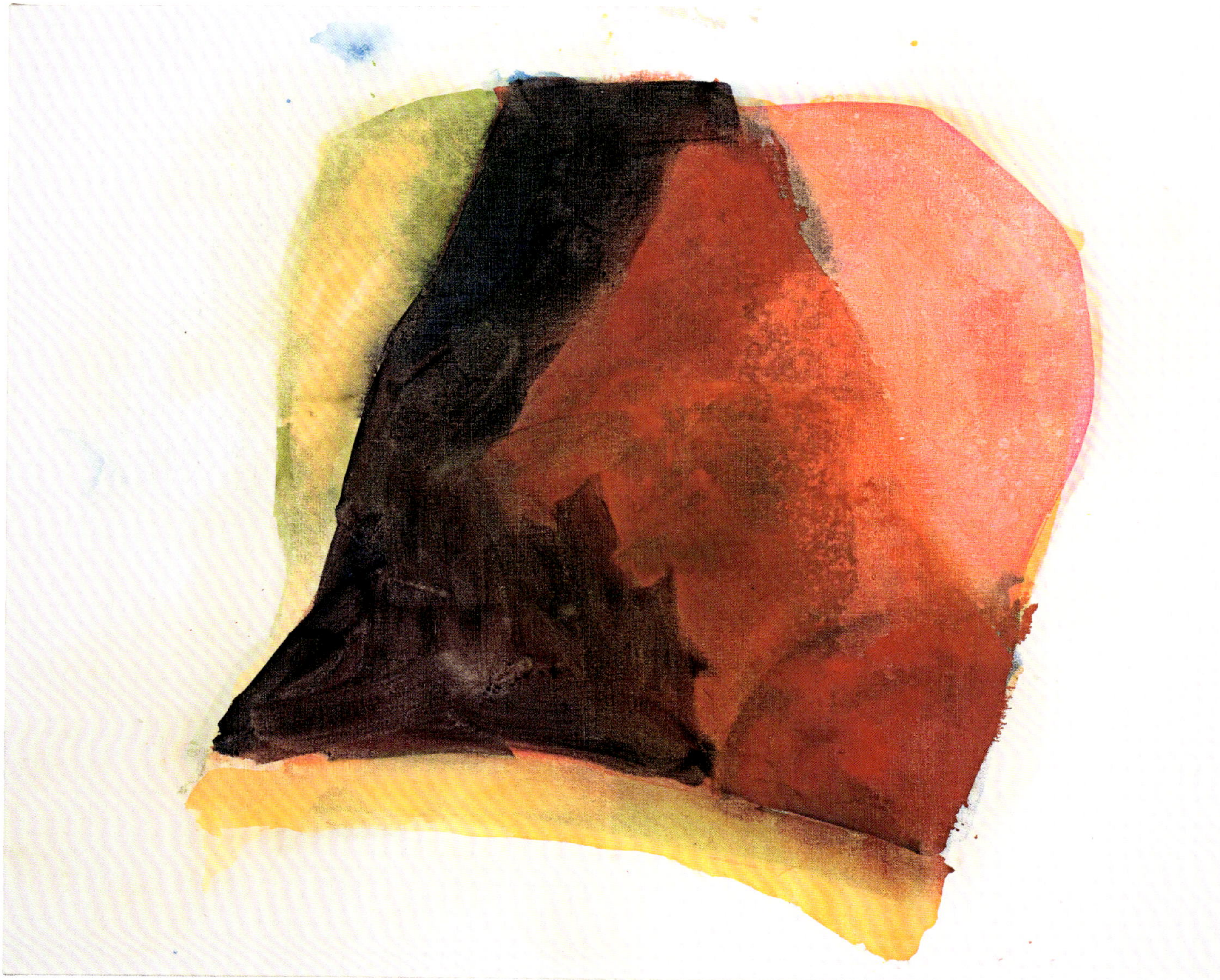

79. Bonnard colors cave 2011

Flashe on linen
162.6 × 198.1 cm (64 × 78 in.)
Private Collection

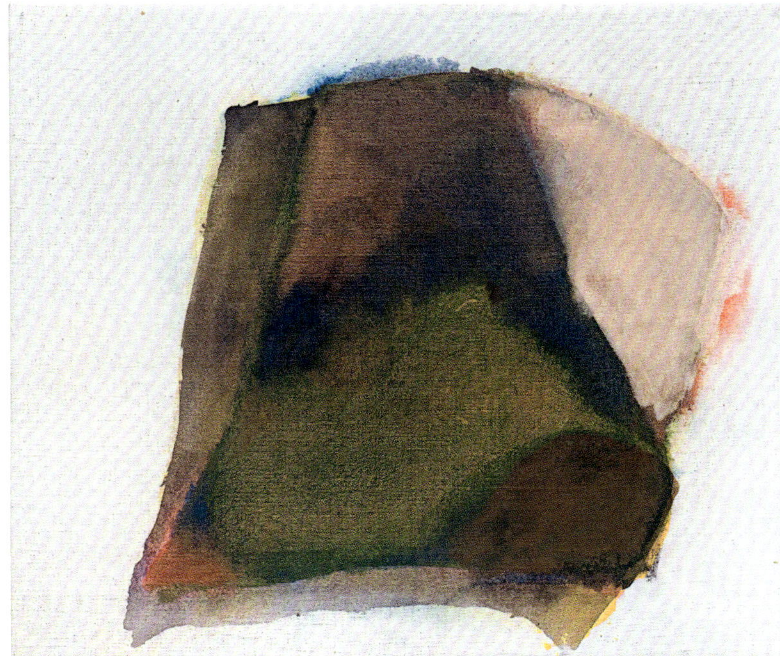

80. Degas colors cave 2012

Flashe on linen
81.2 × 94 cm (32 × 37 in.)
Private Collection

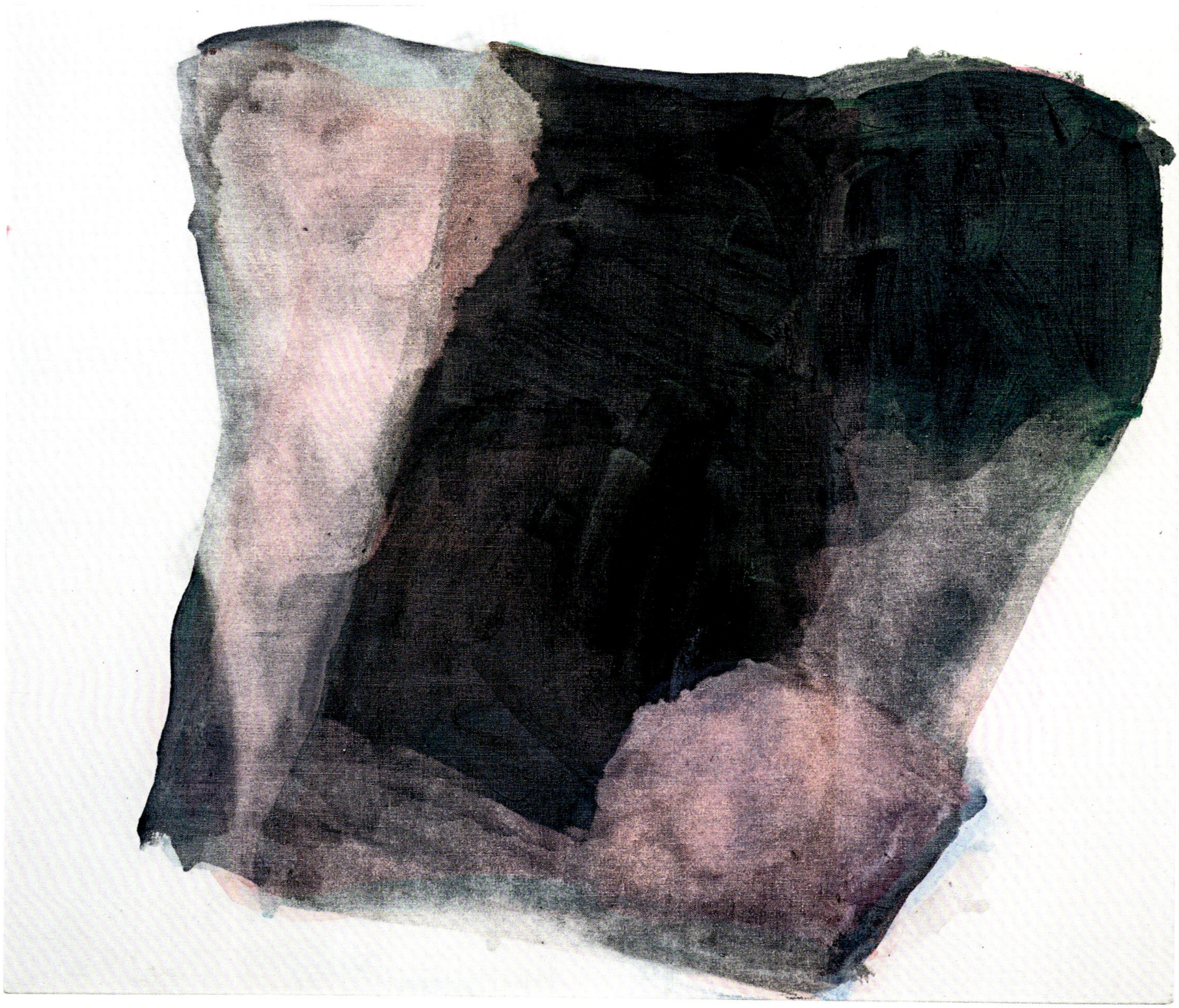

81. black cave 2012–14

Flashe on linen
111.8 × 127 cm (44 × 50 in.)
Private Collection

82. pink cave 2012

Flashe on linen
111.8 × 127 cm (44 × 50 in.)
Private Collection

In 2010 Weatherford decided to take the canvases off the stretcher bars and paint them on the floor. Consequently, she could make her paintings larger because she could walk on them to apply paint instead of reaching in from the sides. She had always painted horizontally, beginning with the targets, which she laid flat on a table; but only with the painting laid directly on the ground could Weatherford physically move into the pictures as she had traversed the immersive coastal landscapes to which they still often referred. (The first unstretched paintings were taped to the floor; in 2012 her assistant built a low wooden platform so that she could staple down the paintings to keep them from shrinking.) One painting, *the sea*, 2017 (fig.103), confesses how she paints in the form of a lone stray footprint perpendicular to one of the syncopated stripes of purple that mark out a horizon as so many points of light scattering on water. More commonly – this tread is a gift – Weatherford erases footprints and handprints by the time she finishes, seeing the work vertically for the first time only when it is restretched. What remains are not so much indexical imprints but a more diffuse immanence that everywhere establishes painting as epistemology – another exodus from the cave, blindness in the act and recognition of a new world only glimpsed in its totality and resolution after, from without.

Cave at Pismo, Weatherford's spring 2011 show at Brennan & Griffin, New York, flaunted what could come of this new method. Every painting contains its own atmosphere, evoking 'shifting time of day and changing seasons',[5] so fully accomplished and non-selfsame does each become. Like the works on paper that she showed in Paris the year before, these paintings use the white ground as a solid rimming a vibrant, multihued void. The show was a hit. *Art and Auction* called it a 'knockout', and on this basis included Weatherford in a list of fifty collectible artists (after noting her 'bad fortune to attract critical notice just before the 1990s art market crash', they crassly predicted a favorable forecast of market success).[6] This would become a leitmotif, wherein her experience over so many years of feast and famine – the *Hollywood Reporter* reminded its readers in 2013 that she was 'no neophyte'[7] – helpfully lends credibility. By 2015 her presence in similar round-ups was nothing less than ubiquitous. No doubt did this restoration have something to do with her inclusion in Laura Hoptman's eclectic *The Forever Now: Contemporary Painting in an Atemporal World* at the Museum of Modern Art, New York, which ran from December 2014 to April 2015. *Coney Island II*, 2012, took pride of place on a prominent wall in MoMA's galleries, while a detail of her painting *la noche*, 2014, served as the cover image for the catalogue. She was made representative of the seventeen artists gathered together on the basis of their ostensibly shared sympathy to pictorializing countless and mutually available data (including styles and genres) – an idea espoused by the post-postmodern theories put forth in the catalogue's pages.

Weatherford's role in *The Forever Now* followed her taking up neon as a medium, and it was this approach to sculptural painting that the show used to suggest her

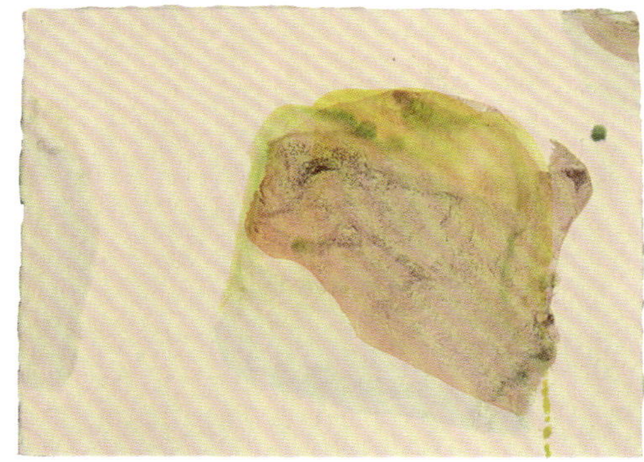

83. cave 2011

Shellac ink on Gampi Torinoko paper
38.1 × 50.8 cm (15 × 20 in.)
Private Collection

84. cave 2011

Shellac ink on Gampi Torinoko paper
38.1 × 50.8 cm (15 × 20 in.)
Private Collection

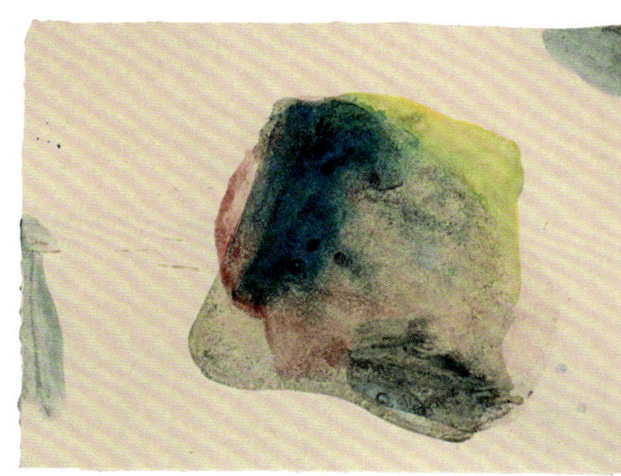

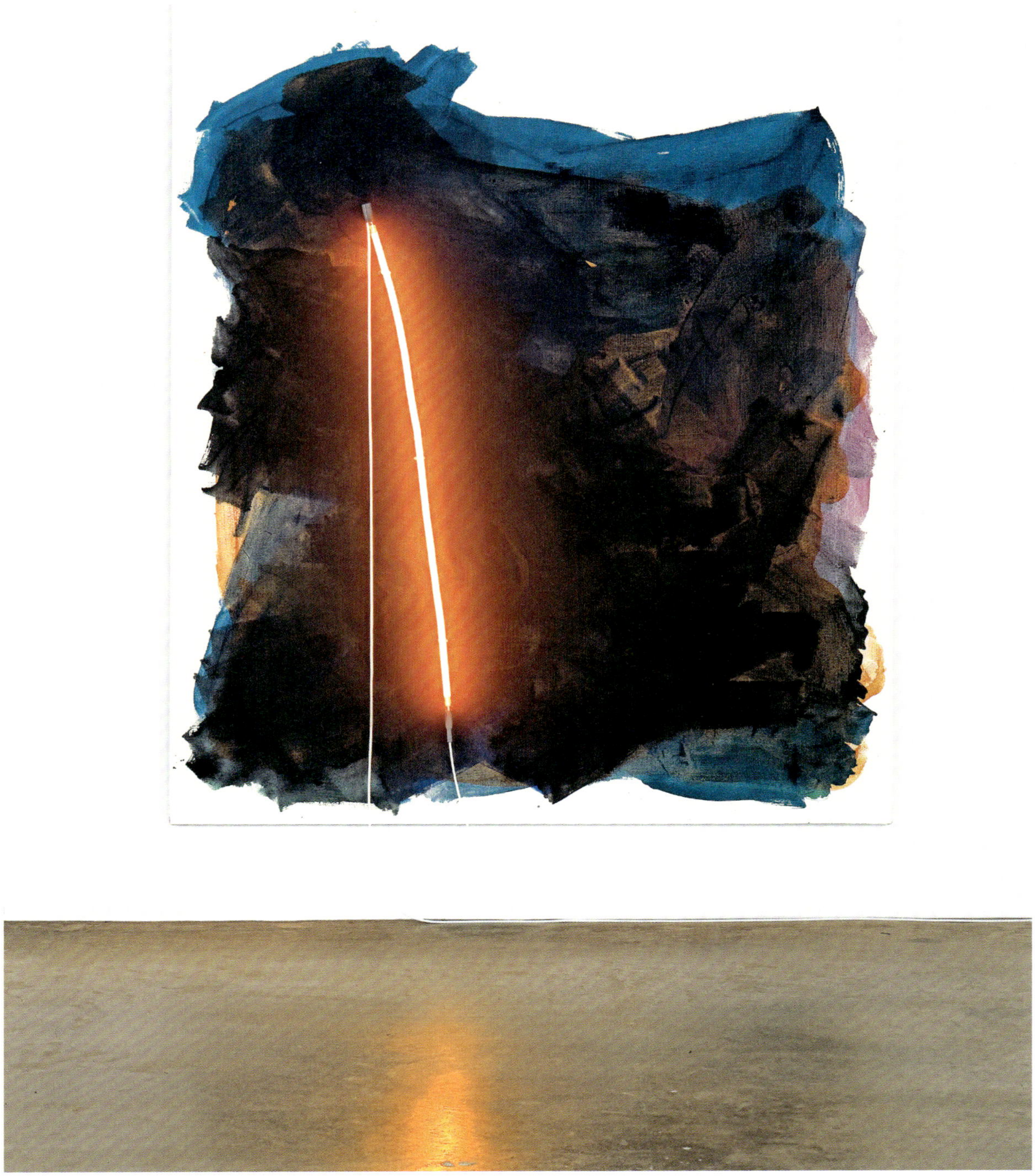

85. Midnight Union Ave. 2012

Flashe and neon on linen
236.2 × 200.7 cm (93 × 79 in.)
Private Collection

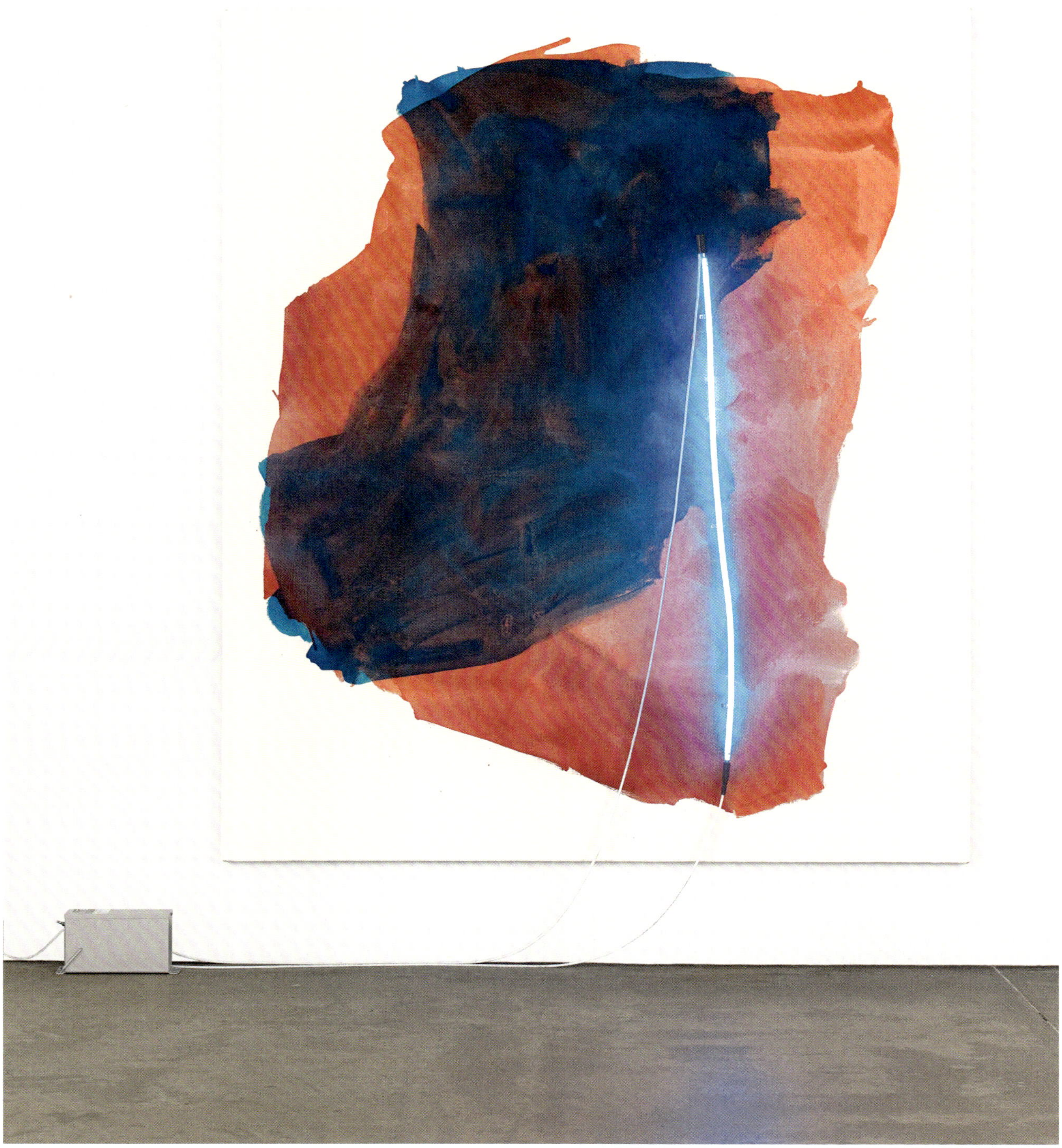

86. California 2012

Flashe and neon on linen
236.2 × 200.7 cm (93 × 79 in.)
Private Collection

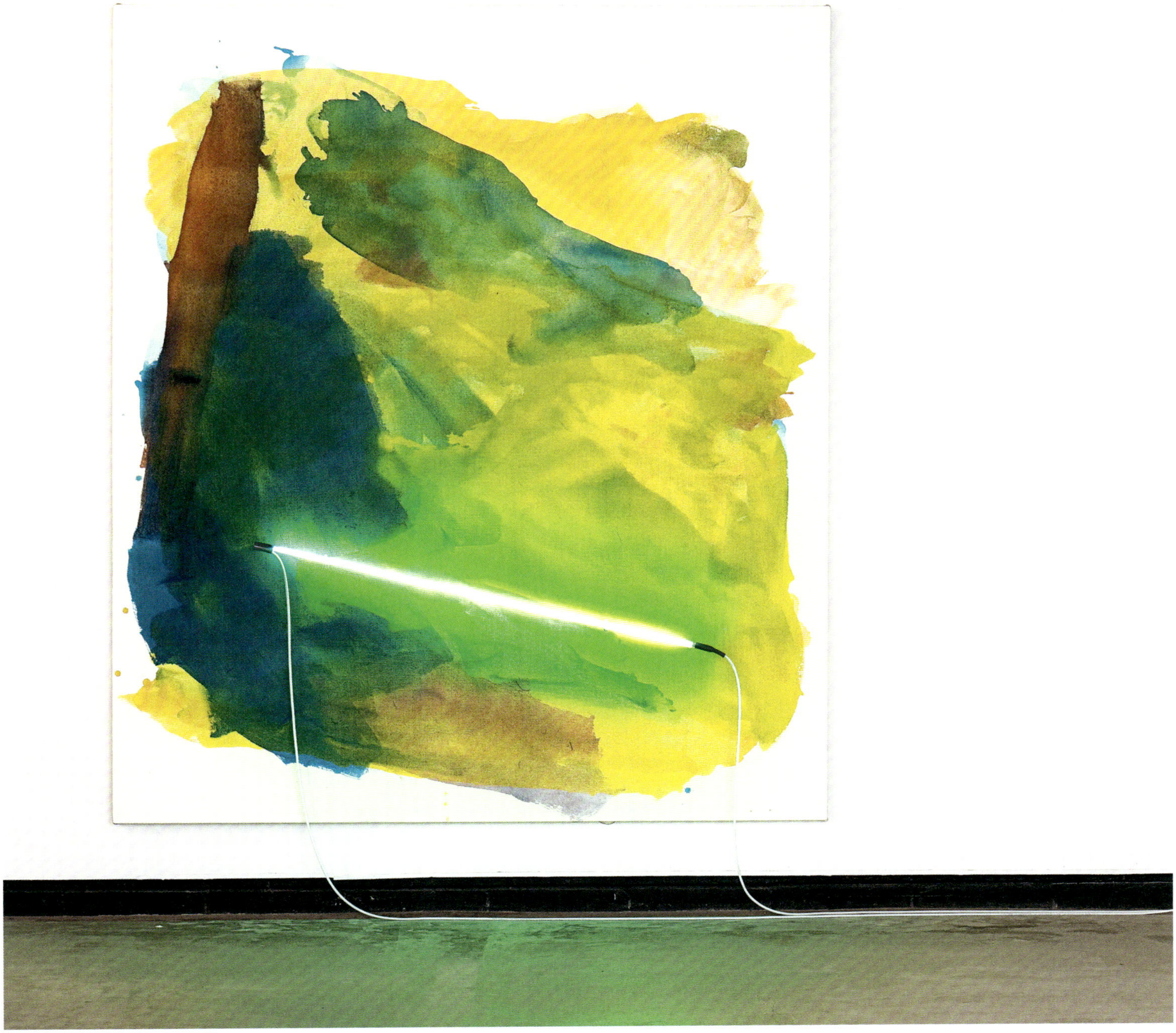

87. North Chester Ave. 2012

Flashe and neon on linen
236.2 × 200.7 cm (93 × 79 in.)
Private Collection

standing in for the zeitgeist, for something larger than herself. The invention came about after she received an offer from friend and painter Joey Kötting for a residency in Bakersfield, California, an agricultural region in the Central Valley known for its pistachios, almonds, and oil fields. Weatherford's brief for the residency, which began in January 2012, included working with students at California State University, Bakersfield (CSUB), to make a spring show for the school's Todd Madigan Art Gallery. *The Bakersfield Project* resulted in seven paintings: *Ruby I (Thriftimart)*, *Ruby II (Thriftimart)*, *Midnight Union Ave.* (fig.85), *Truxtun*, *California*, *North Chester Ave.* (fig.87), and *Panorama Dr.*, all 2012. *Ruby I (Thriftimart)* and *Ruby II (Thriftimart)*, crossed with potent tubes of ruby neon, were inspired by a giant letter *T* from an obsolete Thriftimart sign and are the first neons Weatherford made; *Panorama Dr.*, tinged like cherry ice, recalls a sunset over the valley, a giant Rorschach of paint beside a short pink tube of neon somehow registering the exact moment when city lights come on as night falls. Weatherford's decision to incorporate neon – to cast its three-dimensional brightness on the painted composition, to amplify both through adjustments of color and scale – was a revelation: it extended the flatness and depth of the target, the tactility of the shells and sponges, and concretized the light outside the cave. A readymade phenomenology, it bleeds onto the viewer and cuts a hole in one's vision even as it brings the surrounding marks to the pitch of visibility. Obliteration, while courted, never quite comes.

Interviewed for the CSUB newspaper, Weatherford discussed 'the life of the city and how things change and then change back',[8] in reference to the scenery figured in the vaporous blue cast of *Truxtun*, like morning mists, but also the neon that stands in for the landscape. She was inspired by Union Avenue, a main drag once studded with fancy hotels and businesses; today, so many years after Highway 99 diverted traffic, their derelict shells remain. This single, metonymic sign for shifting fortunes is just one of many in the region, whose modern ups and downs began in the 1860s, when floods wiped away the first American settlements (this before the gold rush ensured the migration of still more seekers in what became Kern County). Two years after her residency, when asked about Bakersfield's significance for her, Weatherford swept up in her accounting 'the Dust Bowl, the oil rush, *The Grapes of Wrath*, Dorothea Lange, Merle Haggard, honky-tonks, the Tea Party, the Ku Klux Klan, and dinosaurs'.[9] Janus-faced, the group of work she made there incorporates all of this, including the forthright acknowledgment of present conditions. As Katy Siegel synopsizes, 'Like the Thrifty Mart [*sic*] itself, Bakersfield feels elegiac, left behind in a new economy of immaterial service jobs, clustering in a few global cities that have been amplified and shined up, filled with money and culture and luxury goods. Weatherford's paintings grasp the vanishing materiality, the feel and the look of the fading short American century.'[10] To this point, the Bakersfield shop Center Neon, where Weatherford saw the defunct Thriftimart sign, and whose proprietors, the McNamee family, fabricated her first tubes, has since shuttered after fifty years.

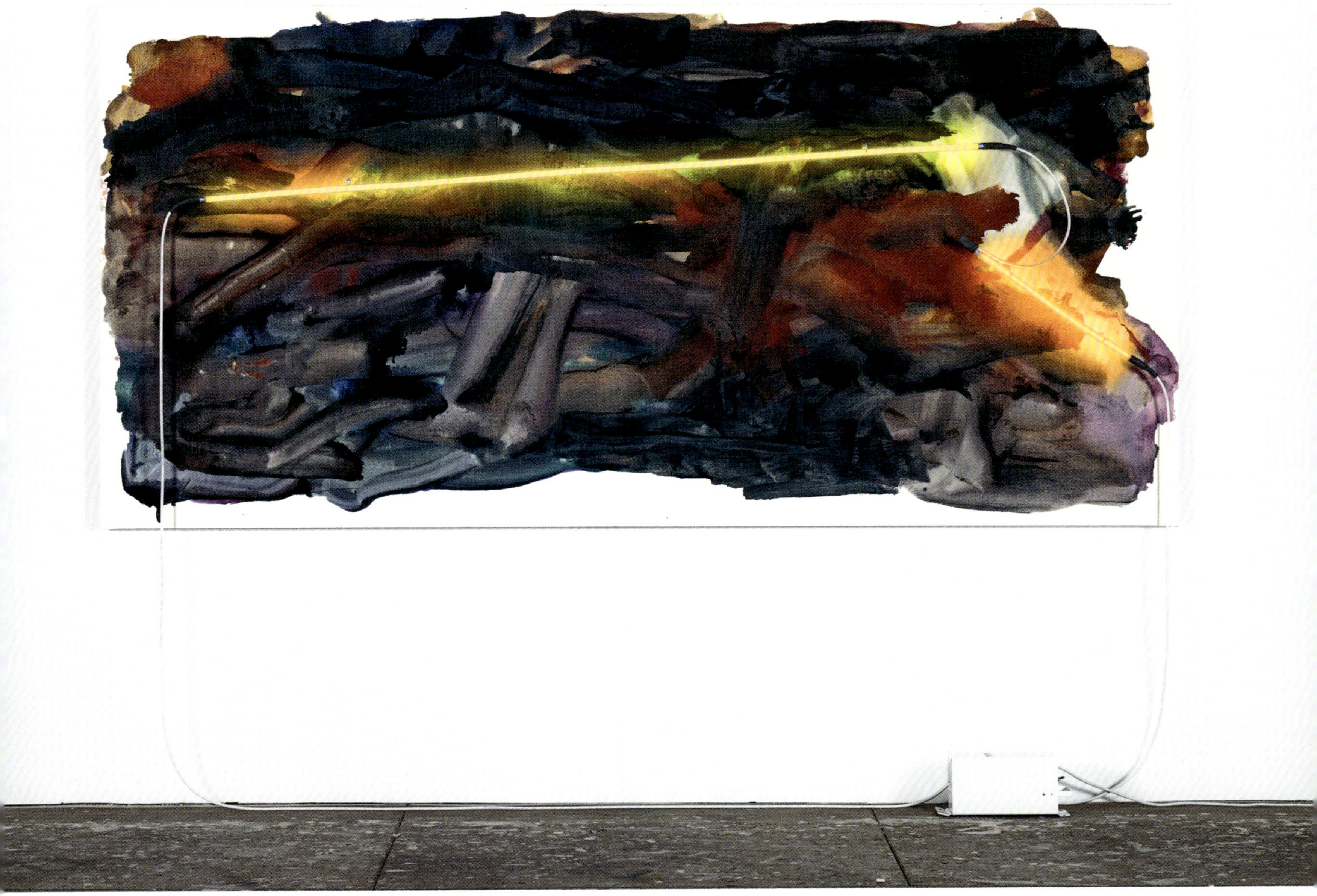

88. Chung King Rd. 2014

Flashe and neon on linen
142.2 × 284.5 cm (56 × 112 in.)
Rubell Family Collection, Miami

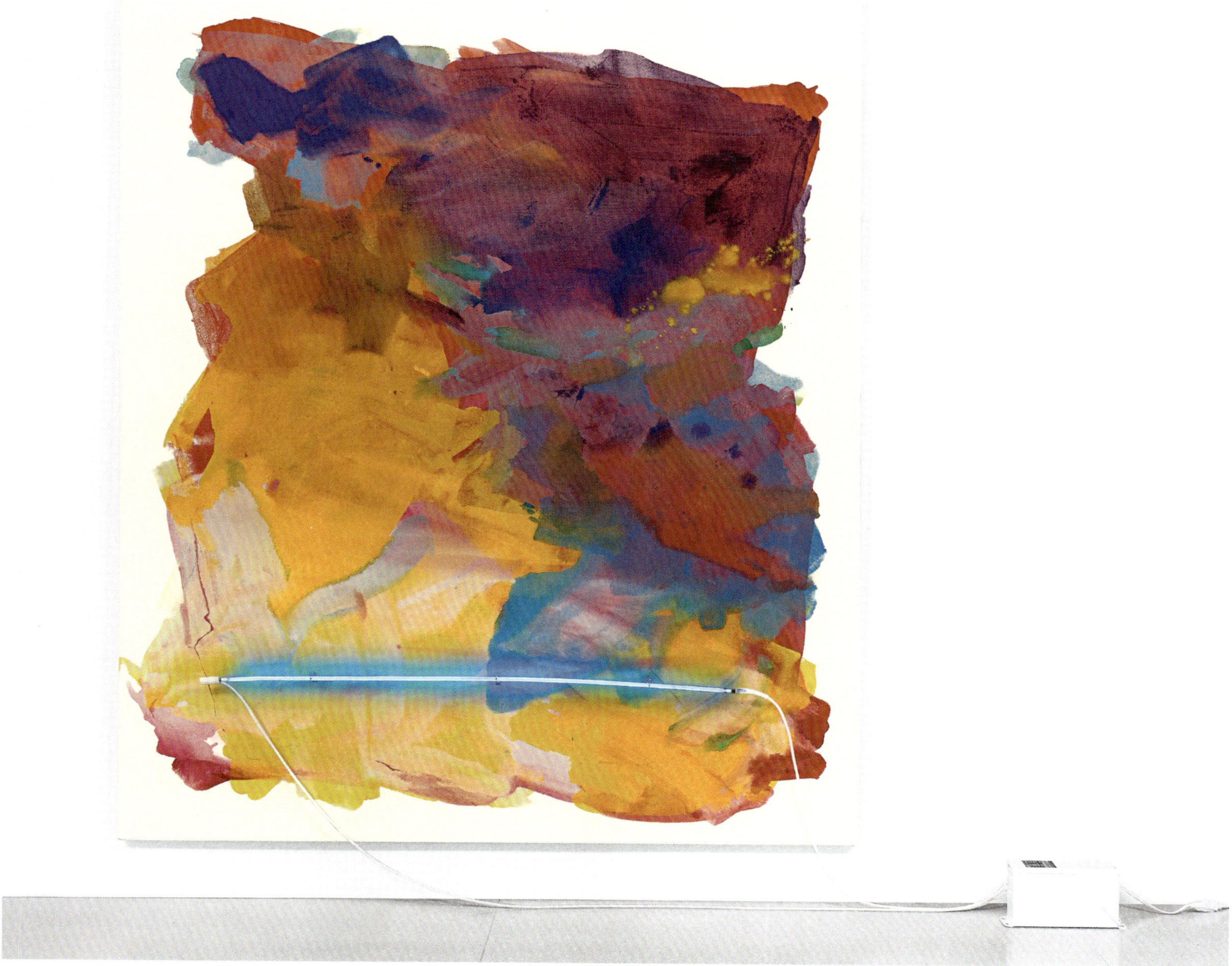

89. Chinatown 2012

Flashe and neon on linen
236.2 × 200.7 cm (93 × 79 in.)
Private Collection

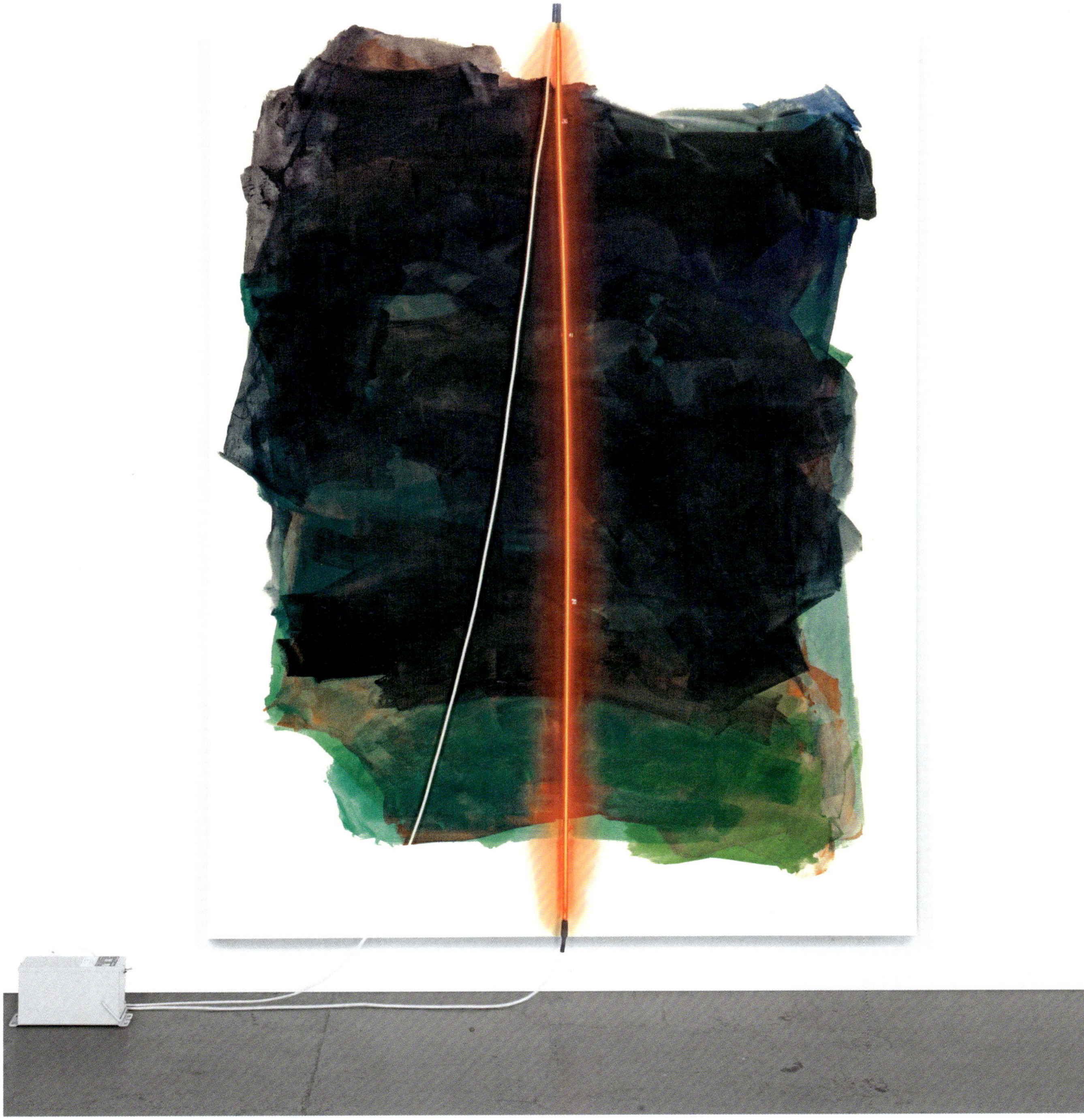

90. Empire 2012

Flashe and neon on linen
266.7 × 200.7 cm (105 × 79 in.)
Private Collection

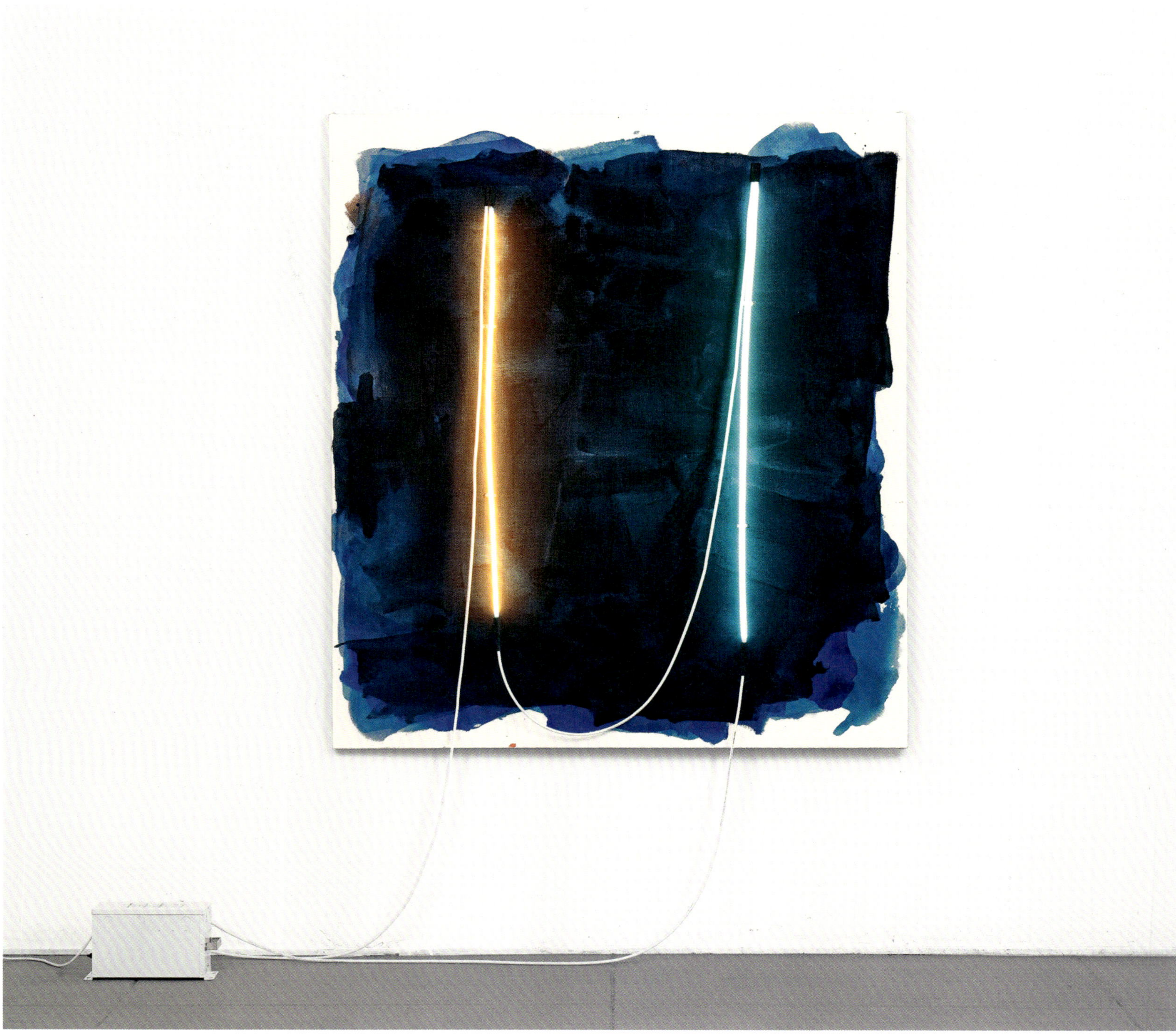

91. Brooklyn Bridge 2013

Flashe and neon on linen
167.6 × 147.3 cm (66 × 58 in.)
Private Collection

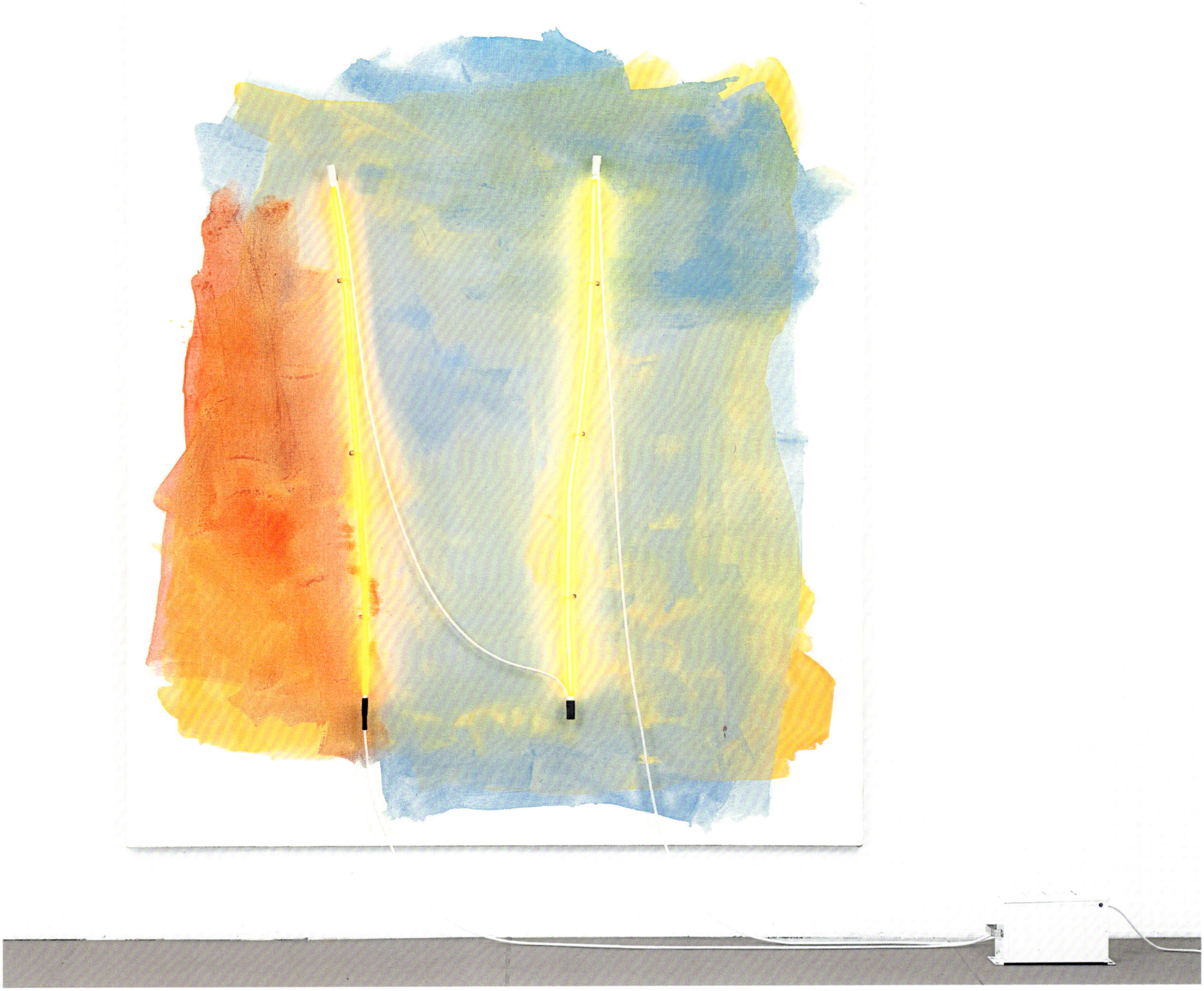

92. Mermaid Avenue 2013

Flashe and neon on linen
236.2 × 200.7 cm (93 × 79 in.)
Private Collection

The Bakersfield Project also marked a transition of a decidedly more personal sort. Weatherford's younger sister, Margaret Weatherford, passed away that March. They had collaborated on the prose miniatures for the Korzelius show in 1998, and again a decade later for Margaret's *East of the 5, South of the 10*, a by turns hilarious and gutting recapitulation of Greek mythology set in Southern California, for which Weatherford hosted a book signing at Cottage Home during her 2008 show there. She and Margaret also produced a performative interpretation of the text using actors sourced from the C. G. Jung Club of Orange County.[11] (The Jungians had staged a previous reading, in which they appropriated the text as a found object.) Weatherford returned to the crying woman iconography for the invitation to the performance, recasting the unspecified countenance of grief as either Demeter or Persephone.

In the printed version of *East of the 5, South of the 10*, Weatherford adjoined photos of flowering vines, matchbooks and single matches – virgin and charred – and a decorative Vera Bradley scarf to her sister's text. The story relies upon territorial mapping: Zeus reigns over Hollywood, downtown Los Angeles, La Brea, the Miracle Mile, Pasadena, Highland Park, and Mount Washington; Poseidon annexes the West Side, its palisades meeting the waves; and Hades rules the realm charted in the title, the edges of Los Angeles that Margaret Weatherford wrote of and Mary Weatherford paints. It goes on to recount the birth of Persephone and then the conditions of her disappearance. In the final act, Persephone's mother, Demeter – here a Marin County earth goddess turned arsonist – avenges her daughter's abduction, flicking matches from a speeding car, igniting the undergrowth in an angry blaze. This is a creation myth where, despite a punctual beginning, tenuousness is cyclical, interminable:

> Even if Zeus and Hades and Poseidon are the gods we struggle so hard to please, it is Demeter who suffers us to live at all. It is she who gives us food. It is she who lets us build our houses on bluffs eroding into the sea; amidst living tinder; on the flood plains of precariously imprisoned rivers; along huge fractures in the crust of the planet itself.
>
> And so, when Persephone's time with Hades rolls around again, as it does every year, and the long, unhappy, oppressive, dreary, stifling months of summer stretch horribly toward Halloween, Demeter reserves the privilege under the terms of the renegotiated agreement, to strike a few matches and watch the Southland burn.[12]

A piece Margaret published in the *Paris Review* in November 2011 could just as well be the companion to Weatherford's paeans to inhospitable topography: those places only arrived at by cars, so often broken (her family's vehicle overheating on trips to Yosemite National Park lurk in these neons conjuring up steaming blacktop roads), and the desolation of I-5 cutting through the state, everything a roadside mirage except the real danger of the elements, or other people. Her exquisite 'Green Car' traverses freeways and deserts, coming to rest with the following passage: 'We were never allowed to take our shoes off in the car. Wherever we were driving, however long it would take to get there, however hot it was, we always had to wear shoes. You could never know, my father said, where or when you might have to get out and run.'[13]

That Weatherford's apotheosis into *Art and Auction*'s pantheon should have come before Margaret's death, and that its prophetic force would be so extreme in the months after, is the grim, oracular stuff of her sister's writing, and, with *Satellite Girl*, her own. Not only did Weatherford show the Bakersfield paintings at LAXART in Los Angeles, she also took five neons to Brennan & Griffin in New York that same fall under the banner *Manhattan*. Sharon Mizota understood *The Bakersfield Paintings* as 'not landscapes per se but more like mood poems',[14] an evocative and sensitive assessment. The New York presentation got equivocal praise from Roberta Smith in the *New York Times*, where she admitted that the gambits of stain plus neon 'should not work, but by some weird function of visual chemistry, they mostly do'.[15] Matthew Higgs christened the likes of *Coney Island* and *Varick St.*, both 2012, 'psychogeography', marked by 'personal experiences and memories of real places',[16] even as the reminiscences were rather tenuous, feelings after things faraway or lost. Barry Schwabsky called this out, underscoring the shift away from working in a location (even if modifying it, or making it anew, in the studio) to picturing in the course of making:

> Weatherford's recent abstract paintings incorporating neon tubes don't quite touch the same chords of sentiment as those beachcomber reveries [with affixed seashells and starfish], but they do compromise the purity of the painted canvas in related and equally debatable ways, and they likewise play on nostalgia – this time for the city she left behind more than a decade ago. But while the show was called 'Manhattan', and the individual paintings bore titles such as *Varick St.* and *Chinatown* . . . you'd have been hard put to make out any specific references to the sights of the city then or now. My guess is that the New York that these works refer to is the one that subsists in the paintings of those who flourished here in the four decades preceding Weatherford's own arrival in 1984, mainly the Abstract Expressionists and Color Field painters, the Pollocks and de Koonings, but also the Frankenthalers and Olitskis – which means, in turn, the art-historically validated together with the critically sidelined.[17]

That the neons were paintings about paintings as well as landscapes allowed the specificity of reference to exist within the tradition of art – of abstract painting as its twentieth-century prize – that it reciprocally reframes. Like the Bakersfield pieces, these New York canvases commemorate things that no longer exist in colonies of

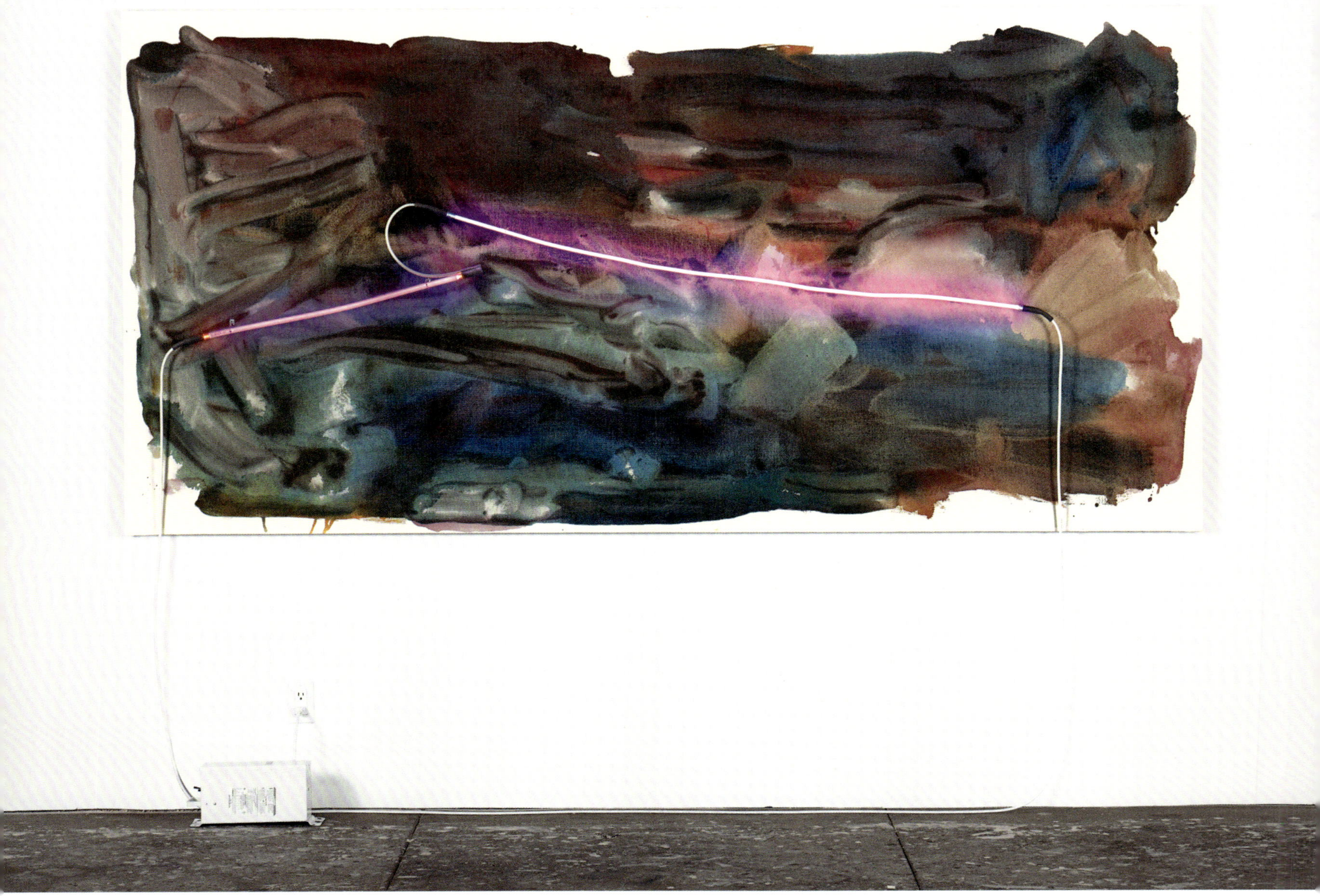

93. Gin Ling Way 2014

Flashe and neon on linen
142.2 × 284.5 cm (56 × 112 in.)
Rubell Family Collection, Miami

community and erstwhile art worlds but also, within the last, her routine, so many years ago, traced along the streets of Tribeca, trips to Coney Island, and spying the Empire State Building walking home late at night. Diaristic, but also obliquely so, they replace nostalgia with a more accessible ambience.

The work with neon proved formally adaptable and transmissible while remaining related to context. In the years since 2012, Weatherford has iterated the seemingly manifold possibilities proffered by the structure of stain on heavy-gauge Belgian linen made to her specifications with an exaggerated warp and weft that creates pockets for the paint, drawn over with linear conduits of neon bracketed by boots on either end of the glass and perched on tiny stands. Furthermore, while she still paints alone, she now has assistants who help prepare the gesso and later, as she completes the work and sets it on the wall, help move the increasingly colossal paintings and hang the neon. For these rods, Weatherford makes templates for the glass blower out of masking tape on butcher paper, creating crooked lines that look like gingerly arcing and imperfect tree branches, later recapitulated as actual tracings of the finished glass. Weatherford has the tubes fabricated in San Diego using Murano and other glass (such as vintage American Ruby and Uranium Green that she tracks down online). She has substituted argon for neon and vice versa, tried out krypton, used boots of different colors and cords of varying gauge, and experimented with dimmers, electrical transformers, and magnetic transformers, all of which factor into the finished piece, the result of so many decisions even after the paint dries.

The epic *from the Mountain to the Sea*, 2014 (fig.94), commissioned by Robert Faggen, Claremont McKenna College's director of the Gould Center for Humanistic Studies, where Weatherford was a fellow in 2013–14, extends this method to a mural of nearly three meters by six. Its amplified horizontality matches the sweep of land from Mount Baldy to the Pacific one hundred kilometers away as a valley of lights. Recalling Helen Frankenthaler, but also Weatherford's 1990s efforts to confound surf and shore, the churning, viscous expanse might also be tempestuous sky. The seven paintings that she presented that same year at David Kordansky Gallery, Los Angeles, in a showing called *Los Angeles*, fought against this orientation, going vertical with invocations of Oxnard, Ventura, and Artesia measuring around two and a half meters tall. These localities and her experiences in them across time are made over into browns and ochers, a dirtier palette than those pellucid glimpses of New York met through crisp air. (As Weatherford explains, 'Los Angeles used to have "smog days," when you didn't have to go to school. I was aware of living in a smog basin from the time I was little. So, what I tried to do in this show was to make the colors dirty.'[18]) This show struck a nerve, with Christopher Knight calling the paintings 'the finest I've seen'.[19]

She inaugurated Brennan & Griffin's satellite space in Red Hook, Brooklyn, in 2015 with eight paintings (fig.95), trapping the light of the Hudson and East Rivers in the massive hall of the former metal-castings warehouse near what once was a

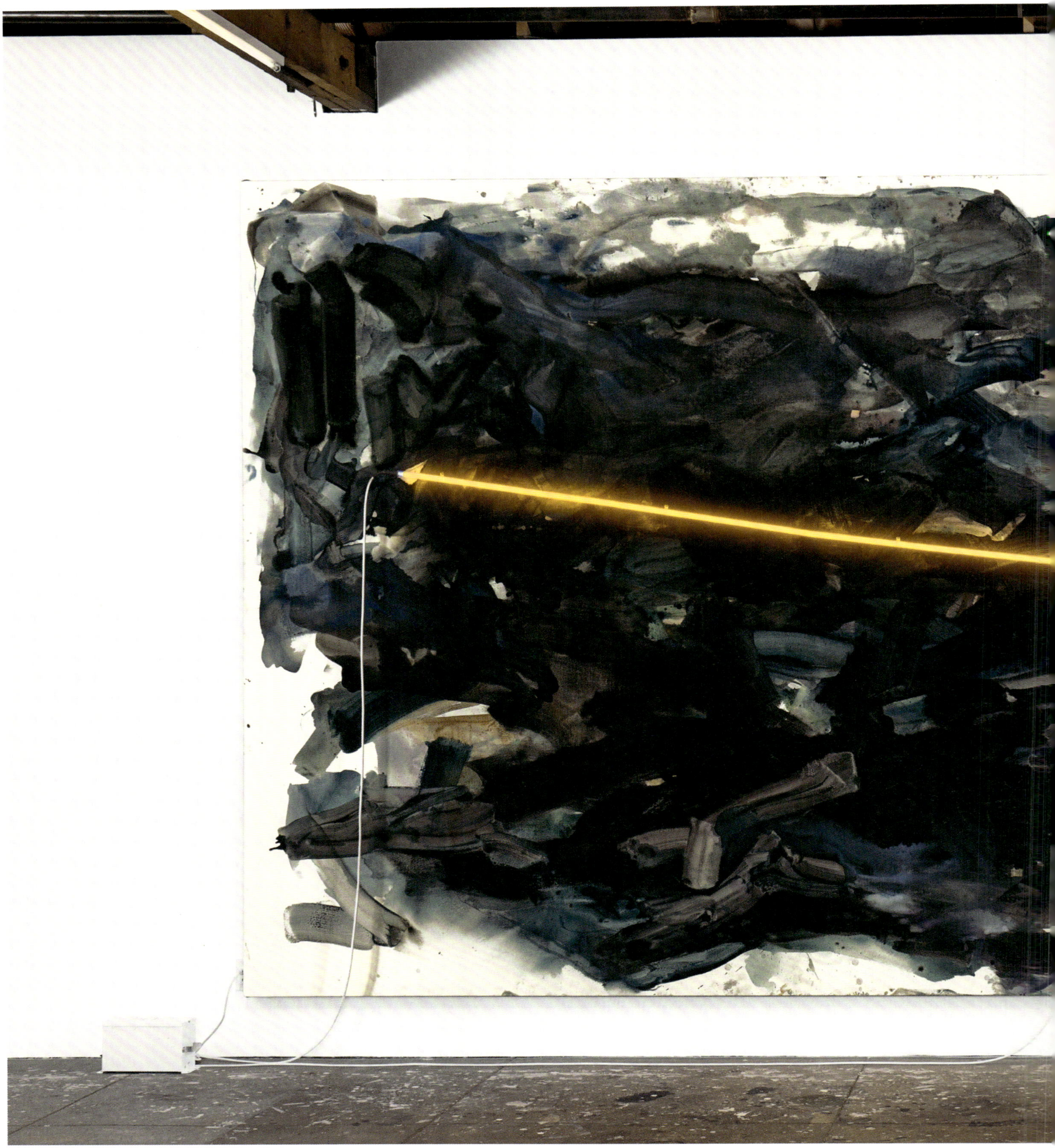

94. from the Mountain to the Sea 2014

Flashe and neon on linen
297.2 × 594.4 cm (117 × 234 in.)
On display at the Marian Miner Cook Athenaeum Collection
of Claremont McKenna College, Claremont

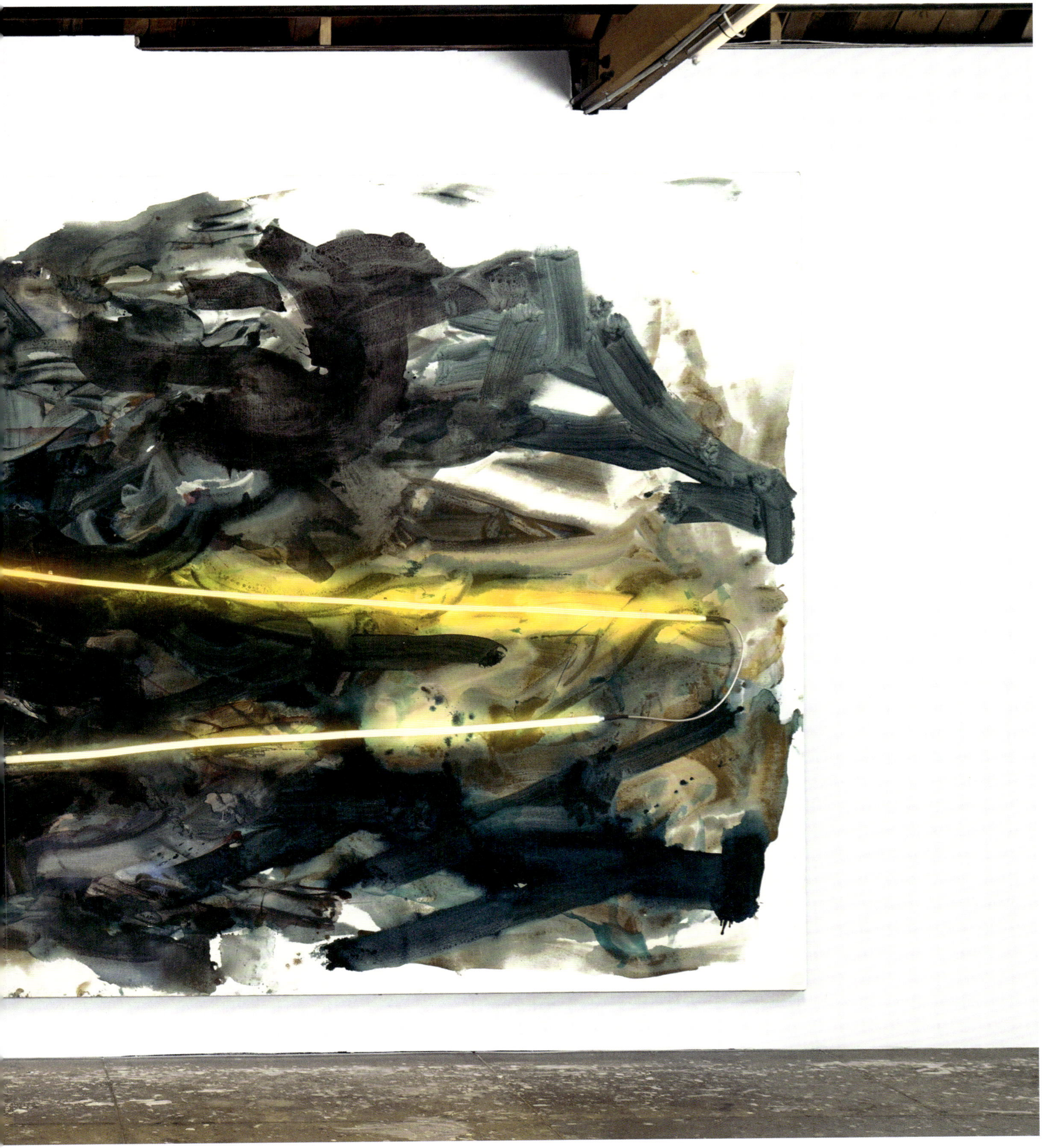

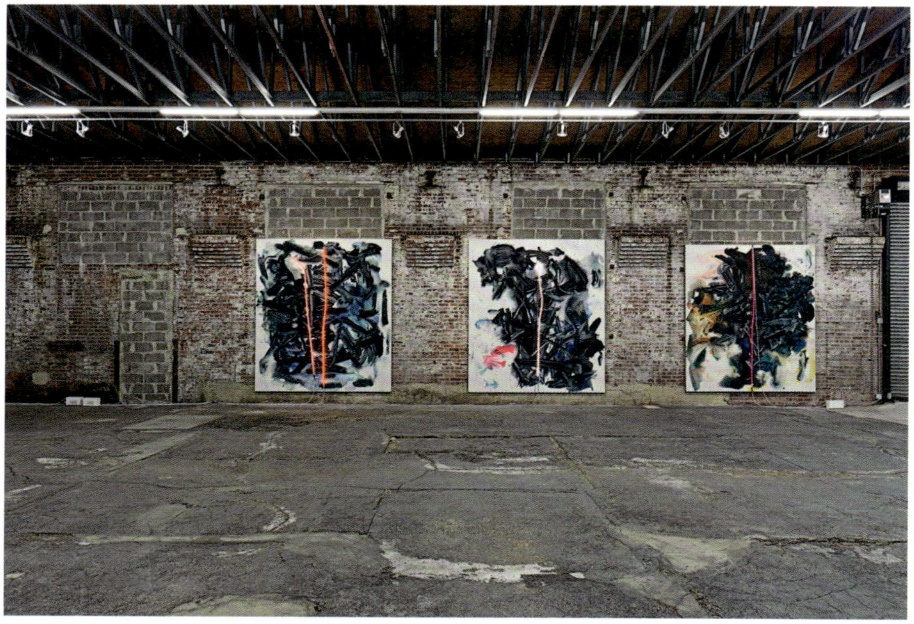

95. *Red Hook*
Brennan & Griffin
Brooklyn, New York
2015

bustling freight port. Weatherford's mother researched the local waterways and their roles within histories of contact, settlement, and trade. For example, the painting *beautiful lake* (2015) references a letter by Giovanni da Verrazzano, the man credited with the 'discovery' of New York Harbor in 1524. The explorer writes of meeting Native Americans, and what a lovely day it was when he encountered the Lenape at the entrance to the Hudson River. Like a sundial, *dawn Channel*, 2015, delivers morning, *Canal*, 2015, midday, and *Something with Bells*, 2015 (fig.98), after nightfall. In the words of Nora Griffin, writing of the paintings in relation to the surrounding neighborhood and the mutable conditions they helped her see:

> As the sun sets at Valentino Pier you can observe, all at once, the Statue of Liberty, the glittery mirage of Wall Street, and the journey of an illuminated Staten Island Ferry. Perhaps it was in moments similar to these that Weatherford found her source material. But more importantly than the artist's own relationship to this area, it is the viewer who will emerge from the show with a more complex appreciation of a city in flux and stillness.[20]

This last line resonates forcefully with *past Sunset*, 2015 (fig.96), a mass of navy sliced with magenta light that underscores the potential for a dissolving sublimity, which has been linked to topography since the capacious and ultimately projective landscapes of Romanticism.

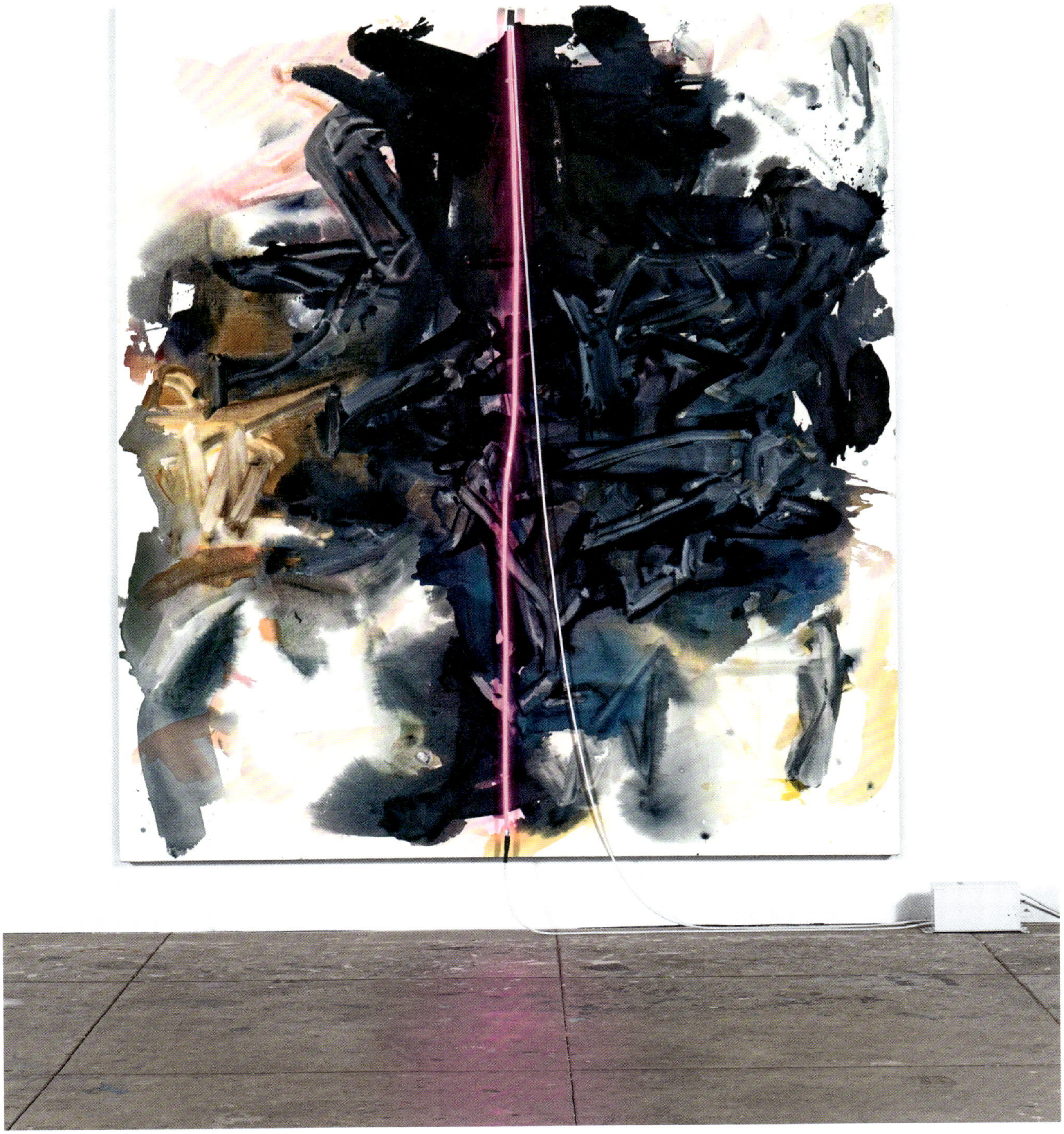

96. past Sunset 2015

Flashe and neon on linen
284.5 × 251.5 cm (112 × 99 in.)
Rubell Family Collection, Miami

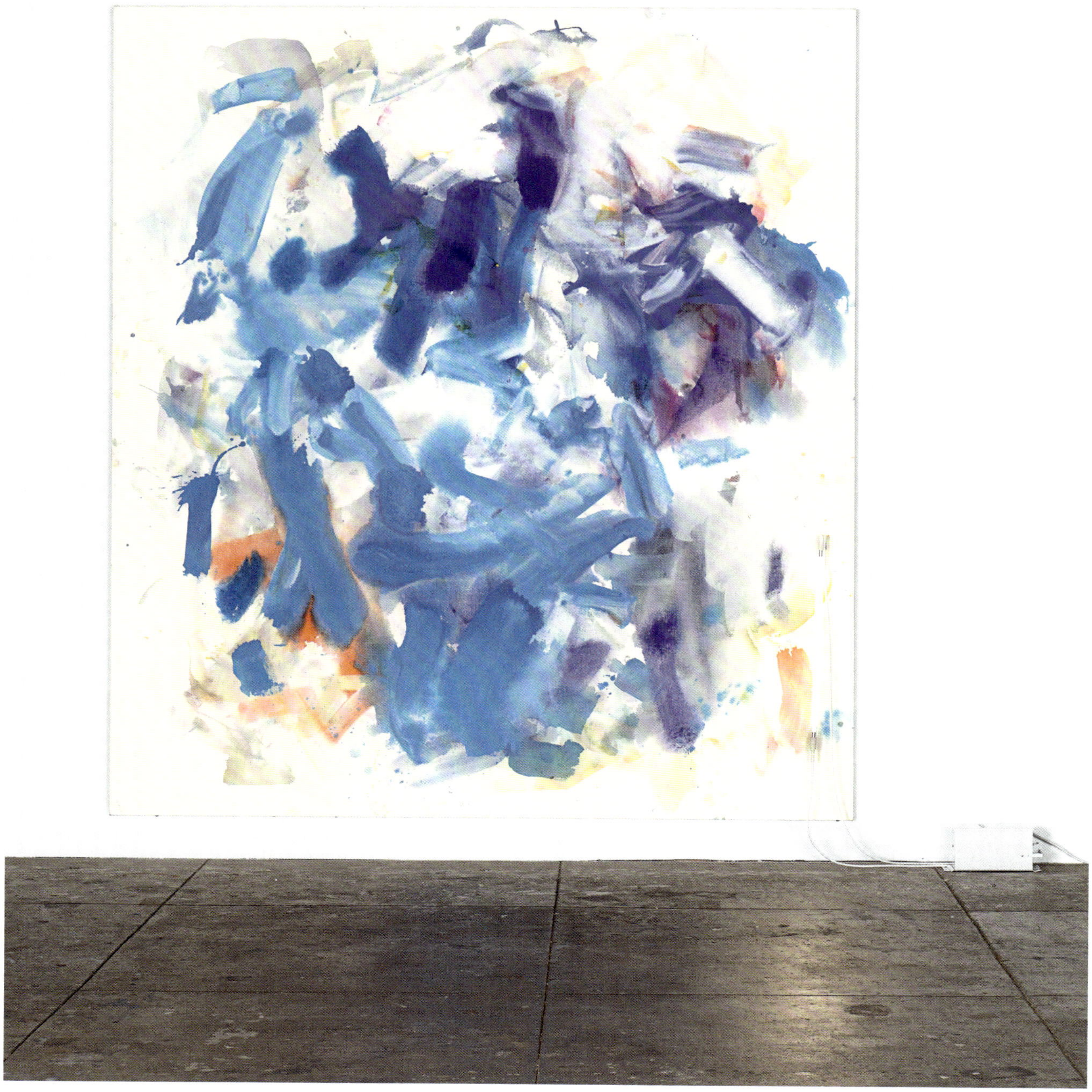

97. beautiful lake 2015

Flashe and neon on linen
297.2 × 264.1 cm (117 × 104 in.)
Collection of the artist

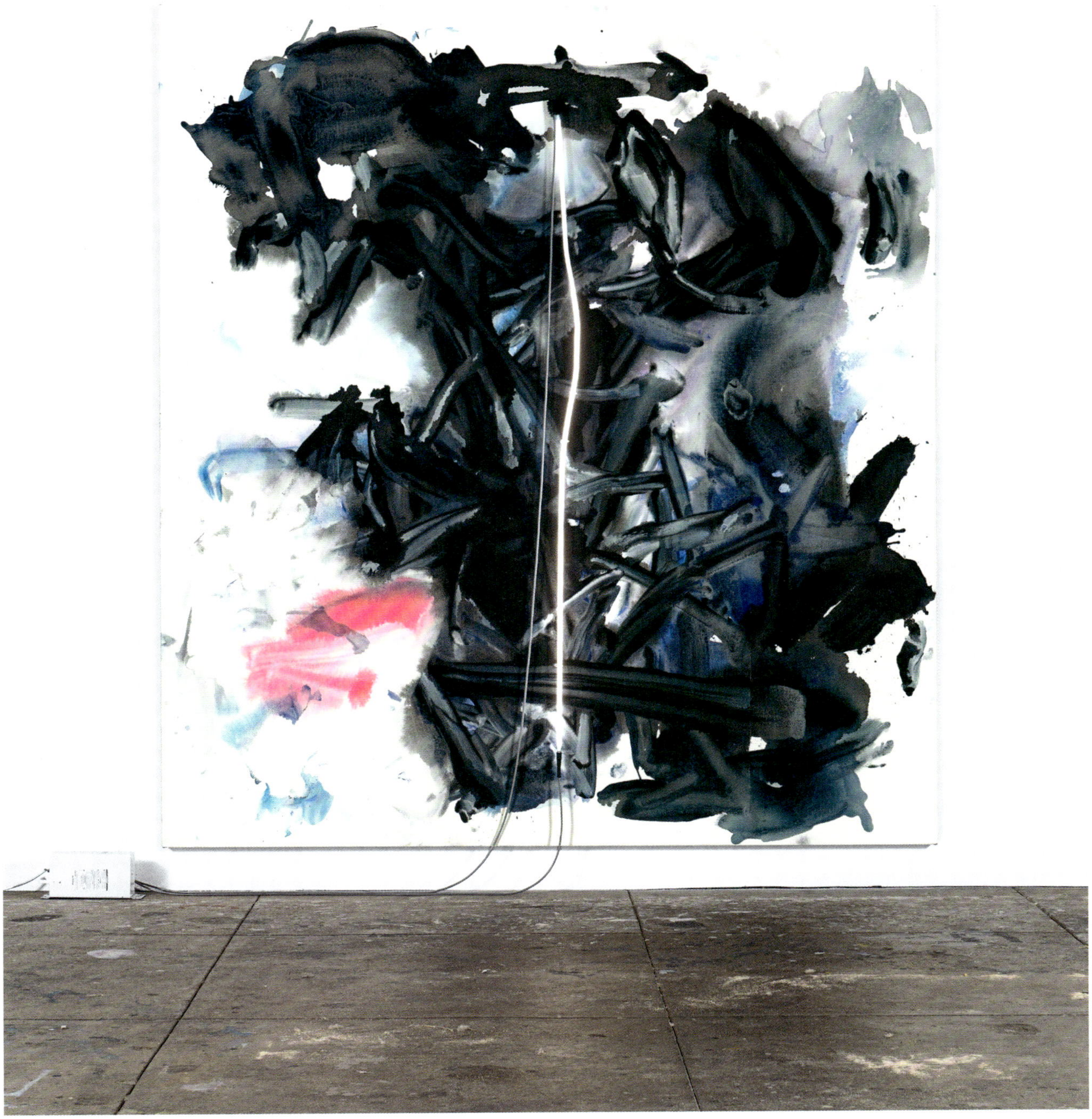

98. something with Bells 2015

Flashe and neon on linen
297.2 × 264.1 cm (117 × 104 in.)
Collection of the artist

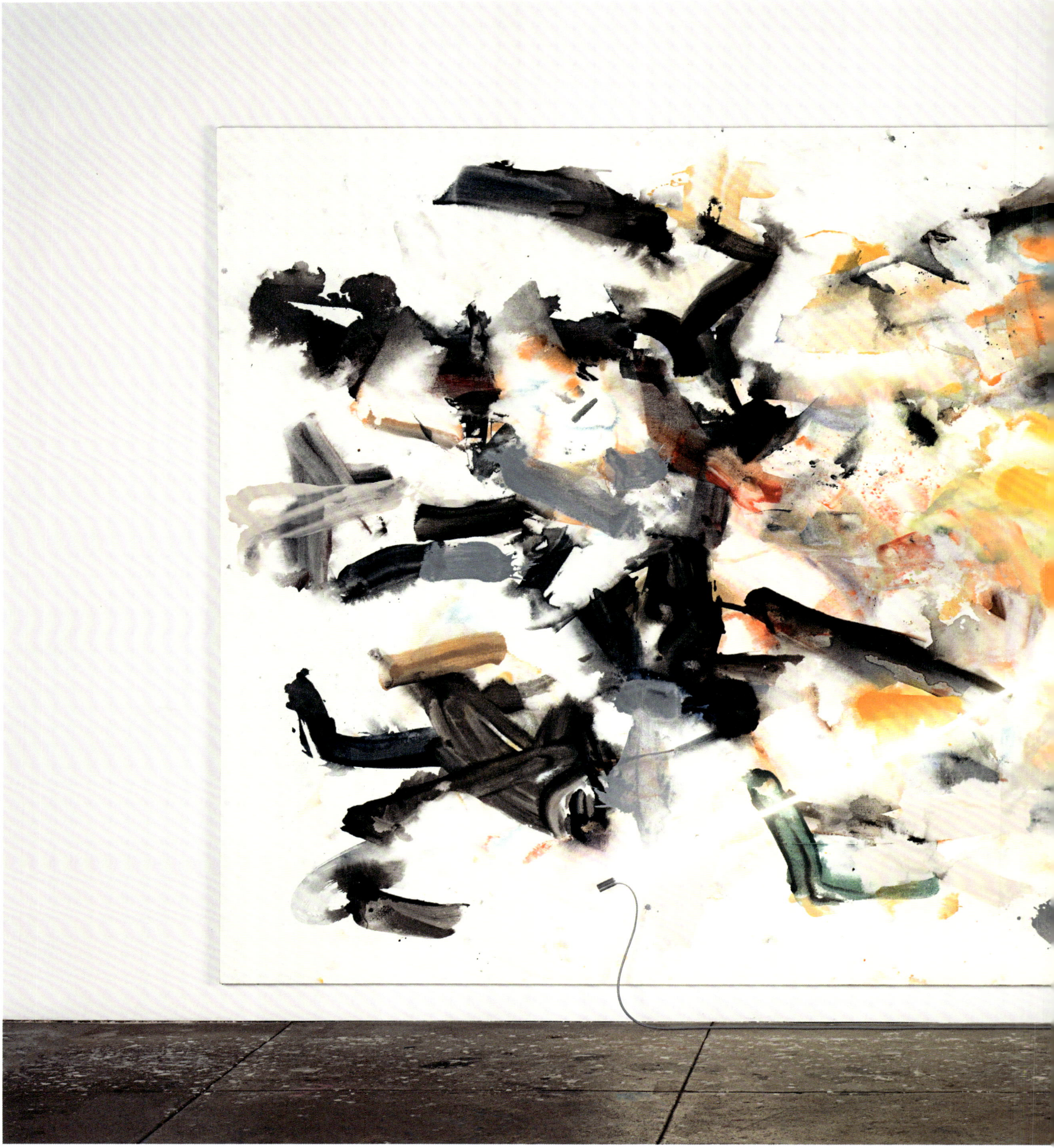

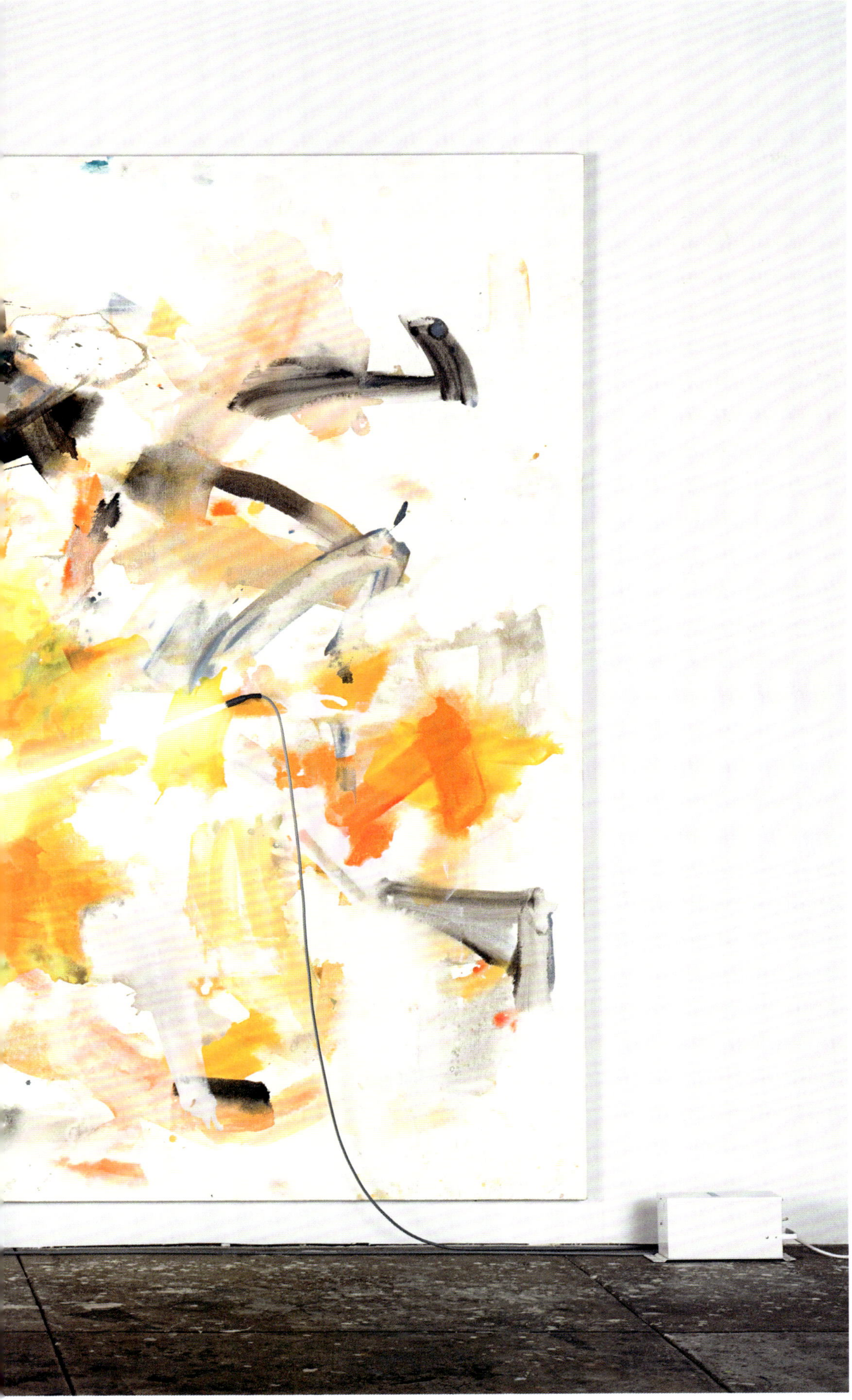

99. Weekend 2015

Flashe and neon on linen
264. 2 × 411.5 cm (104 × 162 in.)
Fondation Louis Vuitton, Paris

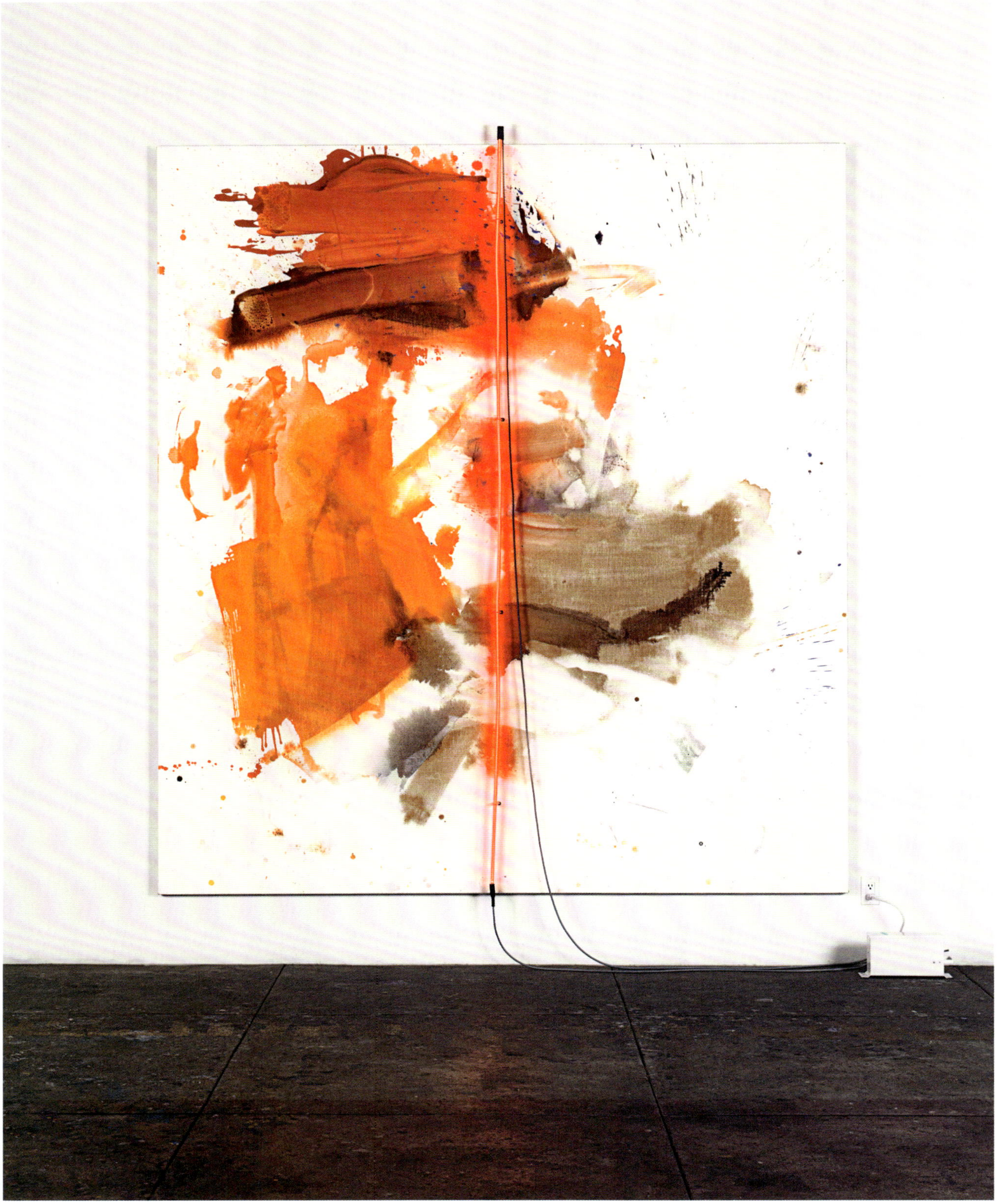

100. sand fire 2015

Flashe and neon on linen
236.2 × 200.7 cm (93 × 79 in.)
Private Collection

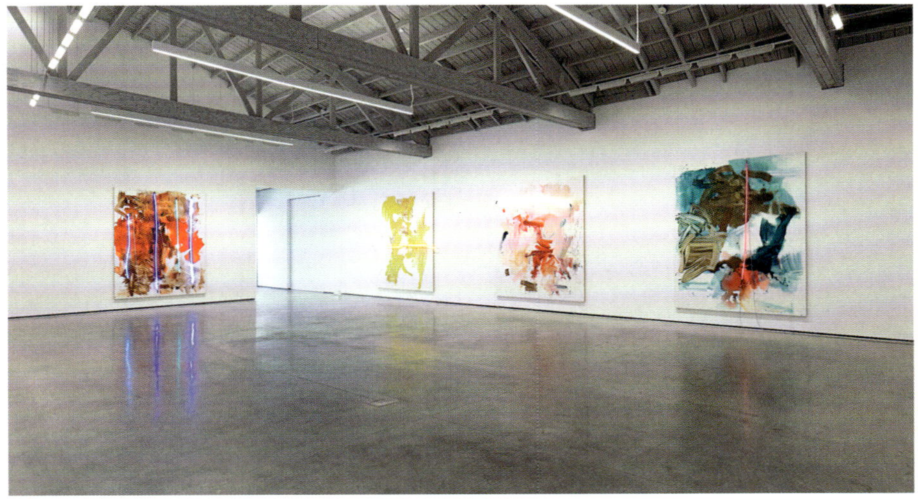

101. *like the land loves the sea*
David Kordansky Gallery
Los Angeles
2017

Perhaps this opportunity for mutual recognition comes from the temporality of the painting now coinciding with its references so wholly. Maxwell Williams recognized something like this in 2015:

> Weatherford is slowly shifting from history-based paintings to the purely experiential side of things. 'It's turning into the summer 2015 highlights', she says of her newest works. 'I went on a hike on Mt. Baldy. We saw some yellow yuccas, and that's what got me into using yellow in my paintings. Then I went swimming at Windansea Beach [in La Jolla, California]. I had to work through the paintings with a backstory, and now I'm up to the present day.'[21]

This came through in *like the land loves the sea*, a presentation of thirteen paintings – four becoming environments at around three by six meters – at David Kordansky in 2017 (fig.101). In one room, Weatherford offered vertical paintings, each notable for a single dominant hue; in the other were the four large murals, testaments to her now rather more literally wrestling control and asserting herself as the maker of something that inevitably slips away from her. So epic were the proportions and the crescendos of roiling color enfolding the white ground that Hunter Drohojowska-Philp dubbed her, consentingly, the 'J. M. W. Turner of Southern California'.[22] Color, once studied and set into careful armatures, here rushed unimpeded and with refined sensitivity, amplified through adjustments of internal and external scale and light.

If the neons had been summonses to places, whether remembered, experienced close to their fabrication, or conjured in the creative act, these murals inscribed place palpably in the event of its witness. As Weatherford put it in an interview after

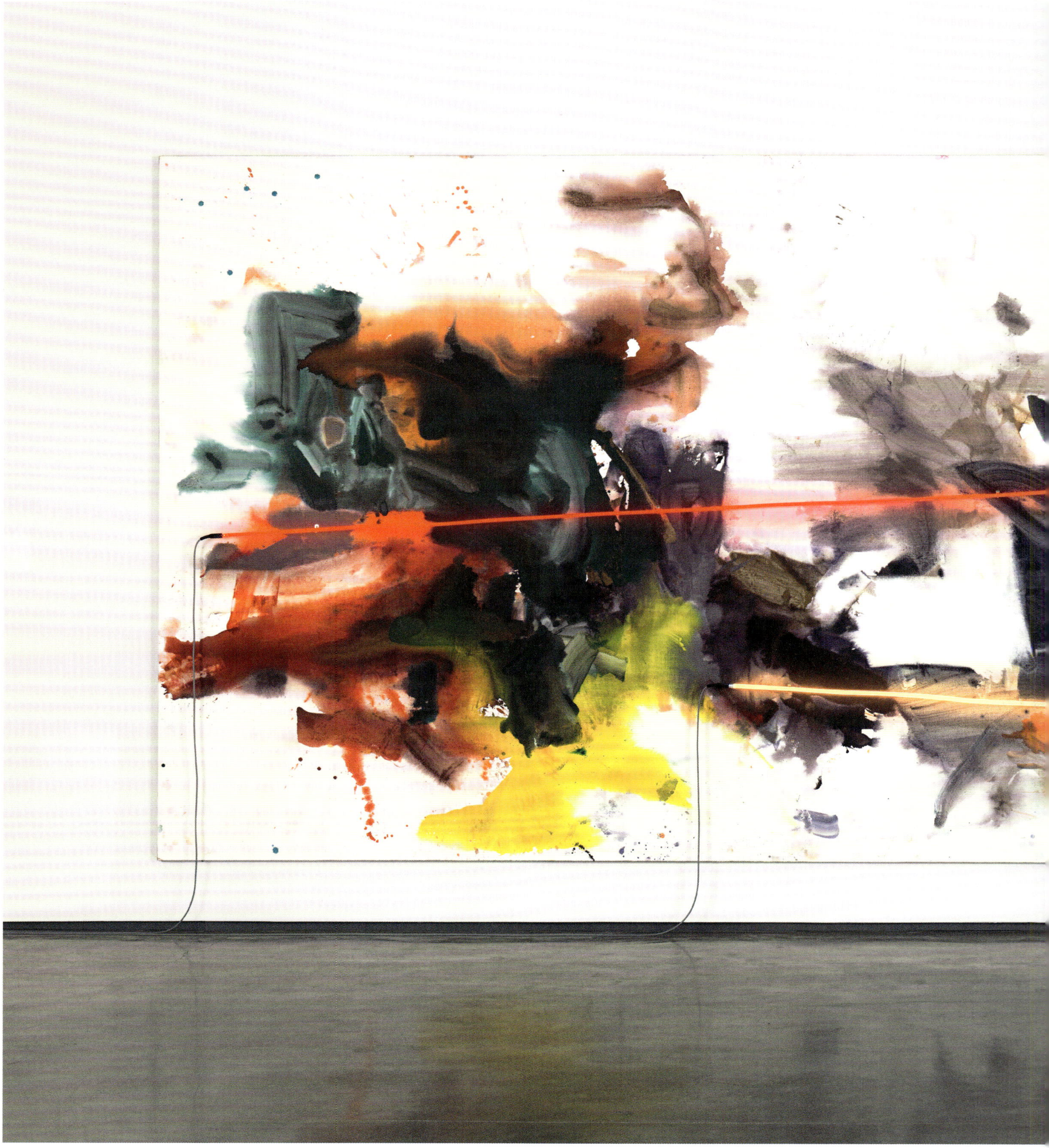

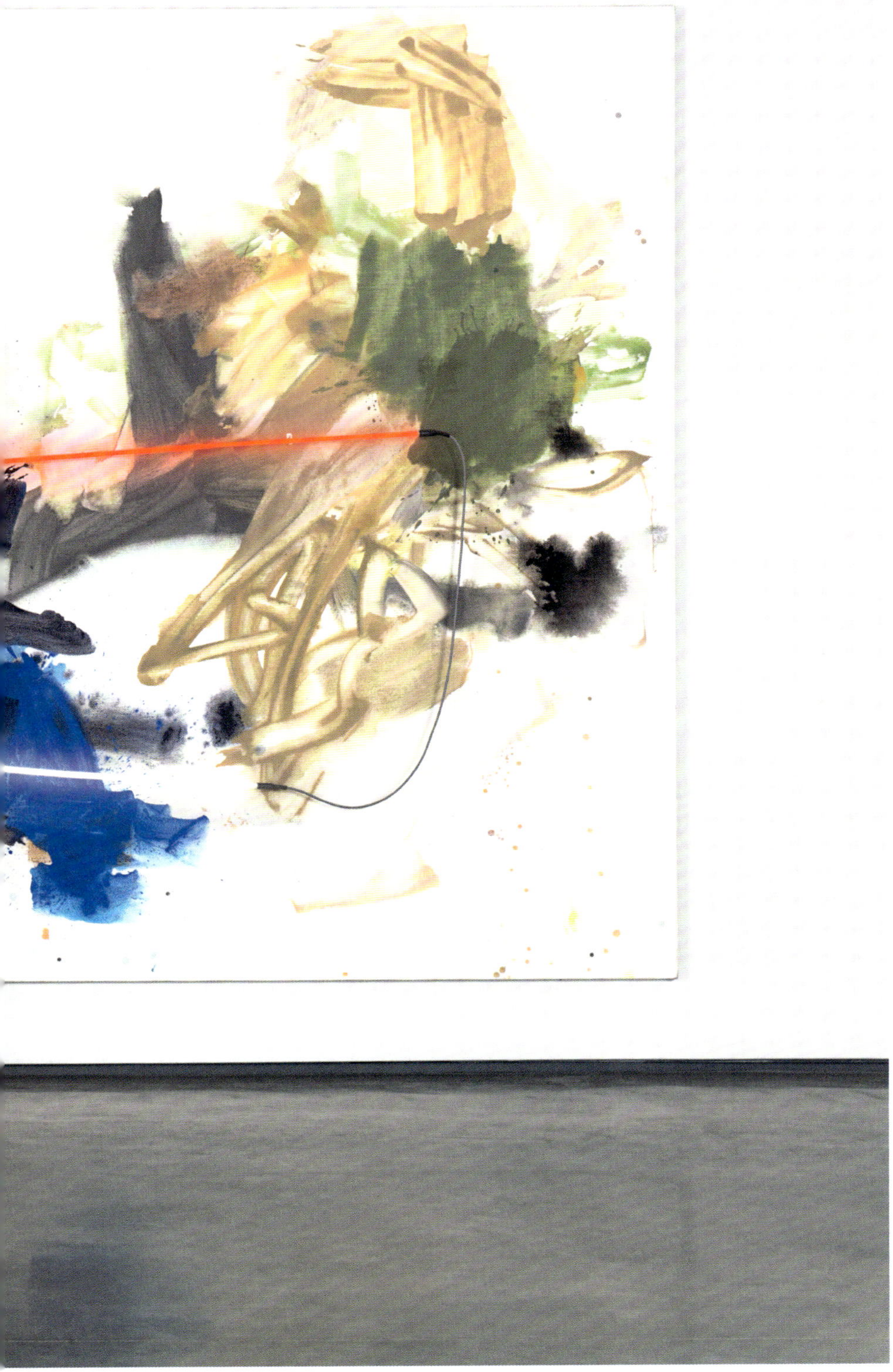

102. City 2017

Flashe and neon on linen
297.2 × 594.4 cm (117 × 234 in.)
Private Collection

Bakersfield, although neon has a history (the 'first neon in the US was purchased in Paris by a Packard dealership on lower Figueroa Street', meaning that it 'bypassed New York and went straight to L.A.'[23]), it forever encroaches upon its present: 'Electric light is always now – it has no past.'[24] The works do, and will, continue to mediate this temporal horizon as the possible limit of representation, forging continuity with the wee shell on *Red, yellow, black*, or in a sort of infinite regress, the character in *Satellite Girl* who stands eternal amidst the currents and times in a moment of knowing where she is:

> She let the next wave wind itself around her ankles and, on its way out, billow around her feet. She did this until her feet disappeared.
>
> Now she was anchored, she became a piling heavy with creosote. Standing forever, forever facing west. She pictured herself as a tiny tiny tiny toothpick on an enormous globe. Which way did she face precisely? To the south seas? to Hawaii? to Vietnam? What land mass was out there beyond the curve of the ocean covered earth, out farther than she could see. Beyond the horizon.[25]

In this passage, Weatherford's language is earnest, shamelessly lush. She describes submission as it approximates command, as it arrives at power.

There is no attempt at denial in Weatherford's recent paintings, but neither is there sentimentality. They are expressive of the self as it meets, and recognizes as continuous with its own subjectivity, the potent and ultimately inviolable phenomena of nature. These paintings are bigger than so much contemporary abstraction, in stakes as well as size. They make clear that Weatherford's ongoing investigations into the properties of the medium – its conventions and tools, histories and tacit assumptions – are less motivated by some belated modernist ambition than underwritten by a liberal, manifold curiosity: about the natural world, pictures and the stories that have been told about them, and sensible apprehension of place and one's implication within it, most intimately but also most broadly. Weatherford's arc, in this sense, is a surprising one, passing through feminist appropriation in other media to arrive at one of the most certifiably painterly of topoi in the abstract evocation of landscape. It bears mention that she did this in the last decades, amid and against a recuperation of the screen and a mode of cool conceptualism that cloaked intention, displaced affect, and mocked labor as material or process legitimated apart from its issuing intelligence. But Weatherford's relation to the vicissitudes of contemporary painting is not exclusively the meaning. However contestatory her work remains (as was the case in the 1980s and 1990s), it is not elegiac, for that would imply mourning for something lost and worth preserving. Rather, each painting exists, fully realized, as though a toothpick planted in shifting sand – hardly a defense against a swell or a riptide, but a statement implying a question about encompassing fate.

103. the sea 2017

Flashe and neon on linen
297.2 × 264.2 cm (117 × 104 in.)
Private Collection
Promised gift to Los Angeles County Museum of Art

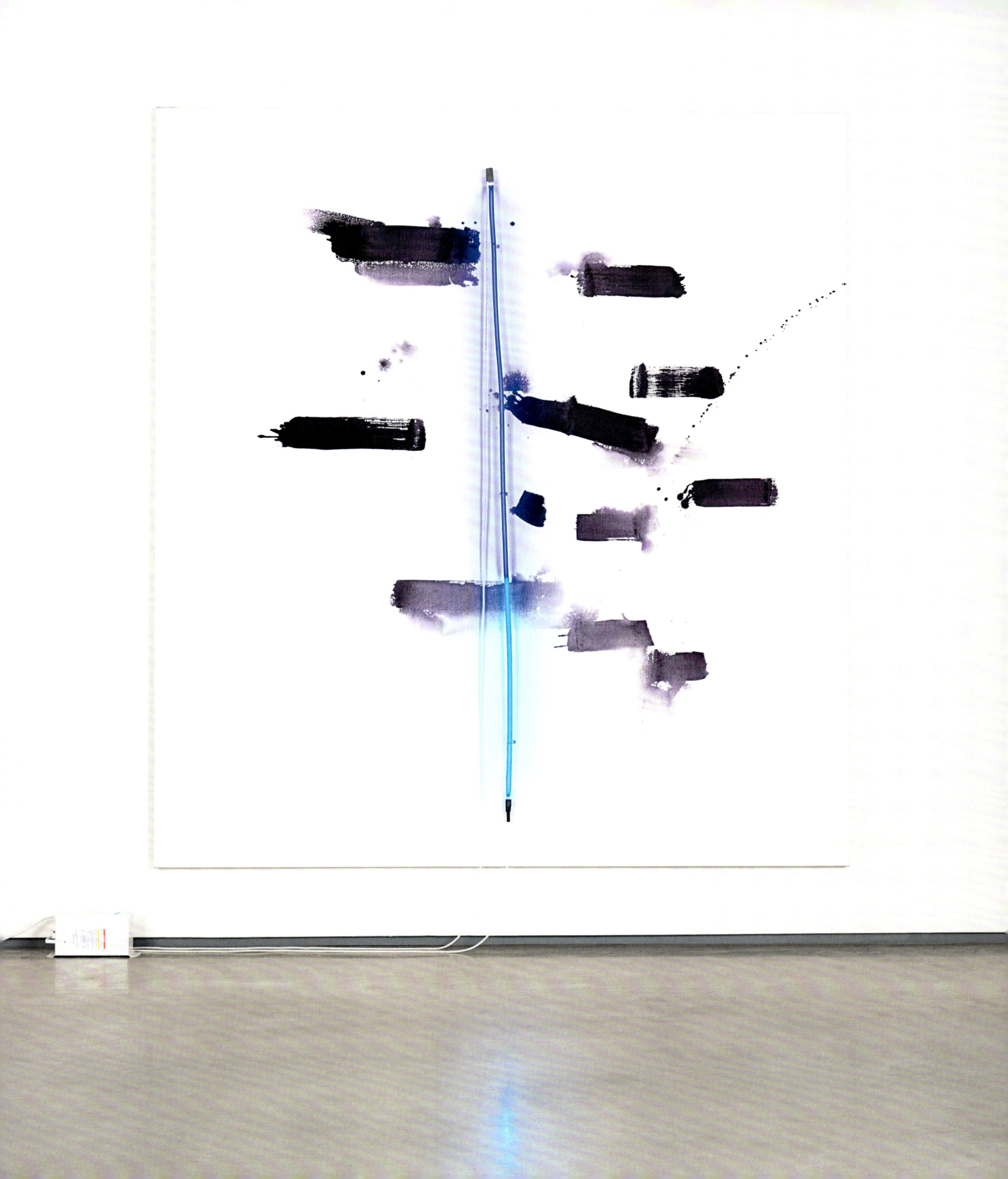

Notes

All uncited quotes of Mary Weatherford are from conversations with the author that took place between fall 2017 and spring 2018.

Introduction

1. Joan Didion, *Slouching Towards Bethlehem* (New York: Farrar, Strauss, and Giroux, 1968), 220–1.
2. Joan Didion, quoted in Michiko Kakutani, 'Joan Didion: Staking Out California', *New York Times*, June 10, 1979, accessed March 4, 2018, http://www.nytimes.com/1979/06/10/books/didion-calif.html.
3. Mary Weatherford, unpublished and undated note, Weatherford archive.
4. The Turner frontier thesis was linked, by Richard Slotkin most prominently, to Indian genocide – an important position during the years of the Vietnam War. Slotkin, *Regeneration Through Violence: The Mythology of the American Frontier, 1600–1860* (Middleton, CT, 1973).
5. Jackson Pollock, in Letters, *Time*, December 11, 1950, 10.
6. Katy Siegel's revisionist work affords an important corrective. See *'The heroine Paint': After Frankenthaler*, ed. Katy Siegel (New York: Gagosian Gallery/Rizzoli, 2015).
7. Harold Rosenberg, 'The American Action Painters', *Artnews*, January 1952, 22. Rosenberg is usually seen as writing this about Pollock, but in fact he was probably describing Willem de Kooning.
8. Clement Greenberg, 'Modernist Painting' (1960), in *Clement Greenberg: The Collected Essays and Criticism, Volume 4: Modernism with a Vengeance, 1957–1969*, ed. John O'Brian (Chicago: University of Chicago Press, 1993), 90.
9. Morris Louis, quoted in James M. Truitt, 'Art-Arid D.C. Harbors Touted "New" Painters', *Washington Post*, December 21, 1961, A20; and later in Gerald Nordland, *The Washington Color Painters* (Washington, DC: Washington Gallery of Modern Art, 1965), 12.
10. Helen Frankenthaler, voiceover in *Frankenthaler – Towards a New Climate*, directed by Perry Miller Adato, in *The Originals: Women in Art* series (1978; WNET/Channel 13,), DVD, as cited in Alexandra Schwartz, 'As in Nature: On Frankenthaler's Painting', in *As in Nature* (New Haven: Yale University Press with the Sterling and Francine Clark Art Institute, 2017), 32.
11. The full group is: William Baziotes, James Brooks, Willem de Kooning, Jimmy Ernst, Adolph Gottlieb, Robert Motherwell, Barnett Newman, Jackson Pollock, Richard Pousette-Dart, Ad Reinhardt, Mark Rothko, Theodoros Stamos, Clyfford Still, and Bradley Walker Tomlin.
12. 'Women Artists in Ascendance: Young Group Reflects Lively Virtues of U.S. Painting', *Life*, May 13, 1957, 74.
13. Harold Rosenberg, 'Art and Words' (1969), in *The De-Definition of Art* (New York: Horizon Press, 1972), 64.
14. Ibid.
15. Michael Fried, 'Art and Objecthood', *Artforum*, 5, no.10 (Summer 1967), 12–23.
16. Arthur Danto, 'Morris Louis' (1986), in *Encounters and Reflections: Art in the Historical Present* (Berkeley: University of California Press, 1997), 49.

1. Origins: 1963–1980s

1. Mary Weatherford and Robert Faggen, 'From the Mountain to the Sea: A Conversation, Claremont McKenna College, September 17, 2014', in *Mary Weatherford: The Neon Paintings*, ed. Robert Faggen (New York: DelMonico Books/Prestel and Gould Center for Humanistic Studies, Claremont McKenna College, 2016), 200.
2. Artist Statement for Fellowship, undated, in Weatherford archive.
3. Ibid.
4. Mary Weatherford, quorted in *'The heroine Paint': After Frankenthaler*, ed. Katy Siegel (New York: Gagosian Gallery/Rizzoli, 2015), 242.
5. Mary Weatherford, email to the author, December 17, 2017.
6. Ron Clark, quoted in *Independent Study Program: 40 Years, Whitney Museum of American Art, 1968–2008* (New York: Whitney Museum of American Art, 2008), 19.
7. Press release, 'Sherrie Levine, May 14–June 5, 1981', Metro Pictures, accessed March 4, 2018, http://www.metropictures.com/exhibitions/sherrie-levine.
8. David A. Ross, 'Preface', in *Endgame: Reference and Simulation in Recent Painting and Sculpture* (Cambridge, MA: MIT Press; Boston: Institute of Contemporary Art, 1986), 6.
9. One significant discussion and critique of this position can be found in Douglas Crimp, 'The End of Painting', *October* 16 (Spring 1981), 69–86.
10. Albers fostered formal experimentation and chromatic interactions within the series' determining structure of concentric squares painted with a palette knife under artificial lighting.
11. Katy Siegel makes a connected point about her use of color also being related to her past: 'Her early work borrowed the flat appearance and the geometric forms of Color Field painting, rhyming them with the Op-art patterns and colors that trickled down from high art into the clothing and décor of her own 1960s childhood.' Siegel, 'Into the Nightlife', in *Mary Weatherford: The Neon Paintings*, 12.
12. Rosalind Krauss, 'Grids', *October* 6 (Summer 1979), 64.
13. Sam Hunter, *New Directions* (brochure) (New York: S. Bitter Larkin Gallery, 1990).
14. Mary Weatherford, quoted in ibid.
15. Some of the early targets on paper are Flashe, but all the target paintings are oil paint. She has also used Flashe for the flowers atop the diluted acrylic grounds of the *Violetta* paintings of the early 1990s, and the roses and chrysanthemums of the early 1990s, all the way through to her large transparent veils behind the neon sticks after 2012.
16. Unpublished notes, Weatherford archive.
17. 'Close Conversation: Mary Weatherford and Katy Siegel', conversation accompanying the exhibition *The Forever Now: Contemporary Painting in an Atemporal World*, The Museum of Modern Art, New York, March 2, 2015.

2. Concentric Circular Timelines: 1985–1991

1. Mary Weatherford, in *Mary Weatherford: Bakersfield Paintings*, ed. Matthew Schum (Los Angeles: LAXART, 2012), 15. In this interview, she also notes Murray's painting with an eraser stuck to its surface as a likely trigger for her pasting materials to the surfaces of her own paintings.
2. 'Fall Fixes', *New York Press*, September 30, 1988, 31.
3. About her own work, she posed: 'It's difficult for women in the art world, and I'm committed to my feminist project. But it's a mistake to talk about discrimination in the art world, since it is really about discrimination in the real world. Women still earn less than men, jobs remain characterized by gender. All sorts of factors contribute to an economic rift based on sex. I felt this kind of difference when I was growing up. That's one of the reasons why I've always worked so hard and, from the beginning, have always been geared towards making a

living . . . I wouldn't call it easy because I've worked really hard. It sounds odd the way it happened. Some artists my age could tell you tales of going door-to-door with their slides. Their histories would seem rockier, but we've achieved similar ends by different routes. After art school, they had the confidence to say they were artists and they were actively being artists. I just refused to let anyone see my work for a long time, so it might seem that it has been faster and easier for me, but I don't think it has been.' Mary Weatherford, in Lilly Wei and Cecile N. McCann, 'Making Art, Making Money', *Art in America*, July 1990, 139.

4. Decter also included Weatherford's work in *Hybrid Abstract* at Usdan Gallery, Bennington College, Bennington, Vermont, in 1991.
5. Marcia Tucker had contributed to this work: She leaned over to Weatherford at a Diane Brown dinner and said, 'So what do you really do?' Weatherford told her that she was an artist, and Tucker offered to come over right away. She visited Weatherford in Brooklyn (this was before Weatherford moved to the East Village), where she saw the Hitchcock piece 'made of the disks' and said, 'How will I know who these stand for?' As Weatherford explains: 'So I made the next director "portraits" with a white screen on the right like a movie screen with names projected on to it.'
6. Robert Mahoney, 'School's Out', *New York Press*, February 3, 1989, 9.
7. Some friends as well as clients from the Diane Brown Gallery found out about the PS1 show and purchased the works from it. It was on the basis of these sales that Weatherford could afford to rent a studio, taking part of a floor above a mosque at 12 Warren Street in Tribeca that she rented from Alfredo Jaar.
8. Alexandra Anderson, 'The Next Generation', *Smart*, no. 5 (September–October 1989), 69.
9. Ibid., 72.
10. Ibid., 76.
11. Roberta Smith, 'Fresh, Hot and Headed for Fame', *New York Times*, January 5, 1990, C1. That year would also see Weatherford participating in group shows, including one at Andrea Rosen Gallery that received less than favorable reviews. The *New Yorker* characterized *Stendhal Syndrome: The Cure*, a show organized around theses of beauty and affliction, as 'a misbegotten, truly sophomoric group show'; 'psychiatric camp' was how Gerrit Henry put it. Henry did single out positively Weatherford's piece, for which she played a tape loop of Diana Ross's 'Love Hangover'. See 'Art', *New Yorker*, July 23, 1990, 9; and Gerrit Henry, 'Stendhal Syndrome: The Cure at Andrea Rosen Gallery', *Contemporanea*, no. 22 (November 1990), 91.
12. Louis Jacobson and Paul Lim, 'Life as a "Rising Star" in SoHo: Alumna's Work Targets Sexism', *Daily Princetonian*, April 25, 1990, 6.
13. Smith, 'Fresh, Hot and Headed for Fame', C1.
14. Ibid.
15. Robert Mahoney, 'New York in Review', *Arts Magazine*, April 1990, 108.
16. Leo Steinberg, 'Contemporary Art and the Plight of Its Public', *Harper's*, March 1962, 3.
17. Sam Hunter, *Emerging Art 1990* (Trenton: New Jersey State Museum, 1990).
18. Sam Hunter, *New Directions* (brochure), (New York: S. Bitter Larkin Gallery, 1990).
19. Participants in the BlumHelman Warehouse show were Weatherford and Polly Apfelbaum, Angela Bulloch, Cathy de Monchaux, Gail Fitzgerald, Sylvie Fleury, Aki Fujiyoshi, Dominique Gonzalez-Foerster, Asta Gröting, Paula Hayes, Rebecca Horn, Karen Kilimnik, Rachel Lachowicz, Liz Larner, Patty Martori, Annette Messager, Rona Pondick, Beverly Semmes, Jessica Stockholder, Rosemarie Trockel, and Andrea Zittel.
20. K. K. Kozik, 'Lyric', *Cover*, 1991, 16.
21. Steven Evans, 'Painting Culture', *NYQ*, November 10, 1991.
22. John Zinsser, 'Geometry and Its Discontents', *Tema Celeste*, no. 32–3 (Autumn 1991), 72.
23. Ibid., 74.
24. Elizabeth Hess, 'Death to the Masters', *Village Voice*, October 22, 1991, 91.
25. Ibid.
26. Ibid. No doubt Weatherford appreciated Kass's support following Hess's criticism. She kept in her files a handwritten note that Kass wrote her as the work traveled to Orange County: 'Your painting looks great in Painting Culture at Irvine . . . Your presence was really important.' Deborah Kass, note to Mary Weatherford, undated, Weatherford archive.
27. Zan Dubin, 'Painting Themselves Out of a Corner: Women's Works at UCI's Fine Arts Gallery Chip Away at Male-Dominated Societies', *Los Angeles Times*, October 10, 1992, accessed March 5, 2018, http://articles.latimes.com/1992-10-10/entertainment/ca-478_1_women-painters.
28. Suzanne Joelson and Andrea Scott, 'The Woman's Side: A Culture to Defend', *Tema Celeste*, no. 37–8 (Autumn 1992), 5.
29. Mary Weatherford, 'Fleur du Mal', *Tema Celeste*, no. 37–8 (Autumn 1992), 65.
30. Ken Johnson, 'Mary Weatherford at BlumHelman Warehouse', *Art in America*, May 1992, 109.
31. Ibid.
32. Anderson, 'The Next Generation', 77.
33. Roger Caillois and John Shepley, 'Mimicry and Legendary Psychasthenia', *October* 31 (Winter 1984), 17–32.
34. Jan Avgikos, 'Toot Toot', *Artforum*, May 1994, 87, accessed March 5, 2018, https://www.artforum.com/print/199405/toot-toot-33391.
35. Ibid.

3. Stains and Starfish: The 1990s

1. Phyllis Braff, 'Collectors' Diversified Choices: Some Ideas Internationally Discussed Get a Venue', *New York Times*, September 9, 1990, 16.
2. Weatherford worked there from 1991 to 1993, sharing a studio in the then-functional Meatpacking District with Josef Ramaseder. She was around the corner from Matthew Barney, upstairs from Cady Noland, across the hall from Peter Schuyff, and down the hall from Glenn Goldberg.
3. Mary Weatherford, *Satellite Girl*, 1992–3.
4. Ibid.
5. Ibid.
6. Ibid.
7. Ibid.
8. Mary Weatherford, in *'The heroine Paint': After Frankenthaler*, ed. Katy Siegel (New York: Gagosian Gallery/Rizzoli, 2015), 242.
9. See Elena Filipovic, *David Hammons Bliz-aard Ball Sale* (London: Afterall, 2017), 71–4.
10. Joyce Carol Oates, 'Foreword', in *Saving Graces*, ed. David Robinson (New York: W. W. Norton, 1995), 10.
11. Nancy Princenthal, 'Mary Weatherford at Debs & Co.', *Art in America*, July 1998, 92.
12. Janet Preston, 'New York Report Card', *Coagula Art Journal*, no. 33 (May 1998), 50.
13. Ibid.
14. Dale Peck, 'Easter', in *Easter* (New York: Debs & Co., 1998), n.p.
15. Ibid.
16. Press release by Thomas Korzelius Fine Art, 'Mary Weatherford: Works on Paper', 1998.
17. Barry Schwabsky, 'Mary Weatherford: Works on Paper, Thomas Korzelius Fine Art, New York', *Art on Paper*, March–April 1999, 64.
18. Margaret Weatherford did not edit her 1992 contribution to *Tema Celeste* or *Satellite Girl*, but she did review everything else, including Weatherford's grant proposals and press releases.

19. Margaret Weatherford, *Miniatures*, entry ii, 1998, n.p.
20. *Supernatural* (brochure) (New York: Dorsky Gallery, 1998), n.p.

4. Rocks, Caves, Weeds, Vines: The 2000s

1. 'Watercolor Techniques for Botanical Painting and Illustration', syllabus, Weatherford archive.
2. Claudine Isé, 'Coughlan, Reeder, Root, Weatherford, chicagoprojectroom, Los Angeles', *Tema Celeste* 8, no. 87 (September–October 2001), 86.
3. Press release, 'Mary Weatherford: recent paintings', Debs & Co., New York, 2000.
4. 'Galleries – Chelsea: Mary Weatherford', *New Yorker*, December 25, 2000, 33.
5. Robert Mahoney, 'Mary Weatherford', *Time Out New York*, January 4, 2001, 46.
6. John Zinsser, 'Painter's Journal', *artnet*, January 16, 2001, accessed March 5, 2018, http://www.artnet.com/Magazine/reviews/zinsser/zinsser1-16-01.asp.
7. Weatherford designates *5:00 a.m.* (1992) as her first cave. The title also references Mary Magdalene approaching Jesus' tomb at sunrise – although she did not assert it as a subject until 2000.
8. William Weatherford, 'Different Kinds of Caves', 2007.
9. This was also the frame for a group show, *Cavepainting*, at the Santa Monica Museum of Art, in 2002, where Laura Owens, Peter Doig, and Chris Ofili showed large-scale paintings. The formal properties of the respective works differed from one contributor to the next, yet their friendship, shared gallery context (they all worked with Gavin Brown's enterprise in New York), and collective curation belied this mythos of the solitary, or at least asocial, producer.
10. William Weatherford, 'Different Kinds of Caves', 2007.
11. Ibid.
12. Unpublished grant proposal, 2009, Weatherford archive.
13. Ibid.
14. Ibid.
15. Press release, 'Mary Weatherford: New Paintings', Sister, Los Angeles, January 14–February 18, 2006.
16. Amra Brooks, 'Los Angeles Round Up: Mary Weatherford', *ArtInfo.com*, January 2006, accessed March 5, 2018, http://www.blouinartinfo.com/news/story/264520/los-angeles-roundup-a-report-on-current-gallery-museum-shows.
17. Christopher Knight, 'Flourishing on Their Vines', *Los Angeles Times*, November 11, 2008, E19.
18. Press release, John Tevis Gallery, Paris, 2010. For this context, Weatherford got a grant to have her father's 'Different Kinds of Caves' translated into French by Youna Kwak.
19. 'Mary Weatherford in Conversation with Alex Israel', in *2008 California Biennial*, ed. Lauri Firstenberg, Joshua Decter, and René Peralta (Newport Beach: Orange County Museum of Art, 2008), 204.

5. Atmospheres and Lights: The 2010s

1. Willem de Kooning, 'The Renaissance and Order' (lecture, Studio 35, New York, Autumn 1949), *Trans/formation* 1, no. 2 (1951), 86.
2. Michael Fried, *Courbet's Realism* (Chicago: University of Chicago Press, 1990), 209.
3. Ibid., 212.
4. Ibid., 217.
5. Press release, 'Cave at Pismo', Brennan & Griffin, New York, 2011.
6. '50 Next Most Collectible Artists: Mary Weatherford', *Art and Auction*, June 2012, 113.
7. Chris Wyrick, 'L.A.'s Hottest Artists Right Now', *Hollywood Reporter*, November 8, 2013, 54.
8. Brian N. Willhite, 'Bakersfield Streets Glow under Neon Lights of Artist Mary Weatherford', *The Runner* (California State University, Bakersfield), February 15, 2012, 5.
9. Fan Zhong, 'Mary Weatherford: Brushes with Greatness', *W Magazine*, December 11, 2014, 92.
10. Katy Siegel, 'Into the Nightlife', in *Mary Weatherford: The Neon Paintings*, ed. Robert Faggen (New York: DelMonico Books/Prestel and Gould Center for Humanistic Studies, Claremont McKenna College, 2016), 11–12.
11. The invitation reads: 'EAST OF THE 5, SOUTH OF THE 10' / An Evening Performance / Thursday, October 30 at 8 p.m. / The myth of Persephone, retold for 21st-century Los Angeles by Margaret Weatherford. Dramatized by Robyn Palmer and Fred Thompson. Music by the Chapin Sisters. Paintings by Mary Weatherford. Produced by Mary & Margaret Weatherford and Jodie Berry.'
12. Margaret Weatherford, 'East of the 5, South of the 10', *Zyzzyva*, 2005, accessed March 3, 2018, http://www.zyzzyva.org/2012/04/05/east-of-the-5-south-of-the-10/.
13. Margaret Weatherford, 'Green Car, Nightfall', *Paris Review*, November 14, 2011, accessed March 8, 2018, https://www.theparisreview.org/blog/2011/11/14/green-car-nightfall/.
14. Sharon Mizota, 'Around the Galleries: A Poetic Mood Captured in Neon', *Los Angeles Times*, October 12, 2012, D14.
15. Roberta Smith, 'Mary Weatherford: "Manhattan"', *New York Times*, September 14, 2012, C27.
16. Matthew Higgs, 'Best of 2012', *Artforum*, December 2012, 237.
17. Barry Schwabsky, 'Mary Weatherford', *Artforum*, December 2012, 277.
18. Mary Weatherford, quoted in Maxwell Williams, 'Mary Weatherford: L.A. Confidential', *Art in America*, May 19, 2014, accessed March 9, 2018, https://www.artinamericamagazine.com/news-features/news/mary-weatherford-la-confidential/.
19. Christopher Knight, 'Review: Mary Weatherford's Seductive Paintings Marvels of Abstraction', *Los Angeles Times*, May 1, 2014, accessed March 9, 2018, http://www.latimes.com/entertainment/arts/culture/la-et-cm-review-mary-weatherford-david-kordansky-gallery-20140429-story.html.
20. Nora Griffin, 'Mary Weatherford *Red Hook*', *Brooklyn Rail*, July 13, 2015, accessed March 9, 2018, https://brooklynrail.org/2015/07/artseen/mary-weatherford-red-hook.
21. Maxwell Williams, 'There's Something About Mary', *Cultured Magazine*, Fall 2015, 172.
22. Hunter Drohojowska-Philp, 'Mary Weatherford and New Digs for Christies', *KCRW.com*, April 21, 2017, accessed March 9, 2018, https://www.kcrw.com/news-culture/shows/art-talk/mary-weatherford-and-new-digs-for-christies.
23. Mary Weatherford, in *Mary Weatherford: Bakersfield Paintings*, ed. Matthew Schum (Los Angeles: LAXART, 2012), 16.
24. Ibid., 13.
25. Mary Weatherford, *Satellite Girl*, 1992–3.

Selected Bibliography

Books and Catalogues

2008 California Biennial, texts by Joshua Decter, Lauri Firstenberg, and Rene Peralta, Newport Beach: Orange County Museum of Art, 2008.

Cottingham, Laura, 'The Feminist Continuum: Art after 1970', in *The Power of Feminist Art: The American Movement of the 1970s, History and Impact*, ed. Norma Broude and Mary D. Garrard, New York: Harry N. Abrams, 1994.

Crockett, Tobey, *A Vital Matrix*, Los Angeles: Domestic Setting, 1995.

Faggen, Robert (ed.), Katy Siegel, Jennifer Peterson, and Mary Weatherford, *Mary Weatherford: The Neon Paintings*, Claremont, CA: Claremont McKenna College; New York: DelMonico Books/Prestel, 2016.

Fyfe, Joe, *Om*, New York: Dorsky Gallery, 1999.

Hoptman, Laura, *The Forever Now: Contemporary Painting in an Atemporal World*, New York: Museum of Modern Art, 2014.

Hunter, Sam, *Emerging Art 1990*, Trenton: New Jersey State Art Museum, 1990.

Hunter, Sam, *New Directions*, New York: S. Bitter Larkin Gallery, 1990.

Kahn, Robin (ed.), *Time Capsule: A Concise Encyclopaedia by Women Artists*, New York: Creative Time and SOS International, 1995.

Liu, Catherine, *Plastic Fantastic Lover (object a)*, New York: BlumHelman Warehouse, 1991.

Oppenheim, Eric, *The Real Thing*, New York, 1992.

Peck, Dale, *Easter*, New York: Debs & Co., 1998.

Rubenstein, Meyer Raphael, *Postcards from Alphaville: Jean-Luc Godard in Contemporary Art, 1963–1992*, New York: PS1 Institute for Contemporary Art, 1992.

Salle, David, *How to See: Looking, Talking and Thinking about Art*, New York: W. W. Norton, 2016.

Schum, Matthew (ed.), *Mary Weatherford: Bakersfield Paintings*, Los Angeles: LAXART, 2012.

Siegel, Katy (ed.), *'The heroine Paint': After Frankenthaler*, New York: Gagosian Gallery/ Rizzoli, 2015.

Steiner, Rochelle, 'Mary Weatherford', in *Vitamin P3: New Perspectives in Painting*, London: Phaidon, 2016.

Stendhal Syndrome: The Cure, New York: Andrea Rosen Gallery, 1990.

Tsatsos, Irene (ed.), *Caught Looking*, Pasadena: Armory Center for the Arts, 2014.

Tsatsos, Irene, *Common Threads, Shared Spaces: Five Years of Fellowships for Visual Artists from the California Community Foundation, 2004–2008*, Los Angeles: California Community Foundation, 2009.

Weatherford, Margaret, *Miniatures*, 1998. Illustrated by Mary Weatherford.

Weatherford, Margaret, *East of the 5, South of the 10*, 2005. Illustrated by Mary Weatherford.

Periodicals and Newspapers

'50 Next Most Collectible Artists: Mary Weatherford', *Art and Auction*, June 2012, 98–9, 113.

'50 Women Artists Worth Watching', *Art and Auction*, September 2014.

Anderson, Alexandra, 'Mary Weatherford at Diane Brown Gallery', *Artnow*, 1990.

Anderson, Alexandra, 'The Next Generation', *Smart*, no. 5, September–October 1989, 69–79.

Auriti, Sandy, 'New York', *Cento Cose*, November 1989, 54.

Braff, Phyllis, 'Collectors' Diversified Choices', *New York Times*, September 9, 1990, 16.

Brooks, Amra, 'Los Angeles Round Up: Mary Weatherford', *Artinfo.com*, January 2006.

Cameron, Dan, 'Don't Look Now', *Frieze*, no.3 (January–March 1992).

Cha, Olivian, 'Critics' Picks: Mary Weatherford', *Artforum.com*, May 6, 2014.

Chandler, Elizabeth Khuri, 'The Originals', *C Magazine*, October 2014, 128–35.

Curtis, Cathy, 'Women's Work: Rich, Shocking', *Los Angeles Times*, October 16, 1992.

Deamer, Julie, 'Sharing Sunsets', Museum of Contemporary Art Tucson, 2002.

Drohojowska-Philp, Hunter, 'Mary Weatherford at David Kordansky Gallery', *KCRW.com*, May 1, 2014.

Dubin, Zan, 'Painting Themselves Out of a Corner', *Los Angeles Times*, October 10, 1992.

Evans, Steven, 'Painting Culture', *NYQ*, November 10, 1991.

'Girls Gone Wild', *New Yorker*, June 30, 2003, 24.

Goldfarb, Brad, 'Stop and Smell the Roses', *Interview*, May 1997.

Gordon, Alastair, '11 Artists "Emerge" at Gallery in East Hampton', *Newsday*, August 31, 1990.

Greenberger, Alex, 'Mary Weatherford', *Artnews*, November 2015, 98.

Griffin, Jonathan, 'The New Dealer', *T Magazine*, September 14, 2014, 124–8.

Griffin, Nora, 'Mary Weatherford *Red Hook*', *Brooklyn Rail*, July/August 2015.

Guadagnino, Kate, 'Bright Spot', *T Magazine*, March 5, 2017, p.58.

Halperin, Julia, 'Mary Weatherford's "Manhattan" at Brennan & Griffin', *Artinfo.com*, December 21, 2013.

Henry, Gerrit, 'Stendhal Syndrome: The Cure at Andrea Rosen Gallery', *Contemporanea*, November 1990.

Hess, Elizabeth, 'Death to the Masters', *Village Voice*, October 22, 1991, 91.

Higgs, Matthew, 'David Korty and Mary Weatherford', *Artforum*, December 2012, 237.

Hoberman, J., 'Jean-Luc Godard: Picasso, Marx and Coca Cola', *Artnews*, February 1993.

Isé, Claudine, 'Coughlan, Reeder, Root, Weatherford, chicagoprojectroom, Los Angeles', *Tema Celeste*, September–October 2001, 86.

Johnson, Ken, 'Mary Weatherford – Chelsea Galleries', *New York Times*, December 22, 2000, B43.

Johnson, Ken, 'Mary Weatherford at BlumHelman Warehouse', *Art in America*, May 1992, 109.

Kalin, Tom, 'Plastic Fantastic Lover (object a)', *Artforum*, January 1992.

Kendricks, Neil, 'Primarily Paint', *San Diego Union Tribune*, February 6, 1997, 17.

Kimmelman, Michael, 'Painting Culture', *New York Times*, November 1, 1991, C16.

Knight, Christopher, 'Watercolors in Sensuous Form', *Los Angeles Times*, March 28, 2017, E2.

Knight, Christopher, 'Review: Mary Weatherford's Seductive Paintings Marvels of Abstraction', *Los Angeles Times*, May 1, 2014.

Knight, Christopher, 'Flourishing on Their Vines', *Los Angeles Times*, November 11, 2008, E19.

Knight, Christopher, 'Don't Take It Lying Down: 2008 California Biennial', *Los Angeles Times*, November 4, 2008, E1.

Knight, Christopher, '45 Painters under 45', *Los Angeles Times*, December 2, 2007, F1.

Kozik, K. K., 'Lyric', *Cover*, May 1991, 16.

Kushner, Rachel, 'The New Blue Chips', *C Magazine*, March 2009, 85–87, 132, 134.

Liberio, Lydia, 'What if Andy Warhol and Roy Lichtenstein Had Been Women?', *Irvine World News*, October 15, 1992.

Mahoney, Robert, 'Mary Weatherford', *Time Out New York*, January 4, 2001, 46.

Mahoney, Robert, 'Mary Weatherford', *New Yorker*, December 25, 2000, 33.
Mahoney, Robert, 'New York in Review', *Arts Magazine*, April 1990, 108.
'Mary Weatherford', *Paper Monument*, no. 4, summer 2013.
'Mary Weatherford', in 'The Artists' Artists', *Artforum*, December 2015, 105.
'Mary Weatherford: "Los Angeles"', *Art and Auction*, July/August 2014.
'Mary Weatherford "Los Angeles" at David Kordansky Gallery, Los Angeles', *MousseMagazine.it*, June 11, 2014.
'Mary Weatherford Receives Artists' Legacy Foundation 2014 Artist Award', *Artforum.com*, September 23, 2014.
Meyer, Megan, 'Light and Space', *C Magazine*, September 2014.
Miranda, Carolina A, 'Artist's Noble Pursuit', *Los Angeles Times*, April 2, 2017, F6–F7.
Mizota, Sharon, 'Around the Galleries: A Poetic Mood Captured in Neon', *Los Angeles Times*, October 12, 2012, D14.
Peetz, John Arthur, 'Critics' Picks: Mary Weatherford', *Artforum.com*, September 28, 2012.
Pincus, Robert L., 'Many Movements Render "Paint" Lively but Random', *San Diego Union Tribune*, March 2, 1997, E4.
Princenthal, Nancy, 'Mary Weatherford at Debs & Co.', *Art in America*, July 1998, 92.
Robinson, Walter, 'Weekend Update', *Artnet.com*, June 25, 2011.
Row, D. K., 'Painter's Paradise', *The Oregonian*, February 3, 1999, E1.
Salle, David, 'Structure Rising: David Salle on "The Forever Now" at MoMA', *Artnews.com*, February 23, 2015.
Saltz, Jerry, '"The Forever Now" Is MoMA's Market Moment', *Vulture.com*, December 12, 2014.
Saltz, Jerry, 'Seeing Out Loud: Jerry Saltz on the Brief, Great Career of Moira Dryer', *Vulture.com*, January 30, 2014.
Schwabsky, Barry, 'Mary Weatherford', *Artforum*, December 2012, 277.
Schwabsky, Barry, 'Mary Weatherford: Works on Paper, Thomas Korzelius Fine Art, New York', *Art on Paper*, March–April 1999, 64.
Sholis, Brian, 'Critics' Picks: Mary Weatherford', *Artforum.com*, June 19, 2006.
Smith, Roberta, 'Review: "Pretty Raw" Recounts Helen Frankenthaler's Influence on the Art World', *New York Times*, June 3, 2015.
Smith, Roberta, 'Art in Review, Mary Weatherford', *New York Times*, September 14, 2012.
Smith, Roberta, 'Art in Review, "Girls Gone Wild"', *New York Times*, July 4, 2003.
Smith, Roberta, 'Fresh, Hot and Headed for Fame', *New York Times*, January 5, 1990.
Solway, Diane, and Fan Zhong, 'Brushes with Greatness', *W Magazine*, December 2014/January 2015, 90, 92.
'Stendhal Syndrome: The Cure', *New Yorker*, July 30, 1990.
'Ten × Ten: 10 Extraordinary People, 10 Random Questions', *Malibu Magazine*, October/November 2012, 74.
Wallach, Amei, '"The Forever Now" vs. Recombinant DNA', *Brooklyn Rail*, March 5, 2015.
Walquist, Grant, 'The Ballad that Becomes an Anthem', *ArtLTDMag.com*, May 2009.
Weatherford, Mary, 'Fleur du Mal', *Tema Celeste*, November 1992.
Wei, Lilly, 'Making Art, Making Money', *Art in America*, July 1990, 139–40.
Willhite, Brian N., 'Bakersfield Streets Glow under Neon Lights of Artist Mary Weatherford', *The Runner*, California State University, Bakersfield, February 15, 2012, 5.
Williams, Maxwell, 'There's Something About Mary', *Cultured Magazine*, Fall 2015, 170–3
Williams, Maxwell, 'Mary Weatherford: L.A. Confidential', *ArtinAmerica.com*, May 19, 2014.
Wood, Eve, 'Killer Pick of the Week: Mary Weatherford', *ArtilleryMag.com*, May 17, 2014.
Wyrick, Chris, 'L.A.'s Hottest Artists Right Now', *Hollywood Reporter*, November 8, 2013, 54.
Zimskind, Lyle, 'Framed: Oxnard Ventura, Abstract and Illuminated', *LAMag.com*, April 25, 2014.
Zinsser, John, 'Painter's Journal', *Artnet.com*, June 16, 2001.
Zinsser, John, 'Geometry and Its Discontents', *Tema Celeste*, Autumn 1991, 72–6.

Biography

1963
Born in Ojai, CA

1984
BA, Princeton University, Princeton, NJ

1985
Whitney Independent Study Program, Helena Rubinstein Fellow, New York

2006
MFA, Milton Avery School of the Arts, Bard College, Annandale-on-Hudson, NY

Lives and works in Los Angeles

Selected Exhibitions

Solo Exhibitions

2019
Survey exhibition, Contemporary Arts Museum Houston, Houston (traveling to Frances Young Tang Teaching Museum and Art Gallery at Skidmore College, Saratoga Springs, NY).

2018
I've Seen Gray Whales Go By, Gagosian, New York.

2017
like the land loves the sea, David Kordansky Gallery, Los Angeles.

2015
Red Hook, Brennan & Griffin, New York.

2014
Los Angeles, David Kordansky Gallery, Los Angeles.

2012
The Bakersfield Paintings, LAXART, Los Angeles.
Manhattan, Brennan & Griffin, New York.
The Bakersfield Project, Todd Madigan Gallery, California State University, Bakersfield.

2011
Cave at Pismo, Brennan & Griffin, New York.

2010
The Cave, John Tevis Gallery, Paris.

2008
Vines, Sister, Los Angeles.
Brick Walls and Sea Life, Cottage Home, Los Angeles.

2007
Paintings of a Cave, Sister, Los Angeles.

2006
New Paintings, Sister, Los Angeles.
Mary Weatherford, Shane Campbell Gallery, Chicago.

2003
Mary Weatherford, boomeditions (Shane Campbell Gallery), Chicago.

2000
recent paintings, Debs & Co., New York.

1999
Mary Weatherford: Works on Paper, Thomas Korzelius Fine Art, New York.

1998
Easter, Debs & Co., New York.

1993
Unfair, Cologne, solo presentation by Galerie Ralph Wernicke.

1992
I Never Promised You a Rose Garden, BlumHelman Warehouse, New York.

1991
Galerie Marc Jancou, Zurich.

1990
Diane Brown Gallery, New York.

Group Exhibitions

2018
Surface Work, Victoria Miro, London.

2017
Masterworks on Loan, Jordan Schnitzer Museum of Art, University of Oregon, Eugene.
LA Invitational, Gagosian Gallery, New York.
Between Two Worlds: Art of California, San Francisco Museum of Modern Art, San Francisco.
Color People, Rental Gallery, East Hampton, NY.
Unpacking: The Marciano Collection, Marciano Art Foundation, Los Angeles.
Unique and Singular, Cirrus, Los Angeles.

2016
The Noise of Art, Soccer Club Club, Chicago.
Accumulations: 5,000 Years of Objects, Fictions, and Conversations, Mead Art Museum, Amherst College, Amherst, MA.
NO MAN'S LAND: Women Artists from the Rubell Family Collection, National Museum of Women in the Arts, Washington, DC.
NEON: The Charged Line, Grundy Art Gallery, Blackpool.
End of Semester, BBQLA, Los Angeles.

Graffiorists, Torrance Art Museum, Torrance, CA.
Nice Weather, Skarstedt Gallery, New York.

2015
NO MAN'S LAND: Women Artists from the Rubell Family Collection, Rubell Family Collection, Miami.
Six Doors, The Other Room, Foundation for Contemporary Arts, New York.
Pretty Raw: After and Around Helen Frankenthaler, The Rose Art Museum, Brandeis University, Waltham, MA.
Pure Paint for Now People, Mary Elizabeth Dee Shaw Gallery, Webster State University, Ogden, UT.

2014
The Forever Now: Contemporary Painting in an Atemporal World, The Museum of Modern Art, New York.
Variations: Conversations in and around Abstract Painting, Los Angeles County Museum of Art, Los Angeles.
Caught Looking, Armory Center for the Arts, Pasadena, CA.
The Moira Dryer Project, Eleven Rivington, New York.
California Landscape into Abstraction, Orange County Museum of Art, Newport Beach, CA.

2013
Selections from the Grunwald Center and the Hammer Contemporary Collection, Hammer Museum, Los Angeles.
CULM, Night Gallery, Los Angeles.

2012
Sam Falls, Mark Hagen, James Hayward, Mary Weatherford, China Art Objects, Los Angeles.
Take Shelter in the World, Boston University Art Gallery, Boston.

2011
A Painting Show, Harris Liebermann Gallery, New York.

2010
LAst Show, Cottage Home, Los Angeles.
Artificial Paradises, ACME, Los Angeles.

2009
These Are a Few, JGM Galerie, Paris.
The Ballad that Becomes an Anthem, ACME, Los Angeles.

2008
California Biennial 2008, Orange County Museum of Art, Newport Beach, CA.

2007
Something about Mary, Orange County Museum of Art, Newport Beach, CA.

2006
Hotel California, Glendale College Art Gallery, Glendale, CA.
The Trace of a Trace of a Trace, Perry Rubenstein Gallery, New York.

2004
Where do we come from? What are we? Where are we going?, Champion Fine Art, Los Angeles.
Eastman, Weatherford & Arnold, Daniel Hug Gallery, Los Angeles.

2003
Still or Sparkling, John Connelly Presents, New York.

2002
Simmer, Echo Park Projects, Los Angeles.

2001
New Angeles, University Galleries, Illinois State University, Normal (traveled to Ewing Gallery of Art and Architecture, The University of Tennessee, Knoxville).
Sharing Sunsets, Museum of Contemporary Art, Tucson.
Chicago Project Room and Laura Owens's studio, Los Angeles.

2000
as i love you you become more pretty, 937 N. Hudson, Los Angeles.

1999
Stars of Track and Field, Debs & Co., New York.
Life in Space, a Three Day Weekend event at California College of Arts and Crafts, San Francisco.
a ball and a bat, Pacific Northwest College of Art, Portland.
Om, Dorsky Gallery, New York.

1998
Bowie, Rupert Goldsworthy Gallery, New York.

1997
Very Large Array, Debs & Co., New York.
Primarily Paint, Museum of Contemporary Art, San Diego.

1994
Don't Postpone Joy, or Collecting Can Be Fun, Neue Galerie am Landesmuseum Joanneum, Graz, and The Austrian Institute, New York.

1993
The Return of the Cadavre Exquis, The Drawing Center, New York.

1992
Postcards from Alphaville: Jean-Luc Godard in Contemporary Art, 1963–1992, PS1, New York.
Painting Culture, University of California at Irvine Fine Arts Gallery, Irvine.
The Real Thing, various locations, New York.

1991
Synthesis, John Good Gallery, New York.
Hybrid Abstract, Usdan Gallery, Bennington College, Bennington, VT.
Lyric: Uses of Beauty at the End of the Century, White Columns, New York.
Painting Culture, fiction/nonfiction, New York.
Plastic Fantastic Lover (object a), BlumHelman Warehouse, New York.

1990
Emerging Art 1990: Commodities Corporation Collection, New Jersey State Art Museum, Trenton.
To Know a Hawk from a Handsaw, Wolff Gallery, New York.
Stendhal Syndrome: The Cure, Andrea Rosen Gallery, New York.
New Directions, S. Bitter Larkin Gallery, New York.
Information, organized by Robert Nickas, Terrain Gallery, San Francisco.
About Round/Round About, Anders Tornberg Gallery, Lund, Sweden.

1989
Drawings, Wolff Gallery, New York.
Special Projects '89, PS1, New York.

1986
Indoor/Outdoor, El Bohio Community and Cultural Center, New York.

Selected Public Collections

Anderson Collection at Stanford University, Stanford, CA
Brooklyn Museum, New York
Brown Forman Corporation, Louisville, KY
The Capital Group Companies, Los Angeles
Fondation Louis Vuitton, Paris, France
Hammer Museum, Los Angeles
Hirshhorn Museum and Sculpture Garden, Washington, DC
Laguna Beach Art Museum, Laguna Beach, CA
Los Angeles County Museum of Art, Los Angeles
Marciano Art Foundation, Los Angeles
Mead Art Museum, Amherst College, Amherst, MA
Museum of Contemporary Art, Los Angeles
Museum of Contemporary Art San Diego, San Diego
The Museum of Modern Art, New York
National Museum of Women in the Arts, Washington, DC
Norfolk Southern Corporation, Norfolk, VA
Orange County Museum of Art, Newport Beach, CA
Progressive Corporation, Cleveland
Rose Art Museum, Brandeis University, Waltham, MA
San Francisco Museum of Modern Art, San Francisco
Tate Modern, London
Walker Art Center, Minneapolis

Acknowledgments

This book would not have been possible without the tremendous support of Sandy Lu and Mollie White. My gratitude extends to Domenick Ammirati, Grant Johnson, Jennifer Knox White and Stuart Krimko. Most of all, I thank Mary Weatherford for the work and the gift of conversation about it.

I dedicate it to Beatrice and Lucian, children of California.

Index

Titles of artworks are *italicized* and are by Mary Weatherford if no other name is included. Page numbers in *italics* are for illustrations

First published in 2019 by Lund Humphries

Lund Humphries
Office 3, Book House
261a City Road
London
EC1V 1JX
www.lundhumphries.com

Mary Weatherford © Suzanne Hudson, 2019
Works, unless otherwise stated, © Mary Weatherford, 2019

ISBN: 978-1-84822-246-5

A Cataloguing-in-Publication record for this book is available
from the British Library.
All rights reserved.

No part of this publication may be reproduced, stored in a retrieval system or transmitted in any form or by any means, electrical, mechanical or otherwise, without first seeking the permission of the copyright owners and publishers. Every effort has been made to seek permission to reproduce the images in this book. Any omissions are entirely unintentional, and details should be addressed to the publishers.

Suzanne Hudson has asserted her right under the Copyright, Designs and Patents Act, 1988, to be identified as the Author of this Work.

Photography of Mary Weatherford's work by Fredrik Nilsen Studio unless otherwise stated. Other photographs (by figure number): Sylvie Ball 39, 42, 51, 53; John Bessler 21; Sheldon C. Collins 75; Genevieve Hanson 95; Pinkney Herbert and Jennifer Secor, courtesy of Public Art Fund, New York 36; Ken Lavey 90; Light Blue Studio, Fairfield (Timothy Pyle) 26; Mancia / Bodmer 18, 19, 20; Bill Orcutt 14, 16, 17; Ellen Page Wilson 27; Adam Reich 82; Special Collections and Archives, University Library, University of California, Santa Cruz, Frank Zwart Papers 5; Tom Van Eynde 65; Simon Vogel 29; Mary Weatherford 3, 32, 63, 66; Robert Wedemeyer 69, 71, 72, 73, 74, 77, 78, 79, 80, 85, 86, 87, 91, 92; Photography © Joshua White 61, 62, 70; Unknown 11, 12, 13, 23, 24

Printed in Italy
Frontispiece: Mary Weatherford in her studio by Katherine McMahon
Cover: *absorbent*, 2000, Flashe and sponges on canvas